THE NAKED GUIDE TO BATH

By Gideon Kibblewhite and Melissa Blease

First published in 2004 by Naked Guides. Second Edition published 2012 by Tangent Books.

Tangent Books, Unit 5.16 Paintworks, Bristol BS4 3EH
www.tangentbooks.co.uk
Tel: 0117 972 0645

Publisher: Richard Jones (richard@tangentbooks.co.uk)
Editors: Steve Faragher, Jonathan Palmer
Contributors: Kate McDonnell, Steve Bradley, Nia Evans, Steve Faragher, Jon Palmer, Richard Jones, Charly Paige
Design/cover artwork: Joe Burt (joe@wildsparkdesign.com)
Map design: Alex Dimond
Print management: Jonathan Lewis (essentialprintmanagement@gmail.com)

ISBN: 978-1-906477-68-4

2nd Edition

Printed using paper from sustainable sources

The Naked Guide to Bath's cover stars

A Marcus Tullius Cicer – see if you can spot him at his post on York Street

B Mr Martin Salter, a Georgian gentlemen, often to be found at the Jane Austen Centre

C Jane Austen at the Jane Austen Centre

D The Rebecca Fountain – she stands outside the Abbey

E Beau Nash, Bath's greatest Master of Ceremonies

F Bath Rugby's Olly Barkley

G A pig – like one of those in the legend of Bath's founding

WELCOME

The Naked Guide to Bath is your comprehensive companion to help you discover Bath old and new. Within these pages you can find out all about the city's amazing 2,000-year history and at the same time get the low-down on the many delights that modern Bath has to offer.

This second edition of the Naked Guide boasts a new *Must-see Bath* section – an in-depth guide to the main highlights of the city. A new street-by-street history guide transports you back in time to the Bath of centuries ago, introducing you to some of the extraordinary people who have lived here.

A bang-up to date listings section guides you through the best restaurants, pubs, museums, shops and more – it's all here plus where to pay golf, where to see an art house film, what to do with the kids when it's raining and much, much more.

Bath is still, as it was designed to be, "a city for the pleasures" – and with the Naked Guide to Bath you can enjoy them all…

Gideon Kibblewhite

FIND US ON FACEBOOK AND TWITTER

Keep in touch with *The Naked Guide to Bath* by liking our Facebook page or following us on Twitter **@nakedguide_bath**. Or you can get in touch with us via the contact form at **www.tangentbooks.co.uk** or call us on **0117 972 0645.**

ABOUT THE AUTHORS

Gideon Kibblewhite enjoyed an almost ridiculously idyllic childhood involving goats and buxom serving maids. Indeed, he thought he might live out the rest of his days in the western bowels of Wiltshire until one day he heard of the fabled city of Bath. It was a place of debauch and indolence, he was told, whose populace did nothing but drink, play cards and generally get carried around in chairs. With nothing but a handkerchief full of sandwiches packed by his mother and handful of beans he unwisely bought from a farmer on the way, he arrived in Bath to discover he was about two hundred years too late. It has been his mission since to seek out those mysterious palaces of the idle and to relive the high life of bygone days.

Born in Liverpool just before Cilla Black topped the charts with *You're My World*, **Melissa Blease** moved to Bath in 1999 and made it hers. This big-haired, big-mouthed, self-styled renaissance woman is a freelance writer currently seeking an agent to represent a massive back-catalogue of fiction; meanwhile, she regularly contributes to several publications including *Folio* magazine and online eating out guide *The Pig* (www.thepigguide.com). What Melissa doesn't know about food, fun and cats isn't really worth knowing, but she's happy to blame any gaps in her knowledge on an over-indulgence of sunshine, good times and boogie.

CONTENTS

MUST-SEE BATH

A-Z

PERAMBULATION

HISTORY

LISTINGS

BATH IN PICTURES

1 The Roman Baths

Welcome to the remains of one of the swankiest temple and health resorts of the Roman Empire...

■ The steamy waters of the 2,000-year-old Great Bath look so inviting. You're not allowed in though

If you only have two hours to spend in Bath, visit the Roman Baths.

Once you're through the grand lobby (formerly the concert hall of the Pump Room), you immediately get a glimpse over the (Victorian!) stone railings of the Great Bath below and you can't wait to get down to it.

But the winding route down (the temperature and the humidity gradually increase as you go) is all part of the experience and a fascinating dawdle. With the help of gadgets like telephone guides and computer reconstructions, you are taken on a tour of a hoard of finds that includes over 8,000 Celtic and Roman coins, carved offerings and curses, pewter vessels, leatherwork and mosaics. And that's forgetting the major discoveries

– a huge network of baths ands saunas, the Sacred Spring, the pediment of the Roman Temple, the Façade of the Four Seasons, the bronze-gilt head of Minerva, the 'Gorgon's Head' and the oldest sewer in Britain. If you wish, human tour guides will show you around – and delight in disgusting you with tales of what the Romans did with their body scrapings.

When they arrived in Britain in 43 AD the Romans would have been very excited to find hot springs. Important assets for the Empire, hot springs were not only great for both drinking and bathing, they were also valued for their powers over ills like gout, rheumatism and skin disease. These were the only known hot springs in Britain.

With typical efficiency, the Romans swiftly built a garrison, made the area a focus of their transport system and built a lead-lined reservoir around the Sacred Spring so that the boggy valley could be drained.

The local Iron Age Celts, the Belgae tribe, had given the

The Gorgon's Head, which stared out from the Temple's pediment. This strange face could be a combination of the snake-headed Gorgon from Greek mythology and the Celtic goddess of the springs Sulis, or it could be some other god

The Temple

There were other temples in Aquae Sulis – for gods like Mars, for example – but *the* deity in town was Sulis Minerva.

Walled within a sacred precinct, the temple of this Roman-Celt goddess of the springs stood high on a stepped podium where Stall Street now lies. Look from the Abbey's Great Doors down Abbey Churchyard and you are looking over what was once the temple courtyard, where worshippers prayed. The temple's altar – a two-metre-high slab of stone on which animal sacrifices were made, their entrails read by augurers – stood roughly at the Pump Room's corner.

The richly decorated temple was built in the classical style with many pillars (you can see a replica of it in Sydney Gardens). This shows the importance that the Romans attached to it, for the only other temple like it in Britain was in Colchester. Amazing, the temple's pediment – with its carved 'Gorgon's Head' with hair of snakes and fierce Celtic warrior's face – has survived along with part of the altar and also the Minerva Head, part of a beautiful statue that quite possibly looked out from the temple.

A building on the south side of the courtyard – now beneath the Pump Room – housed the Sacred Spring. The Spring was revered for its healing powers and pilgrims believed that by making offerings they could receive aid from the goddess of the underworld. Thousands of coins as well as gold and silver treasures have been found near it.

The Roman writer Solinus gives us a teasing hint of what the scene for worshipers was like in the temple's heyday…

In Britain are hot springs furnished luxuriously for human use. Over these springs Minerva presides, and in her temple the perpetual fire never whitens into ash, but as the flame fades, turns into rocky balls.

The "rocky balls" indicate that the eternal flames were fuelled not by wood but by Somerset coal – a novelty to the Romans.

By 391 AD the Christian emperor Theodosius had shut down the Empire's pagan temples and Aquae Sulis, like its baths, fell into ruin to be buried by mud and forgotten.

It is possible that the temple in Aquae Sulis was deliberately destroyed by Christians – and that the Minerva Head was hacked off. The Roman pool near the present day Cross Bath might also have been vandalised, for a carving dedicated to Sulis Minerva was found at its bottom.

Romans little trouble during the conquest. However, the brutally crushed rebellion of 60-61 AD led by the northern warrior queen Boudicca underlined the need to 'Romanise' the Celts. So as part of this strategy, the Romans merged the Belgae's goddess of the springs Sulis with their own god Minerva. Around 70 AD, a temple to "Sulis Minerva" was built and the town and baths that grew up around it the Romans named Aquae Sulis – the Waters of Sulis. It would grow and develop for three hundred years.

Aquae Sulis' bathing complex was simply huge for such a small town and it was huge for a reason: Aquae Sulis had millions of gallons of free hot water and the Romans were determined to use it. Expensive to produce, hot water was rare in the Roman Empire. Ordinary Roman baths might boast a modest hot tub, but certainly not a vast, warm swimming bath surrounded by pools and saunas of varying temperatures such as the hot springs allowed.

As the baths increased in fame they also increased in size and complexity until they covered roughly an acre of the 23 acre town. Smaller bathhouses also sprang up near

The gilt bronze head of Sulis Minerva, part of a statue that probably stood in the temple and surely the most beautiful of the thousands of remarkable objects found on the site

Where Does The Water Come From?

Bath is built around three natural hot mineral springs. Nowhere else in Britain has hot springs. The King's Spring (which was called the Sacred Spring by the Romans) surfaces by the Roman Baths. The Cross Spring and Hetling Spring are under the Cross and Hot Baths respectively. The new Spa facilities use water from all three springs, fed by new boreholes to ensure its purity.

The three hot springs gurgle up a total of 1.3 million litres of water each day. The King's Spring supplies about 80 per cent of this, while the Hetling Spring is, just, the hottest.

King's Spring: 45°C (113°F)
972,000 litres per day
Hetling Spring: 45.3°C (113.5°F)
86,400 litres per day
Cross Spring: 43.7°C (110.7°F)
192,000 litres per day

The most commonly accepted theory about the source of the hot water is that it is rain that fell up to 10,000 years ago on Somerset's limestone Mendip Hills. This rain then soaked in and sank to a depth of two kilometres, where it was cooked to temperatures of up to 69°C before being forced through faults back to the surface.

Early Bathers

The Romans were not the first to enjoy the hot springs. Flint remains discovered around the Hot and Cross springs suggest that hunter-gatherers visited the springs as long ago as 8,000 BC. After about 100 BC the Belgae, an Iron Age Celtic tribe of farmers and craftsmen, built shrines to the goddess Sulis around the springs. From coins that have been found near the King's Spring we know that these Celts were still worshiping their local goddess of the springs at the time of the Roman invasion of 43 AD.

the Hot and Cross springs. Who would have bathed there? Legionnaires stationed in Britain, many of whom would have come from sunnier climes, would certainly have enjoyed the facilities. The Romanised Celts would have too, and wealthy visitors from Europe. Villas sprang up around the town, many housing Romans who were able to retire to the area. In short, Aquae Sulis became one of the top pleasure resorts of the Roman world.

But as the Roman Empire eventually went into decline, so too did Aquae Sulis. The once great baths were already in a state of decay by 410, when the Roman Empire, under attack by barbarian hoards from all sides, officially abandoned Britain to its own defences. The last Roman coins found in the area date to 400 AD.

The precise fate of Aquae Sulis is unknown. After the last Roman troops withdrew some people appear to have remained in the town, but it was not long before they faced Saxon raiders. A Roman house unearthed by archaeologists in Abbeygate Street contained the severed head of a young girl of this period. Gruesomely, it had

The statues of the Roman emperors and generals on the terrace above the Great Bath were all erected in 1897 – except one. The statue of Julius Caesar only dates back to the late 1980s. The original was vandalised

The Discovery Of The Roman Baths

You might have though that Bath would have been very excited at news of the discovery of major Roman remains in the very centre of the city – but it took a while for the idea to catch on.

The first discovery came in 1727, when workmen building a sewer in Stall Street found a tiled floor. It was part of the west end of the Roman Baths complex. Another clue came in 1755 with discovery of the East Baths under York Street, where the new Kingston Baths were being built. None of this created much of a stir except among archaeologists. Then in 1791, during the digging of the foundations for the present day Pump Room, bits of the Roman Temple were dug up. Admittedly this did cause some excitement, but it didn't last long.

Over the following 80 years the northern and southern limits of the Baths were discovered and a hypocaust, a semi-circular bath and further temple remains were found. Eventually, in 1871, during work to repair a leak in the King's Bath, the Great Bath was discovered. And when this was swiftly followed with the discovery of the Sacred Spring, the city council was forced to act and a major excavation of the area was launched by city architect Major Charles Davis.

It didn't all go smoothly after that. Major Davis was criticised for his handling of the dig (finds were left in the rain and they were poorly recorded) and he also became embroiled in an argument about who actually 'discovered' the remains. Meanwhile, local businesses sued the council for holding up the building of new continental-style massage and douche baths, which they saw as essential to the city's flagging fortunes as a spa.

But in 1889 the Roman Baths were finally opened to the public and in 1892 the Pump Room was extended after it was decided that the antiquities, already damaged by being left out in the elements, could have a place within the complex. And visitors flocked to see it all.

Bath's fortunes were on the mend, revived by the baths it had for so long forgotten.

been thrust into an oven. The Saxons finally took control of the town after a great battle with the Celts in the year 577, but it was deserted well before then.

What happed to the baths? It was the beginning of the Dark Ages. The secrets of grand building and public sanitation went with the Romans and Aquae Sulis crumbled and sank. In the 8th century, a Saxon monk's lovely poem called "The Ruin" describes all that was left:

Wondrous is this masonry, shattered by the fates. The fortifications have given way, the buildings raised by giants are crumbling. The city fell to earth.

Amid the ruins, though, the Saxons continued to use the hot waters. We know this because the same poem also tells us:

There stood courts of stone and a stream gushed forth in rippling floods of hot water. The wall enfolded within its bright bosom, the whole place which contained the hot flood of the baths.

The Saxons renamed the city "Hat Bathu" (hot baths), but they used only a small part of the crumbled Roman complex, probably diverting the Sacred Spring from the Great Bath into the tiny Circular Bath, which they called the "Alron" Bath.

However, when Normans arrived and built the King's Bath over the site of the Great Bath in 1106, the last traces of the once great Roman bathing complex were buried and, eventually, forgotten.

■ **In Roman times bathers in the Great Bath would have been sheltered by a vaulted ceramic roof supported by pillars**

The Roman Rendezvous

From 1961 through the 1970s, the Great Bath and the King's Bath would be thrown open for public bathing during the Bath Festival. Priced £4 a ticket, the first, unofficial "Roman Rendezvous" was held in 1960. To Bath Festival director Yehudi Menuhin's horror, it took the form of a "Roman Orgy"-themed Festival Ball. Guests wore togas and were fed roast boar, swan, dormice, nightingales' tongues, sows' udders and thrushes. To get rid if the last revellers – still in the water at 4am – the authorities were forced, literally, to pull the plug. Menuhin later said: "To see a lot of rich people get together and find some excuse for getting drunk – that attitude to the festival was at odds with my own feeling about it." However, 1,400 people enjoyed the chance to swim in the baths during the four-day event, which was reported worldwide. The Roman Rendezvous was ended, though, by the poisonous amoeba scare of 1978.

2 The King's Bath

Next to the Roman Bath is the 12th century King's Bath – also an extraordinary place in its heyday

■ The King's Bath. Once the scene of steamy bedlam, today you have to go through the Roman Baths complex to visit it

After the Roman occupation of Britain officially ended in AD 410, the Roman's bathing complex in Bath gradually fell into rack and ruin and was slowly consumed by mud.

The Saxons wrested control from the Celts in the year 577 and they built a Benedictine monastery on the site in 676. The Saxons did bathe amid the Roman ruins, however the monks might have shown little interest in the waters, for in the 6th century Saint Benedict, in response to the debauchery of the Roman baths, had told his order: "To those that are well, and especially to the young, bathing shall seldom be permitted."

Around the time Edgar, the first King of all England, was crowned in Bath in 973 a real interest in the upkeep of the baths appears to have caught on. The Saxon kings had "royal lodgings" near the Roman's Sacred Spring, where a small bath known as the Alron Bath was in use. Even the monks joined in, building a new bath over Roman remains where the Hot Bath now stands.

But large scale organised bathing in the city only really took off again with the arrival of the Normans and the appointment of John de Villula as Bishop of Bath and Wells in 1088. Bishop de Villula, who also built the now long-gone cathedral, was an enthusiastic physician and he prized the three springs for their healing powers. So, around 1106, in the grounds of the monastery and right on top of the Sacred Spring reservoir, he built what was then known as the "Bishop's Bath".

■ Admission to the Pump Room is free. A tour of the Roman Baths complex – which includes the Sacred Spring and King's Bath – costs £12 at the time of going to press

Queen's Bath

On the south side of the King's Bath, from 1576, stood the Queen's Bath. Half the size of and slightly cooler than the King's Bath, which fed it, it was originally used by the diseased poor, who were granted the right by a royal charter to travel to the city for free treatment.

It was originally known as the "New Bath". It was renamed the "Queen's Bath" after the visits of Anne of Denmark, James I's wife, in 1611 and 1615. The story goes that the Queen, who had come for a cure for her dropsy, was bathing in the King's Bath when she thought she saw a gout of flame spring from the 'sulphurous' water. It was probably an optical illusion yet she fled in terror to the New Bath next door, which was later renamed in her honour. She never bathed in the King's Bath again. To commemorate the royal drama, the newly christened Queen's Bath had a tower topped with a globe and crown built in its centre.

In 1678, travel writer Celia Fiennes journeyed to Bath and wrote in her journal:

The Queen's Bath is bigger than the other three but not nearly so big as the King's, which do run into each other and is only parted by a wall and at one place a great arch where they run into each other; the Queen's Bath is a degree hotter than the Cross Bath, and the King's Bath much hotter…

You can still see the arch in the King's Bath today.

In 1749, John Wood described the bath as being a "perfect square of four and twenty feet nine inches" that was "tolerably well screened from the wind and idle spectators". The water temperature was apparently more "agreeable" than that of the hotter King's.

In 1889, the Queen's Bath was demolished to make way for the enlargement of the "Private Baths", which had stood between the King's Bath and Stall Street since 1788. The Private Baths were extended as far as York Street (where the Roman Baths shop now stands) to include the "New Queen's Baths", which offered fashionable 'continental' douche and massage treatments. The new facilities were installed after a fact-finding tour of money-spinning European spas and were a big hit with visitors. Both the Private Baths and the New Queen's Bath were demolished in 1970 for the excavation of the Roman Circular Bath. Now the only reminder that the original Queen's Bath ever existed is the carved sign over the Roman Baths' Stall Street entrance.

In 1235, the new bath was renamed the King's Bath, probably after King John, who, soon after he ascended the throne in 1199, took a house in the monastery grounds close by. In 1256, Henry III visited the city and as a joke had one of his knights thrown into the King's Bath fully clothed. Such events only added to the city's growing fame as a place of healing.

Bathers in the King's Bath were soon sat in seats, being pickled up to their necks in the water. By 1578, a tower with a spire stood in the middle of the bath where the hot spring rose. This tower was fitted with recessed seats that were so hot to sit in it became known as the "Kitchen". By 1664 the King's Bath was advertising three different rooms where bathers would be protected from the elements. There were no changing rooms, though, just draughty passageways or "slips", where a sedan chair would wait to carry you to your lodgings – little wonder that not everyone bothered to take any clothes off. The whole scene – one of bedlam, according to a famous picture by Thomas Johnson of 1675 – was looked down on by the public from a balcony.

Various writers since have painted vivid descriptions of what it was like to bathe. John Leland, writing in 1530, noted that the water "reeketh like a seething pot continually, having somewhat a sulphurous and somewhat a pleasant flavour". Describing a King's Bath fitted out with 32 seats, in 1628, Dr Tobias Venner lavished praise on the facilities, declaring: "The King's Bath is the hottest, and it is for beauty, largeness, and efficacy of heat, a Kingly Bath indeed, being so hot as can be well suffered." In 1668, diarist Samuel Pepys noted that the bathers in the King's bath were "of a mixed sort, of good and bad" and that the Cross Bath (where he bathed) was by then reserved for the gentry. Before he left town, though, he observed a local tradition and "went to make a boy dive in the King's Bath" for a shilling. It's a tradition they should bring back!

These steps leading from the King's Bath once took you to the adjacent Queen's Bath

The Prior's and Abbot's Baths

Bishop John de Villula also built two other, smaller baths when he established the King's Bath around 1106. The "Abbot's Bath" and the "Prior's Bath" were sited somewhere close by east of the King's Bath, which fed them. Little else is known about them; they were probably just for the use of the monastery and its visitors. By 1536 they were no longer in use.

Commenting how the area around the "Kitchen" was scalding on the feet, in 1678 one Celia Fiennes wrote how the King's Bath water was "very hot and tastes like the water that boils eggs" and that the nearer the pump you drank it "the hotter and less offensive and more spirituous". She also mentions how, though the baths were emptied twice a day, scum was hosed off bathers less they got spots… Nice.

The unsavoury nature of the facilities was given the full treatment by Tobias Smollett in his 1771 satire *The Expedition of Humphry Clinker*, in which the not very brave Mathew Bramble is absolutely horrified by the King's Bath…

The first object that saluted my eye, was a child full of scrophulous ulcers, carried in the arms of one of the guides, under the very noses of the bathers. I was so shocked at the sight that I retired immediately with indignation and disgust. Suppose the matter of those ulcers, floating on the water, comes in contact with my skin, when the pores are all open, I would ask you what must be the consequence? Good Heaven, the very thought makes my blood run cold.

For John Wood, who arrived in Bath in 1725, the bath was a disgrace, and its slips like "cells for the dead… cold stone, and eternally sweating with the steam of the baths, dark as dungeons…"

It was high time, thought the Georgians, that the bath was made more salubrious and civilised and so in 1780 it was rebuilt by Thomas Baldwin. It was not until the late 1870s – just before Major Charles Davis rebuilt the King's Bath in its present form – that it was discovered that the bath was sitting right on top of the Roman's Sacred Spring reservoir. The reservoir was properly excavated in 1979.

On the south side once stood the Queen's Bath. Demolished in 1889 to make room for the (now also demolished) New Queen's Baths, it was fed by the overflow from the King's and was slightly cooler. The statue of King Bladud in the niche has been there since 1699, according to the inscription. It is thought to be older than that, though, and it may have originally have guarded the city's North Gate.

The 17th century stone seat on the south side is the Master of the Baths' chair – from where strict order was kept over the bathers. John Wood wrote of seeing one

■ This statue of King Bladud, mythical discoverer of Bath, is dated 1699 but many believe it to be earlier

■ The stone seat from where the Master of the Baths would keep order

"certain gentleman…hurled over the rails into the water" for merely commenting on the beauty of his own wife.

Regular bathing in the King's Bath ended, alas, in 1939, so there will be no more hurling, parboiling or anything else in it. We can but imagine the many bizarre scenes it has witnessed in its 900-odd eventful years.

■ **Changing areas called "slips" led to steps down into the water…**

How To Enjoy A Typical Day In Georgian Bath

In Georgian times, important visitors to Bath would sometimes be met by the Master of Ceremonies himself, and, if you were very aristocratic indeed, muffled bells and a band would also greet your arrival. Once you were safely lodged and had been subscribed to the Baths, coffee houses and walks (you had to pay to use some exclusive paths), a typical day for some holidaying toff was, we imagine, a bit like this…

- Breakfast
- Quick trip to the Baths, just long enough to get jostled and to pay a boy to jump in for you
- Call for your chair and get taken home for a cup of tea and a bite to eat
- Off to the Pump Room for a pose, a chat with the 'Company' and a quick glass of the foul stuff
- Lunch
- Off to your coffee house (there were separate coffee houses for men and women), where you could maybe read the papers, rubbish the French and play cards
- Afternoon idle, maybe taking in a walk or a ride by horse or carriage
- More food and drink
- A tedious ball (and a game of cards if you can slip away to a side room)
- Eleven o'clock and home to bed – or to some other assignation

It sounds rather dull (especially for children) – a bit like a posh Butlins, really, and very much up its own Union Passage. But Oliver Goldsmith assures us that his and Beau Nash's Bath "yields a continued rotation of diversions", and that "people of all ways of thinking, even from the libertine to the methodist, have it in their power to complete the day with employments suited to their diversions."

3 Bath Abbey

There have been not one but three great churches on this site. In fact, this one's rather small…

The last great medieval church built in England, the "Lantern of the West" has 52 windows covering about 80 per cent of its wall space

The Saxon king Osric founded a convent in Bath in 675. This later became a monastery that King Offa of Mercia took control of, adding an Abbey Church in 781. It became very important religious centre and Edgar the first King of all England was crowned in Bath in 973 at what his brother Eadwig called the "marvellously built" church.

After the Norman conquest of 1066, the church was swiftly promoted to cathedral status. In 1090, John of Tours became the first ever Bishop of Bath and Wells by transferring his seat of power from Wells to the wealthy Bath Abbey. He immediately began work on a massive new cathedral dedicated to Saints Peter and Paul – and set about transforming the baths. After the half-finished cathedral was gutted by fire in 1137, it was finally finished about twenty years later. About 330 foot (100 metres) long and stretching as far as what is now Parade Gardens, the current Abbey would stand in its nave. The paved area south of the Abbey, known as Kingston Parade, covers part of its cloisters.

By the end of the 15th century the cathedral was in ruins. The present Abbey church was founded in 1499 by Bishop of Bath and Wells Oliver King. The building was funded by the monastery, whose laxness King blamed for the state of the cathedral. King, though, died before his smaller church was finished – just a few years before Henry VIII's Dissolution of the Monasteries in 1536… The new church was immediately stripped of its lead, iron and glass and left roofless to decay.

After her visit to Bath of 1573, Elizabeth I ordered a nationwide collection to raise funds to repair the damage done by her father and the result is the extremely grand parish church you can see today. St Peter and St Paul flank its great oak doors – the statue above guarding them, ironically, Henry VIII.

There are many things to look for within – the East Window, the magnificent vaulted ceiling, the remains of the previous Norman Cathedral, the plaques honouring the lives of Beau Nash, Isaac Pitman (the inventor of shorthand) and Bishop James Montague (who finally got the Abbey's roof mended), and not least, the window commemorating the crowning in 973AD of Edgar.

The ten bells of the Abbey Tower (which you can

The west doors bear the Montague family arms in tribute to Bishop James Montague, who re-roofed the Abbey before his death in 1617. He is buried within. The Latin inscription reads: "Behold how good and pleasing it is."

The olive trees, crowns and mitres either side of the West Doors supposedly remember Bishop Oliver King's legendary dream inspiring him to replace the crumbling Norman cathedral

Scareway To Heaven

The angels climbing Jacob's Ladder on the west front of the Abbey have not been loved by everyone. When he was four, the historical novelist Sir Walter "Ivanhoe" Scott was sent to Bath in 1775 for a water cure for his polio. He later wrote: "No ancient iconoclast or modern Calvinist could have looked on the outside of the Church with more horror than the image of Jacob's Ladder presented to my infant eye…"

Oliver King: A Man Of Vision

In 1496, the new and very devout Bishop of Bath and Wells, Oliver King, was horrified to find the cathedral in ruins through neglect and the monks feasting or idle (when they weren't cavorting with women).

Then in 1499 the good Bishop supposedly had a vision in which he saw angels climb up and down ladders to Heaven and heard voices crying: "Let an Olive restore the Crown, and let a King restore the Church!" He took this to mean that he should build the present Abbey. The images of angels on ladders and olive trees encircled with crowns with a mitre over them were carved upon the Church's west front to commemorate King's dream.

It's more likely, though, that the dream was made up by the Elizabethans to explain the carvings, which actually just signified the good bishop's mission to speed souls on their way from Purgatory to Paradise.

Sorry Sermons

The great diarist Samuel Pepys visited Bath in 1668. He apparently enjoyed walking Bath's "many good streets" but was rather less impressed by his experience of the Abbey. There a "vain pragmatical fellow preached a ridiculous affected sermon that made me angry," he complained. Unwisely, perhaps, he went back that same evening for more: "I slept…"

Houses Of God?

The magnificent Abbey used to have houses stuck to its flanks. Indeed, there were buildings attached to its north and south sides as late as 1750. It hardly seems fitting, but at least it wasn't far to walk home after a late service…

Angels climb the ladder to Paradise

Roof With A View

In 1603, Sir John Harington – poet, courtier, "saucy Godson" of Elizabeth I, and a champion of the neglected church, is supposed to have lured the Bishop of Bath and Wells, James Montague, into the Abbey nave, on the pretext of sheltering from a shower...

"Sir John," observed the Bishop after some time, "we are still in the rain."

"How can that be," artfully answered Sir John, looking about him, "seeing that we are within the church?"

"True, Sir John, but your church is unroofed," replied the Bishop.

"The more is the pity," Sir John nimbly replied, "and the more doth it call for the munificence of your Lordship…"

Montague is swayed by this clever plea, and fronts much of the money needed for a new roof.

inspect on a tour) were the gift of a Lady Hopton. On the great tenor bell – which was recast in 1870 and which weighs as much as a small car – is the same inscription you could read on the original 1700 bell: "All you of Bathe that heare me sound Thank Lady Hopton's Hundered Pound…" There were few thanks, though, but rather a chorus of complaints, and the tower was eventually shuttered to muffle the apparently infernal racket.

■ **King Henry VIII – who pillaged the Abbey – stands guard above the great doors**

OLD BATHONIANS

MARY & PERCY SHELLEY

(1797-1851 & 1792-1822)

5 ABBEY CHURCHYARD

Mary and Percy Shelley stayed at 5 Abbey Churchyard in 1816.

The original three-story building is now gone though, demolished in the 19th century to make way for the extension of the pump room. During this time, Mary Shelley began writing *Frankenstein*, Fanny Imray (Mary's half sister) committed suicide, and distraught that Shelly had left her for Mary, Shelley's first wife, Harriet Westbrook, drowned herself in Hyde Park's Serpentine. Lord Byron's estranged lover Claire Clairmont gave birth to their daughter Allegra at New Bond Street in Bath.

FIELD-MARSHAL GEORGE WADE

(1694-1773)

14 ABBEY CHURCHYARD

A popular MP for Bath and a road-building soldier, Wade blotted his copybook by failing to stop the Scots using the roads he had so helpfully built to invade in 1745. A supporter of Ralph Allen, who married his illegitimate daughter, he also famously gave a hundred pounds to a down-on-his luck Bath private who was caught making off with a chicken from a banquet.

4 Thermae Bath Spa

This way for a dip in the hot water… You're in good company – they've been doing it here for 2,000 years!

The New Royal Bath's fantastic open-air rooftop pool boasts a great view of the city

Before we go and rent a towel from the glossy receptionists at the Thermae Bath Spa complex, we'd like to quickly remind you of the mythical origins of Bath's reputation as a leading spa town.

In Bath in 860 BC Prince Bladud (some say the father of King Lear, and later to become the first King of England) catches leprosy. As a result, he's banned from the court and forced to take a lowly job tending the town's pigs. Bladud notices that the pigs show similar symptoms to his own. But after they wallow in the warm mud moistened by the water that gushes from a nearby spring, they are completely cured. Bladud follows their example and voila! Bye bye leprosy, hello Spa town…

Now this little tale may well, of course, be nothing

more than tittle-tattle legend, especially as the same sources would have you believe that, using powers harnessed from the dead, Bladud later grew wings and flew… but around 200 years later (circa AD43), the rollickin' Romans discovered Bath for themselves. Coming across what turned out to be the warmest natural geothermal mineral springs found in the UK, they swiftly built a temple dedicated to both Celtic god Sul, and Minerva, the Roman goddess of healing – and the spa town hotspot originally known as Aquae Sulis was established.

Since then, Bath's natural spring waters have been largely responsible for the prominence of the city on the UK map. However the old municipal hot pools were closed in 1978. A spa town with no spa? That can't be right. So, a couple of decades later, cash from the National Lottery-funded Millennium Commission was made available to fund a major project to create a commercial, contemporary spa at the heart of a city that existed as a spa in name only (nobody's been allowed to take a dip in the pools within the Roman Baths complex itself for years). With the coffers supplemented by local authority funding, the scheme was originally planned to open in 2002 but – despite a grand,

■ Also responsible for the domes of the Eden Project in Cornwall, Grimshaw Architects designed the award-winning Thermae Bath Spa

Austen Watch

In Jane Austen's time the rich and fashionable went to the Cross Bath while less fortunate people used the Hot Bath. In *Persuasion*, poor, widowed Mrs Smith lives nearby in Westgate Buildings, in the unfashionable lower part of Bath, where it is easy for her to get to the Hot bath for treatment for the rheumatic fever in her legs. We know that Jane's brother Edward bathed in the Hot Bath too.

The Leper's Bath

Around 1576 the small "Leper's Bath" was stuck onto the west side of the Hot Bath, fed by the Hot Bath's overflow. A special Leper's Hospital was also built beside the bath by John de Feckenham, a former Abbot of Westminster.

Before this, from around 1100, there was a leper house in Bath, but this was on the outskirts of the city, safely across the river. Leprosy had almost completely died out in this country by the 16th century, but Bath's waters drew in those sufferers that remained. A separate bath was the safest way of treating them, according to Dr William Turner's 1562 treatise on the waters.

Triangular in shape and draughty, John Wood described the bath as "mean, obscure and small" and "the place of resource [of] the most miserable objects that seek relief from the healing fountains". The hospital he called a "hovel". Nevertheless, many people were also successfully treated at the bath for conditions like scabies and psoriasis before it was demolished in 1773, along with the hospital and the medieval Hot Bath, to make way for John Wood the Younger's new Hot Bath.

Mmm. The Cross Bath sounds an awful lot nicer…

formal opening gig courtesy of The Three Tenors in 2003 – the project was beleaguered with legal disputes, ending up seriously behind schedule, while costs spiralled from an estimated £13 million in September 1996 to a final cost of £45 million when the Thermae Bath Spa finally opened its doors in 2006. Many Bath residents blamed the hullabaloo for an increase in local tax, while the actual look of the building itself (basically a huge glass cube designed by prominent 'modernist' architect Sir Nicholas Grimshaw) has proved to be an ongoing controversial talking point. But whether you're a long-term Bath resident or a day-tripper in search of a bit of pampering, you can't really join the debate until you've taken to the waters.

Today the Thermae Bath Spa combines several pools (including a magnificent rooftop pool – surely the icing on the cake) with various steam rooms, waterfall showers, treatment rooms and a restaurant. Impressive though the

The Hetling Pump House is now the home of the Spa Visitor Centre

Austen Watch

Jane Austen's uncle, James Leigh Perrot, and also her brother Edward drank the water at the Hetling Pump Room – James twice a day regularly and Edward for his suspected gout. Jane wrote of her brother in a letter to her sister Cassandra in May 1799:

He drinks at the Hetling Pump, is to bathe to-morrow, and try electricity on Tuesday. He proposed the latter himself to Dr. Fellowes, who made no objection to it, but I fancy we are all unanimous in expecting no advantage from it…

Clearly, though, the water did him no harm. A month later, she wrote:

Edward has been pretty well for this last week, and as the waters have never disagreed with him in any respect, we are inclined to hope that he will derive advantage from them in the end. Everybody encourages us in this expectation, for they all say that the effect of the waters cannot be negative, and many are the instances in which their benefit is felt afterwards more than on the spot…

Hetling Pump House

The Grand Pump Room by the Abbey was not the only place in Georgian Bath where you could take the waters. In 1772, the City Corporation bought wine merchant William Hetling's 'Hetling Guest House' and turned it into the Hetling Pump House, which served water from the Hot Bath.

By 1875 fewer people were taking the waters and the pump room closed. It is now the Thermae Bath Spa Visitor centre.

Troubled Waters

The building of Thermae Bath Spa was dogged by setbacks and controversy. After what *Private Eye* magazine called a "saga of delays and cock-ups", it finally opened in 2006 – five years late and, with a price tag of £45 million, nearly two and a half times over budget. And the row about who was to blame was very public indeed. In 2004, after a heated argument on BBC TV's *Breakfast Time*, presenter Dermot Murnaghan suggested that then MP Dan Norris and Bath council chief Paul Crossley should both take a 'cold' bath…

complex is (and it is, albeit in a rather sterile, state-of-the-art way), detractors accuse the overall experience of being a bit too 'municipal swimming pool' in ambience – tiny changing rooms and the need to share the space with far, far too many people for comfort at peak times all support such indictments.

On the plus side, if you're in the mood for a bit of pampering, you've definitely come to the right place. Signature treatments delivered by experts in the field include the stress-relieving Watsu massage, the Tropical Salt Mousse Glow and the Kraxen Stove experience from a menu that runs to dozens of enticing options. Be warned, though: such supplementary treatments don't come cheap, and aren't included in the basic admission price (2 hours/£26; 4 hours/£36; full day £56, at the time of going to press). Fancy a budget-friendly quick fix instead? Pop into the Cross Bath – an ancient, standalone facility with its own open-air thermal bath – for an hour (£7.50) and experience instant nirvana [see more below].

The main entrance of the New Royal Bath

Bedlam At The Baths

The behaviour in Bath's baths has been, well, "boisterous" at times down the years and the authorities faced a long battle to banish nakedness, lewdness – and animals. It was a battle, though, that would eventually be won.

In 1449 the custom of bathing naked was officially forbidden by the Bishop of Bath and Wells Thomas Beckington, who was shocked to discover that when bathers "through modesty and shame try to cover their privy parts" other bathers "barbarously and shamelessly strip them and reveal them to the gaze of bystanders". In 1664 animals were also banned from the baths (there was a Horse Bath available from 1598, after all).

Despite the threat of Hell, damnation and fines, these rules took a while to catch on. A writer in the *Guardian* in 1713 noted that "the physicians were not more busy in destroying old bodies than the young fellows in producing new ones", and around the same time, John Wood, Bath's apparently prudish great architect, was aghast at what he saw at the baths…

The baths were like so many bear-gardens, and modesty was entirely shut out of them; people of both sexes bathing by day and night naked; and dogs, cats, and pigs, even human creatures, were hurled over the rails into the water, while people were bathing in it…

But times were changing and by the mid 18th century Dr Johnson was exercising his famous diction by complaining that nakedness in the baths at Bath was "an instance of barbarity unparalleled in any part of this world".

The notion spread and by the turn of the century the baths had become somewhat more genteel places. Jane Austen was probably never forced to endure seeing a bare bottom or a dog hurled in, alas…

THE HOT BATH

ONCE IT WOULD "SCALD THE FLESH", BUT DIDN'T HAVE A JET, WHIRLPOOL NOR 'LAZY RIVER'...

■ A small Roman bath stood very close to this spot

✻The present day Hot Bath uses water from all three of Bath's hot springs, but previous baths on the site drew water from just the nearby Hetling Spring, the hottest of the springs.

The Romans built an extensive bath and temple complex just south of the Hetling spring, but only fragments of that have ever been found.

In the 11th century, a new bath was built over the ruins of the Roman one. It was named Alsi's Bath after its builder Abbot Aelfsige, the last Saxon abbot of Bath. (Aelfsige, who died in 1087, was succeeded by the Norman bishop John de Villula, builder of the cathedral and the King's Bath.)

Because of its warm temperature, after the 14th century the bath became known as the "Hot Bath". According to traveller John Leland, writing in 1530, the bath would "scald the flesh on first coming into it". In 1678, Celia Feinnes described the bath as being "but small, and built all around, which makes it the hotter".

It was not the most popular bath, but the eminent Bath physician Dr Tobias Venner was a keen admirer, declaring it "convenient for cold moist and diseases". Venner rented rooms near the Hot Bath and built up a large practice treating both rich and poor patients. He was made honorary physician to Bellott's hospital in 1652 at the age of 75, becoming the first doctor to hold a hospital position in Bath.

Joseph Gilmore's map of Bath of 1694 shows the Hot Bath, like the Queen's Bath, as having a tower in its centre, a tower that John Wood described as appearing to be "floating in the middle of the water"... It sounds like an eerie place.

The medieval Hot Bath stood in front of the present Hot Bath's site, in the middle of what is now Bath Street. It was demolished (along with the adjoining Leper's Bath) and rebuilt for the City Corporation in 1777 by John Wood the Younger. This was in response to the building of the swish, private Duke of Kingston's Bath just south of the Abbey. The new-look new Hot Bath's octagonal pool had entrances on all four of its sides, each of which led to a pair of changing rooms with discrete stairs (or 'slips') going down into the small pool. The west side of the building also had a "pauper's pump" which was free for the use of the public.

The Hot Bath had another facelift in 1829 when the "Tepid Pool" – Bath's first 'spa swimming pool' – was included behind it and the whole complex was christened the "Royal Baths". The Tepid Bath was demolished in 1923 to make way for the Beau Street Bath, which remained in use until the meningitis scare of 1978, which closed all of the city's spa facilities.

The Hot Bath received a new lease of life in 2006 when it was incorporated into the Thermae Bath Spa development. The Beau Street Swimming Bath was demolished to make way for the "New Royal Bath".

TAKING THE CURE

IF YOU HAVE PALSY, FEAR NOT – YOU'VE COME TO JUST THE RIGHT PLACE!

Since Roman times Bath's naturally occurring hot water has been revered for its healing properties. The Romans themselves thought hot spring water good for gout, rheumatism and skin disease. Since then a dip in the waters has been recommended for just about every illness going.

A separate Leper's Bath was deemed the safest way of treating the country's few remaining lepers. Leprosy had almost died out in his country by Elizabethan times, but many people were also treated at this time for conditions like scabies and psoriasis – and with some success.

Another condition effectively treated was the paralysis-inducing palsy. How? Palsy, it is now known, was caused by lead poisoning – and it has also since been discovered that prolonged immersion in water speeds up the rate at which the body can get rid of lead…

After John Jones' 1572 treatise *The Bathes of Bathe's Ayde*, which suggested you should actually drink the stuff, the fashion for "taking the waters" caught on. The rich and the famous would visit the city with their own doctors in their retinue. On arrival, other visitors would be beset with offers of lodgings and even personal physicians. The healing waters had become big business.

William Oliver, the 18th Century doctor and inventor of the Oliver Biscuit, weighed in by declaring that the water contained an "aetherial essence which cannot be contained in bottles as it will pass through the corks". It was a theory that was good for Bath business. If patients had to actually *visit* the city they could be relieved of their money…

Tobias Smollett, witty novelist, failed doctor and author of *An Essay on the External Use of Waters*, was often bitterly critical of Bath medical men (partly, it has to be said, because his own medical reputation wasn't exactly respected in the city). His 1751 novel *Peregrine Pickle* jealously, but perhaps not whole inaccurately, attacked Bath's doctors as "so many ravens hovering round a carcass".

For a brief period in the early 20th century Bath's spa water was even being advertised for its slightly (and completely safe, by the way) radioactive properties. A "Radon Inhalatorium" room was added to the New Queen's Bath and one Bath baker even offered "radium bread".

But this was a brief fad. Even by the second half of the preceding century the waters were being used for physical applications rather than for their ingredients, showing the way for the future. Immersion up to the neck, mud, sprays, douches and massages were the doctors' orders of the day. Soon the bathing complexes were jammed with machines that could provide jets of water and even electric currents.

Injured service men and women were sent to Bath for rehabilitation after The First and Second World Wars, and between 1948 and 1976 Bath water-cure treatments were available on prescription through the new National Health Service. Buoyancy and heat therapies were used to help joint and muscle mobility. Children with polio were also treated during the 1950s at the Old Royal Bath.

Today, musculo-skeletal pain, arthritis and sports injuries are among the many ills given spa treatment. And if you want to drink the water, do. It contains over 42 minerals and trace elements, and won't do you any harm!

Water… Bath's fortunes are built on it

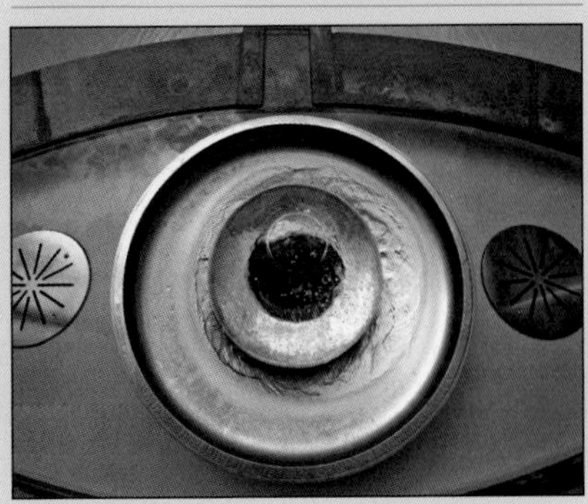

THE CROSS BATH

WELCOME TO THE "DAINTY BATH FOR YOUNG, WEAK, AND TENDER BODIES"...

■ **Lewdness in the Cross Bath is less common today**

The Cross Bath, which has undergone many facelifts during its colourful history, is fed by the coolest of Bath's three hot springs, the Cross Spring.

The Celts first built a shrine at the Cross Spring and then the Romans built a well here. It is not clear exactly clear when the first Cross Bath was built, but a "Bath of the Cross" was in use by the time Bishop Reginald Fitz Jocelyn's St John's Hospital (behind the Cross Bath) was founded in 1180. It may well have been specially built for the hospital.

In 1533, traveller John Leland observed the cross, stone arches and commented that the bath was "much frequentid of people diseased with lepre, pokkes, scabbes, and great aches, and is temperate and pleasant".

Just after Leland's visit the Cross Bath fell into disrepair, but in the 1590s it was restored and a new central cross with built-in seats was erected at its centre. For eminent Bath physician Tobias Venner, writing in 1628, the Cross Bath was very good for certain ailments:

It is a dainty bath for young, weak, and tender bodies, that cannot endure the heat of the hotter baths, or for whom the hotter baths may not be convenient... This bath, by reason off the mildness of its heat, is of a notable, mollifying, and relaxing faculty; good, therefore, in contractions of any member, in obstructions of the breast, spleen, liver, and kidneys; and effectual also for aches...

Just before Georgian times the Cross Bath was the most exclusive (you had to pay top penny) of all the baths. It was the one used by royalty, music was played from a gallery – and everyone got cups of hot chocolate.

Steaminess in the Cross Bath...

Daniel Defoe's *Tour Thro' the Whole Island of Great Britain* gives us a steamy impression of what it was like to be a Cross Bath bather in 1724:

The whole time indeed is a round of the utmost diversion. In the morning you (supposing you to be a young lady) are fetch'd in a close chair, dress'd in your bathing cloths, that is, stript to the smock, to the Cross-Bath. There the musick plays you into the bath, and the women that tend you, present you with a little floating wooden dish, like a bason; in which the lady puts a handkerchief, and a nosegay, of late the snuff-box is added, and some patches; tho' the bath occasioning a little perspiration, the patches do not stick so kindly as they should.

Here the ladies and the gentlemen pretend to keep some distance, and each to their proper side, but frequently mingle here too, as in the King and Queens Bath, tho' not so often; and the place being but narrow, they converse freely, and talk, rally, make vows, and sometimes love; and having thus amus'd themselves an hour, or two, they call their chairs and return to their lodgings...

Samuel Pepys described in his diary in 1668 how he saw "very fine ladies" at the Cross Bath. He did doubt, though, the cleanliness of "so many bodies together in the same water", adding that those who spent the whole season in the waters "cannot but be parboiled, and look like the creatures of the bath…" Despite his misgivings, he allowed himself two hours in the water before being "carried away wrapped in a sheet, and in a chair home".

In 1687, Celia Fiennes described the bath's central cross with its "seats around it for gentlemen to sit", adding that "round the walls are arches with seats for the ladies". She also noted that the bath was "much the coolest and is used mostly in the heat of summer". Sounds rather nice, doesn't it?

That same year, in 1687, the bath was the scene of a famous, or infamous, 'miracle'... James II's wife, Mary of Modena, found herself pregnant with a Catholic heir after bathing in the waters. Whether it was a miracle or just plain adultery (the King hadn't hung around long enough to so much as wet his beak), the event sparked a Protestant uprising. A much decorated new cross at the bath – built at huge cost by the Catholic Lord Meltfort – was eventually attacked by a mob of Protestants, and as a result of the pregnancy James Stuart, would spend his life in exile in France as The Old Pretender. A cherub that belonged to the vandalised "Meltfort Cross" can now be seen looking up Milsom Street from a niche at the end of No 5 New Bond Street (now Mallory the jewellers).

In Beau Nash's day the bath was still very much for the gentry, very much the bath to cavort in and be seen in rather than get better in. Strict order was meant to be kept, mind, by a Sergeant of the Baths, and the sexes were supposed to be segregated, but according to Ned Ward in 1700, "wanton dalliances" could not be stopped in this bath "more famed for its pleasures than its cures".

He's now to be found at the bottom of Milsom Street

Stricter times came, alas. By the time the Cross Bath was rebuilt in 1784 by Thomas Baldwin, and once more in 1798 by John Palmer, it was a much duller and more gentrified place.

The Cross Bath remained open right up until the meningitis scare of 1978. Now tastefully restored, today it is enjoying a new lease of life as part of the Thermae Bath Spa.

Demand hot chocolate! And tell them you want to be serenaded by musicians.

Dalliances are up to you.

Duck trouble

❋ "Beatrice" the mallard duck hit international headlines in April 1999 when she held up the hugely expensive renovation of the Cross Bath at the top of Bath Street. The bath had been closed and left to crumble since the 1970s and in 1998 Beatrice and her drake "Arthur" decided that the natural jacuzzi was the ideal place in which to hatch a clutch. The following year they returned to the site and built a new nest – only to find the City Council moving in to tear the place apart. Netting was the first idea the Council came up with to scare off the innocent ducks. But Beatrice and Arthur would not so easily be kept out of their centrally heated love nest: eyewitnesses saw the pair of them bouncing up and down on the evil roof until they'd made a hole big enough to squeeze through. But even plucky Beatrice might have eventually succumbed under the onslaught of a City Council army of men in yellow hats had not wildlife campaigners intervened and pointed out that the removal of or deliberate interference with her nest contravened the Wildlife and Countryside Act of 1981. In a fairly happy ending, Slimbridge Wetlands and Wildfowl Trust in Gloucestershire hatched Beatrice's family, which was then placed with a foster duck.

ENJOYING THERMAE BATH SPA ROMAN-STYLE: DOS & DON'TS

A DAY GETTING WET AND PAMPERED IS GREAT AND AS YOU'RE IN AQUAE SULIS, WHY NOT DON A TOGA AND DEMAND TO DO IT ROMAN-STYLE?

✖ **Don't... worry about the entrance fee.** Walk loftily through the entrance lobby, perhaps tossing the slaves (sorry – staff) a few coppers with a curt nod. If anyone protests, explain to them that baths were dirt cheap for the Romans, who wanted to *encourage* the public to bathe. Tell them that baths are at the centre of your society, a vital bit of social glue. You are expecting to rub shoulders (and perhaps other bits) with people from all walks of life, from generals to shopkeepers to prostitutes. This is the place where, as an ambitious social climber, you are hoping to meet some of the more influential folk of the world and do your career a bit of good (and get a ticket out of rainy Britain).

✔ **Do... demand all mod cons.** As a Roman citizen on holiday in Aquae Sulis, you can expect the very latest in spa treatments and bathroom design. Demand that the slaves lead you through the following rooms in turn:

Tepidarium – a warm room where you will be massaged with scented oil; laconicum – a hot, dry sauna; caldarium – a really hot room with a warm plunge pool, where you will have the filth scraped off you with a curved metal instrument called a strigil; frigidarium – a cold plunge pool, where you will finish your ablutions.

All your water must be filtered, of course, and the baths should be colourfully painted – and have lovely mosaic floors (ideally depicting things like dolphins and sea monsters).

Be sure to point out any lacks in the new Spa's offerings – but remember too that a big *heated* swimming pool (natatio) is a rare treat indeed, even for a Roman. Water doesn't normally heat itself, you know!

✔ **Do... eat well.** Demand to be able to buy food. At the very least, fruit, sausages, oysters and roasted dormice should all be on the menu.

✖ **Don't... arrive at the baths without your bathing kit.**
If you're a patrician (a Roman aristocrat), you needn't worry about this. Your private slave will bring all your bathing implements, which will include such things as brushes, a scented oil flask, a flat dish for scooping water and, of course, a strigil. All of these things will be attached to a ring for easy carrying. If you're poor, you can get away with flour of lentils in lieu of oil – and you can get a mate to scrape your back.

✔ **Do get the full treatment** If you are a gentleman, demand that your armpits, back, chest and genitals are stripped of hair by expert pluckers (try saying that after a glug of Roman wine). Your slave can then give you a massage and then – once you've got a proper sweat on – get to work on your oiled body with the strigil. If you are delicate you may eschew the strigil and opt instead for a sponge.

If all this sounds rather lovely but a bit time consuming, here's the secret – you only go through it all once every nine days...

✖ **Don't... forget the other half.** Emperors Hadrian and Marcus Aurelius tried to ban mixed bathing. Officially, not even husbands and wives were allowed to go the baths together – women went in the mornings, and men in the afternoon. But not to worry – the rule was widely flouted anyway.

■ What would the Roman's have made of all this space-age splendour...

✔ **Do... enjoy yourself in the pool.**
You are perfectly within your rights to get drunk, break into song and then plunge naked into the steaming waters. Wrestling, writhing, fornication and philosophising are positively encouraged. Think of the spa as a sort of debauched leisure centre. After all, as the old Roman graffiti joke goes: "Baths, drink and sex corrupt our bodies, but baths, drink and sex make life worth living." However, if you are backward when it comes to being forward, you can stick to complaining about the British weather and rubbishing the chances of the barbarians hordes against the Western Empire. You are welcome to play board games and also ball games. Trigon (catch with three balls), anyone?

✖ **Do not, whatever you do... steal anything!**
About 130 "curse tablets" have been found at Aquae Sulis – and many of them relate to thefts from bathers... These texts, invoking help from gods like Minerva, were typically scratched on thin sheets of lead in tiny letters, which were then rolled or folded and tossed into the Sacred Spring or nailed somewhere close by. The really powerful curses were written backwards, like one Basilica's, which demands that whoever stole her silver ring – or who merely knew something but wasn't telling – should be "cursed in their blood, eyes and every limb – and have all intestines eaten away". Nice. So if you're left alone in the apodyterium (changing room), leave that towel alone!

✔ **Do... hit the town afterwards.**
You're feeling great, if a little red. You've been steamed, stewed, plucked and scraped, you've had your various fancies ticked during something approaching an orgy. You've even been to the temple! So it's time to hit town, Roman style.

Aquae Sulis is, remember, a famous Roman leisure resort, so you should avail yourself of all its delights. There are other bathhouses to visit, taverns, shops and a theatre to enjoy, so enjoy! You're on holiday!

✔ **Do say...** Pass me the strigil!

✖ **Don't say...** Oooh, saucy! Mind what you're doing with that sponge!

5 The Pump Room

They've been "taking the waters" in this grand building since the end of the 18th century. Join them...

■ The dining room, where a range of meals is served daily (including a pretty great breakfast) under the watchful gaze of a bust of Beau Nash

Before the 18th century you could only drink the waters from pumps in the baths, but in 1706 the first 'Pump Room' was built and it swiftly became the beating heart of Georgian Bath.

Part of the daily social routine, the Pump Room was where the great and the not so great came to 'take the cure', mingle, gossip, plot, court, and complain about their gout. Any ill folk would be armed with the latest advice from a doctor, new arrivals in the city would be introduced to the 'Company' by the Master of Ceremonies – and all the while nothing short of a social revolution was taking place because people of different classes were socialising with one another.

This social revolution was helped by rules set down – a sort of a code of urban manners – by Beau Nash, Bath's most famous Master of Ceremonies. It was also a revolution that Tobias Smollett mocked mercilessly in his 1771 novel *The Expedition of Humphry Clinker*…

Yesterday morning, at the Pump-room, I saw a broken-winded Wapping landlady squeeze through a circle of peers to salute her brandy-merchant, who stood by the window, propped upon crutches; and a paralytic attorney of Shoe-lane, in shuffling up to the bar, kicked the shins of the

The Pump Room's imposing façade

Austen Watch

In Jane Austen's day, new arrivals in the city would sign a Subscription Book kept in the Pump Room. Having your name in the book meant that you could subscribe, for a fee, to events in the Pump Room and the Assembly Rooms and to libraries and bookshops. It meant that your name would be published in the local press and that the Master of Ceremonies would call on you.

Jane's descriptions of the Pump Room make it sound extremely busy – unpleasantly so – as in the scene in Northanger Abbey when Catherine searches in vain for Tilney…

Every creature in Bath, except himself, was to be seen in the room at different periods of the fashionable hours; crowds of people were every moment passing in and out, up the steps and down; people whom nobody cared about, and nobody wanted to see; and he only was absent…

Later the Pump Room's crowd is described as "insupportable" and eventually Catherine decides it is simply "odious" to parade about the place.

Full Bodied Water?

Georgian doctor-turned-author Tobias Smollett gleefully poured cold water on the reputation of the Pump Room. In his novel *The Expedition of Humphry Clinker*, Mathew Bramble is far from convinced that the water is fit to drink at all…

I am now as much afraid of drinking, as of bathing; for after a long conversation with the Doctor about the construction of the pump and the cistern, it is very far from being clear with me that the patients in the Pump-room don't swallow the scourings of the bathers.

I can't help suspecting that there is, or may be, some regurgitation from the bath into the cistern of the pump. In that case, what a delicate beverage is every day quaffed by the drinkers; medicated with the sweat and dirt, and dandruff; and the abominable discharges of various kinds, from twenty different diseased bodies, parboiling in the kettle below.

And there are even worse tidings for Mathew to come…

Upon inquiry, I find that the Roman baths in this quarter, were found covered by an old burying ground, belonging to the Abbey; through which, in all probability, the water drains in its passage; so that as we drink the decoction of living bodies at the Pump-room, we swallow the strainings of rotten bones and carcasses…

You may rest assured, however, that there are neither bones nor carcasses in today's Pump Room water. Though admittedly it does taste like there could be…

chancellor of England, while his lordship, in a cut bob, drank a glass of water at the pump…

The original Pump Room of Beau Nash, built in 1706 by John Harvey, is now gone. The rebuilding of the present-day Pump Room was begun in 1789 by the fiscally uncompromising Thomas Baldwin, who was sacked by the Corporation in 1792 when he refused to let them see his books. The interior was then finished in 1799 by John Palmer.

A great bust of Beau Nash stands at one end of today's main Room, surveying everything with an imperious eye. He's only made of stone, yet you get the feeling you wouldn't get away with much if you started misbehaving. Indeed, you feel slightly uncomfortable if you're wearing jeans. ("Why, Sir," you almost hear his admonishing voice, "your trousers look like so many bags of grain!" et cetera.)

You can still sample the (completely safe!) waters in the Pump Room, of course. And if it tastes that bad it must be good for you. Of course one shouldn't wonder that rainwater cooked in the bowels of the Earth for 10,000 years and served still warm should be rank. Enjoy!

The Pump Room Fountain, from which you are served warm and, to be honest, foul tasting and smelling water. The fountain looks ancient but was in fact made in 1985

The entrance hall was built in 1897, originally as a concert hall extension to the Pump Room. The domed ceiling is decorated with images of the four seasons

What The Dickens?

In Dicken's *The Pickwick Papers* Sam Weller famously describes the Pump Room's waters as "particklery unpleasant," with "a wery strong flavor o' warm flatirons". Mr Pickwick drinks the water "systematically" – though his friends don't know why…

He drank a quarter of a pint before breakfast, and then walked up a hill; and another quarter of a pint after breakfast, and then walked down a hill; and after every fresh quarter of a pint, Mr Pickwick declared, in the most solemn and emphatic terms, that he felt a great deal better, whereat his friends were very much delighted, though they had not been previously aware that there was anything the matter with him.

OLD BATHONIAN

RICHARD BEAU NASH

(1674-1761)

Beau Nash in his trademark black wig and white hat

The son of a moderately successful bottle maker from Swansea, Nash had unsuccessful careers as a student at Jesus College, Oxford, an army officer and a lawyer before he came to Bath. A great wit, adept social organiser and a gambler, he was born for the role of Master of Ceremonies. He arrived in Bath in 1705 and quickly became noticed as the very able aide to the incumbent Master of Ceremonies, Captain Webster.

The job of Master Of Ceremonies involved arranging the events of the social calendar – balls and dances and other gatherings – and making sure they ran smoothly and in a seemly fashion. The Master Of Ceremonies would also meet and greet new arrivals in the city and introduce them to the 'Company', the people who thronged events at the Pump Room and Assembly Rooms.

When Captain Webster was killed in a duel fought over a disputed card game, Nash was immediately elected to the vacant post and fast became the face of the resort. In his own unique, self-inflating style he not only managed the entertainments at assemblies but also set down rules dictating conduct and even dress. A natural party thrower, he strove to keep people at official gatherings rather than disparate parties.

In a growing resort filled with hundreds of strangers trouble could easily brew, and to help ensure the safety and the reputation of the city as place to come for the Season (the winter months in Bath) he banned the wearing of swords. Duelling fell as a result.

Never a shy man, Nash would enforce his rules using rudeness without a second thought for who he was addressing. Woe betide anyone guilty of lapses in dress code or etiquette. Whether you were an incorrectly attired squire or an impudent princess you could earn rebuke in public by the "King", for whom Bath was his own domain.

Happy with the economic and social benefits that Nash's rule brought, the corporation granted Nash the freedom of the city in 1716. By 1720 his salary, winnings from gambling and his other income allowed him to live it up in style in a fine house in St John's Place. But it was scrutiny of his 'other income' that would lead to his fall from grace.

At the height of his fame, in 1735 Nash appointed himself Master of Ceremonies in Tunbridge Wells, where he became involved in sharing profits from gaming tables. Nash's reputation was forever tainted when the exact nature of his profiteering, both in Tunbridge and Bath, was revealed in court after Nash sued for monies owed him.

Nash's pursuit of money through the courts also revealed how little money he had, despite his social position. By the late 1750s he had become so in debt he was forced to sell many of his possessions and move from his St John's Place mansion to a smaller home in Saw Close. In 1760 the Corporation granted him a monthly pension of 10 guineas but it is believed that he still owed over £1,200 at his death in 1761.

HOW TO BE A REGENCY GENTLEMAN: DOS & DON'TS

OUR ESSENTIAL GUIDE FOR ANY ACCIDENTAL TIME TRAVELLERS AMONG YOU

The Regency Period is, strictly speaking, the period of British history from 1811 to 1820, when King George III was ill (or mad, as was throught at the time) and his son (the future King George IV) ruled as Prince Regent in his stead. More broadly speaking, the world of Regency is the world in which Jane Austen's books are set.

As Austen makes abundantly clear in her writing, if you're to make a convincing Regency woman while in Bath you must learn to forget all modern ideas about equality and opportunity. Gentlemen, though, you can look forward to a much more exciting life. But to cut a decent dash as a Regency gentlemen and sweep some lady off her feet like some smouldering Mr Darcy you need to first pick up some vital skills and attainments.

The 'gentle' part of being a Regency gentleman is not too difficult. You must simply display exquisite manners at all times and be able to bluff like mad on subjects ranging from art, music and literature to the health of the vicar's wife. Pull this off and you mark yourself out as a true aristocrat and not some fake from the emerging class of rich merchants.

The 'man' part of being a Regency gentleman is a little trickier – unless of course you are already expert with horse and sabre…

✖ Don't… Forget your homework

Before anything else you must remember that you come from a wealthy family. This means that you will have a grounding in Greek and Latin, which you will have received from a private tutor and then at school at either Eton or Harrow (not Winchester, obviously, which is a right dump), where you will also have learnt French and geography. During your youth you would also have grown proficient at cricket, fishing, and shooting birds and animals. If you try telling people that you went to university, remember that there were only two in Regency times – Oxford and Cambridge. Don't, whatever you do, say Sussex.

✔ Do… Get some wheels

You really should be able to handle a horse. It is inconceivable for a Regency gentleman not to be able to ride. But don't panic. You could get around this by instead getting yourself a pair of horse and a four-wheeled carriage with a coachman – a mode of transport that also has the advantage of displaying your wealth to great effect. Such displays don't come cheap, though. Renting such a setup would cost you between £200 and £300 a year in Regency times (roughly, £10,000–£20,000 today). You must also add into your budget maintenance, stabling and perhaps even, if you're feeling like really pushing the boat out, liveries for your coachman and grooms. If all that sounds a bit beyond your means, you could just make do with a two-wheeled carriage with a single horse – but this is no good if you're out to impress, because these types of carriages were known as 'bankrupt carts'…

✖ Don't… Take cutthroats lying down

True, today Bath doesn't face the threat of 40,000 French troops massed on the other side of the Channel. Also, having a police force, as a rule our roads paths and alleyways no longer crawl with robbers, bandits, highwaymen, pickpockets, conmen and cutthroats. Yet as a Regency gentlemen you would be trained to defend yourself against such threats with a sabre. Indeed, starting from boyhood you will have been taught all about 'cuts' and 'parries' and the right footwork to go with them – 'retreats', 'attacks' and 'lunges'. You would also have learned how to wield a sabre from horseback. It being a bit late in the day for you to learn such tricks, if trouble does come your way it's probably best to stick to hacking desperately at your attackers from the back of your bankrupt cart.

✔ **Do… Read "Duelling: Do's and Don'ts"**

Though you are unlikely to have to deal with with either 40,000 French soldiers or hoards of footpads and cutthroats, as a Regency gentleman you must certainly be ready to "defend your honour" in response to any slight, injustice or threat to your chances with a lady. Between Regency gentlemen even the tiniest differences could lead to a duel – so find out what to expect in such sticky situations on page 64…

✔ **Do… Enjoy a wager**

While in Bath, enjoy a good bet or two. Regency gentlemen loved gambling on all sorts of things, especially sports. One of the strangest sports gambled on was 'pedestrianism' – walking challenges and competitions. Famously, one Captain Robert Barclay, a celebrated pedestrian, won a bet of 1,000 guineas for walking "a thousand miles in a thousand successive hours at the rate of a mile in each and every hour".

Barclay won the bet by leaving nothing to chance. He had a well-lit, well-surfaced illuminated ring-shaped track built that was exactly one mile long. Every hour he would complete a circuit of the track and then rest in a house situated just next to the track. Teams of security guards were also hired to prevent foul play and to keep at bay large crowds that gathered to see him win his 1,000 guineas. If you fancy such a bet yourself, be warned that during his 42 day walk Barclay lost 2.3 stone (14.5 kg) in weight.

✖ **Don't… Be afraid to give it a go**

Luckily, the most important thing to remember about playing the part of a Regency gentleman is that most of the skills required you surely already have. Though your knowledge of poetry, art, music and literature may be severely limited, your inbuilt sense of style will also mark you out to the ladies as a true gentleman.

You will display your wealth ostentatiously yet with style. Your outfits will be impeccably fashionable. You will, despite testing the patience of the landlady at your bed & breakfast (who for some weeks has been waiting on your promises of "monies from London"), know how to throw lavish parties and entertainments for your new Bath acquaintances, at which gatherings you will nimbly sidestep and put off all requests to hear your much vaunted (by yourself, admittedly) virtuoso skills at the piano forte. You will also display unusual though elegant and masterful deportment on the dance floor at Bath's nightclubs. And when a certain young lady's father has learned that his daughter has been "ruined by that scoundrel", wanting to avoid at all costs a duel (given your lack of skill with a sabre), you will be able to make your escape from Bath swiftly and cross-country on horseback, having wisely become a master equestrian.

6 Royal Crescent

However long you're in Bath, visit the Royal Crescent. It's what Georgian Bath is all about – showing off...

■ Marlborough Buildings, just visible on the far left of the picture, acts as a windbreak for the Crescent

John Wood the Younger's gloriously massive Royal Crescent, the first crescent built in Britain, is the grandest example of Georgian Bath's "urban palaces" for the landed gentry and wealthy middle classes. Indeed, it is so ostentatiously impressive that when Bathonians refer to 'the Crescent' they always mean Royal Crescent and not another of the city's seven great curved terraces.

Huge to the point of being almost cliff-like, its curvature, which spans over 500 feet, increases towards the two end houses, which face each other and which were actually built first. As a centrepiece it has merely two sets of paired columns guarding an unassuming round-headed window – the one flaw in Wood's design according to some architectural critics. Others, though, point out that the Crescent's focal point depends on where you are standing. Try looking up at it from various vantages and you'll see what they mean.

Wherever you stand though it is the sheer staggering scale of the thing that most impresses – and the deliberately understated architecture of Brock Street, which connects his Circus to the Crescent, heightens the sense of awe you experience when it finally comes into view.

It was literally all fields when Wood the Younger and his brother-in-law Thomas Brock bought the site in 1766. He hired a small army of builders to work, under the strictest guidelines, on the 30 houses and 114 Ionic

■ The Crescent is almost scarily big close-up but its pavement offers a very pleasant stroll

It's Not True!

It's thought by some that the 1968 film *Oliver!* used the Crescent for the "Who Will Buy" song sequence. The scene was, however, actually filmed on a massive purpose-built set built at Shepperton Studios in Surrey…

Funny Ha-Ha?

The sunken fence, or 'ha-ha', at the front was designed to keep animals grazing on what is now Victoria Park off the front lawn without spoiling the view. According to Horace Walpole, author of the landmark essay On Modern Gardening, "Common people called them ha-has! to express their surprise at finding a sudden and unperceived check to their walk"… Who said they didn't have a sense of humour in those days! During the Second World War a 'Dig for Victory' vegetable patch covered the lawn. (Bombs in the air raids of 1942 gutted two houses in the Crescent, No. 2 and No. 17.)

Quite The Picture

Not only huge but also hugely influential, the Royal Crescent was a forerunner of the Picturesque movement, which sought to harmoniously blend buildings with the landscape…

Burning Embarrassment

The late Princess Margaret once visited the museum at No. 1 and was so enamoured of the ancient piano there that she insisted on playing it. Unfortunately, the piano sits on an equally ancient carpet and – to the silent horror of the curators – during the performance the Princess apparently balanced a cigarette on the piano's edge, which dripped ash and embers onto said carpet, burning it. Oops. "What's that?" "Nothing, your Highness! We were just remarking how well you played…"

columns that make up the Crescent. They started the work on the east side, No.1, in 1767 and finished the last house just eight years later. Buyers of each house plot had to stick with Wood's exact design for the frontage, which also dictated the level of each floor. They were free, though, to plan the interiors as they liked. The result is that no two houses are the same inside – or at the back (stroll around to the rear and take a look).

Some wealthy families would occupy a house permanently. However, some plots on the Crescent would be let out for the city's "Season". The Season, which took place in Bath over the winter months, was when the landed gentry and emerging wealthy middle classes gathered to dance, gossip, plan marriages, play cards and take the waters for their gout and rheumatism.

What were these houses like inside? You can find out at No. 1 Royal Crescent, which is now a museum run by the Bath Preservation Trust. On show are a series of furnished 18th century rooms illustrating just how fashionably fashionable society lived. If you want to treat yourself, you can book yourself morning coffee, lunch, afternoon tea or dinner at the super-posh Royal Crescent Hotel, which occupies Nos. 15 and 16 in the very middle of the Crescent.

What you should definitely do is simply enjoy a gentle promenade along the wide pavement in front of the Crescent (which was made for promenading, after all), perhaps nodding stiffly to passers-by, just as the gentry would have in Georgian times. If you feel a little scruffy, well never mind. You'll set the building off nicely, anyway, and as you stroll you'll be able to consider meditatively how fashions have changed down the years.

You can both look behind the façade and step back in time at No. 1 Royal Crescent

The posh Royal Crescent Hotel

Austen Watch

The Royal Crescent was completed in 1775, the year of Jane Austen's birth. Jane's aunt, Jane Leigh, and her well-to-do husband the Reverend Edward Cooper swiftly moved into No. 12. In *Northanger Abbey* we discover that the writer herself probably thought a parade along the Crescent a great way of getting way from things:

As soon as divine service was over, the Thorpes and Allens eagerly joined each other; and after staying long enough in the pump-room to discover that the crowd was insupportable, and that there was not a genteel face to be seen, which everybody discovers every Sunday throughout the season, they hastened away to the Crescent, to breathe the fresh air of better company. Here Catherine and Isabella, arm in arm, again tasted the sweets of friendship in an unreserved conversation; they talked much, and with much enjoyment; but again was Catherine disappointed in her hope of reseeing her partner… Sniff!

OLD BATHONIANS

GEORGE SAINTSBURY
(1845-1933)
1A ROYAL CRESCENT

George Saintsbury was a professor of English literature, reactionary Tory, writer, critic, journalist and wine connoisseur. After retiring from his seat at Edinburgh University in 1920 Saintsbury made Bath his final abode. Asserting that he could tell the difference between a freshly opened bottle of sherry to one opened at lunchtime, the same year his celebrated book *Notes On A Cellar* was published. Shortly afterwards the famous 'Saintsbury Club' – a clique for wine-swilling literary types such as GK Chesterton – was formed in his honour. Though a private man (he gave no interviews and refused to provide photographs for the local press on his 80th birthday), in Bath he continued to write prolifically and could often be spotted about town carrying bundles of books. Indeed, the playwright JB Priestley, hardly a slacker himself, remarked at the time how Saintsbury "makes the more indolent of us wonder what we do with our time".

PRINCE FREDERICK
"THE GRAND OLD DUKE OF YORK"
(1763-1827)
1 & 16 ROYAL CRESCENT

The popular second son of George III, Prince Frederick's stylish duel fought on Wimbledon Common with a Colonel Lennox, afterwards the Duke of Richmond, cemented his place in the hearts of the public, as did his opposition to the plot to supplant George III with the Prince of Wales. However, during the French Revolutionary Wars, as the famous nursery rhyme tells, he famously "marched his men to the top of the hill and he marched them down again" – a reference to the disastrous retreat of English forces under his command in Flanders. Despite his incompetence, he was made a Field Marshal and became Commander in Chief of the army. He led another calamitous expedition to the Netherlands before resigning his command after being accused of selling army commissions through his mistress, Mary Anne Clarke. He was, of course, cleared, reinstated and given the Freedom of the City of Bath.

CHRISTOPHER ANSTEY
(1724-1805)
5 ROYAL CRESCENT

MP, poet and writer Christopher Anstey wrote the 1766 *New Bath Guide*, an affectionate but satirical portrait in verse of Georgian Bath, based around the adventures of the Blunderheads, a family of innocents new to the city. The book takes the form of a series of letters to family and friends describing the Blunderheads' progress, their pleasures, and their misfortunes at the hands of various swindlers, gamblers, charlatans, fops and dandies. It was a bestseller when published (there were more than 30 editions between 1766 and 1830) and still makes fascinating reading today. Simkin Blunderhead notes, for example, that though patients would be "boil'd at the Command of an able Physician", Bath doctors themselves didn't dare go near the waters themselves. Though his book was a hit, Anstey was a private man and the novelist Fanny Burney thought him "shyly important, and silently proud". A portrait of Anstey by Bath painter William Hoare hangs in the Guildhall banqueting room and a plaque devoted to him can be found in Poets Corner in Westminster Abbey.

JEAN-BAPTISTE DU BARRE
(1749-1778)
8 ROYAL CRESCENT

In 1778, French soldier Jean-Baptiste du Barre came to Bath with an Irish soldier friend called Captain Rice. One night, du Barre and Rice won of £600 from a Colonel Champion, who lived at No. 29. The ensuing argument

OLD BATHONIANS

between du Barre and Rice over how best to divvy up the loot ended up with the pair priming pistols on nearby Claverton Down. Du Barre shot first in the duel and wounded Rice in the thigh, but Rice's aim was truer: Du Barre took it right square in the chest and was killed almost instantly. Unlucky Du Barre, the real loser that night, is buried at Bathampton.

CAPTAIN PHILIP THICKNESSE

(1719-1792)

9 ROYAL CRESCENT

A bullying army commander, quack, gossip, swindler, blackmailer, gold digger, opium eater and writer who specialised in upsetting people, Thicknesse's lasting legacy is his vivid and acidic account of life in Georgian Bath, the *New Prose Bath Guide*. His books weren't successful but he still used them to write gossip he was paid not to publish, feud with enemies and pass on his ideas about health and wellbeing – for which he prescribed opium and "partaking of the breath of young virgins" (an idea that sparked a riot in which he was burnt in effigy). Thicknesse got through three wives during his career, earning himself the nickname Dr Viper and a (probably untrue) reputation for sleeping in a coffin. Contrary to his boast that he "brought Gainsborough to Bath", it was Thicknesse's bullying that drove the painter away to London. After failing in a legal attempt to obtain money he felt due to him from his first marriage, and facing a growing queue of angry people accusing him of cheating them out of money, he emigrated to France, where he died. Had he stuck around he would have been forced to fight a duel at the tender age of 72. Quarrelsome to the last, he left his right hand to his son "to remind him of his duty to God after having so long abandoned the duty he owed to a father, who once so affectionately loved him". The playwright Samuel Foote concluded that the good captain had "the heart of an assassin and the cowardice of a dunghill cock".

LORD EDWARD BULWER LYTTON

(1803-1873)

9 ROYAL CRESCENT

A friend of Dickens and a bestselling author himself, Lytton wrote his celebrated historical novel *The Last Days Of Pompeii* in Bath. Coining the phrases "the great unwashed", "pursuit of the almighty dollar", "the pen is mightier than the sword" and the famous opening line "It was a dark and stormy night", he made a considerable fortune from his writing. After separating from him, his wife famously used a novel of her own to publicly castigate him. He lived out his days in the city, apparently content, thinking the place like "those tranquil ponds in which carp, forgotten by the angler, live to a fabulous age"...

ELIZABETH LINLEY

(1754-1792)

11 ROYAL CRESCENT

Famous beauty Elizabeth Linley eloped with the dashing playwright Richard Brinsley Sheridan from this address. Elizabeth was not only a beauty but, of a talented musical family (her father arranged concerts in Bath), she also sang like an angel. She could have had any 'suitable' man (even George III was observed drooling over her at an opera) but she wanted the dashing playwright. After he fought two extremely unpleasant duels with a rival suitor, Sheridan married her. But Sheridan was unfaithful and Elizabeth contracted tuberculosis and died aged 38.

ANGELA BURDETT-COULTTS

(1814-1906)

16 ROYAL CRESCENT

The wealthy philanthropist daughter of Sir Francis Burdett, baroness Angela Burdett-Coutts became known as "the richest

OLD BATHONIANS

heiress in England" when she inherited her grandfather's fortune of nearly three million pounds. She established the National Society for the Prevention of Cruelty to Children in 1883 and was closely involved with the Royal Society for the Prevention of Cruelty to Animals. When she was 67 she shocked polite society by marrying her 29-year-old secretary. Fictionalised, she appears in George MacDonald Fraser's Flashman novel *Flashman's Lady*.

ELIZABETH MONTAGU
(1720-1800)
16 ROYAL CRESCENT

Writer and society hostess Elizabeth Montagu threw highbrow parties and launched a revolutionary women's literary discussion group known as the "Bluestockings". Her guests included Hester Thrale, the formidable Methodist campaigner Countess Huntingdon (what parties they must have been), Fanny Burney and Christopher Anstey.

SIR FRANCIS BURDETT
(1770-1844)
16 ROYAL CRESCENT

This baronet, radical MP and campaigner against corruption and for parliamentary reform served two jail sentences for his views. However, in his later years his blue blood got the better of him and, after arguing that the 1832 Reform Bill went too far, he promptly joined the Tories. He lived at No. 16 from 1814 to 1822.

MARY, COUNTESS OF BELMORE
(1755-1841)
17 ROYAL CRESCENT

Widow of the Northern Irish peer Armar Lowry-Corry, the first Earl of Belmore. After her husband's death, the countess moved into No. 17 Royal Crescent, where she lived for 30 years, presiding as hostess over balls held in the Assembly Rooms and becoming the inspiration for Lady Snuphanuph in Dickens' *The Pickwick Papers*.

SIR ISAAC PITMAN
(1813-1897)
17 ROYAL CRESCENT

The inventor of Pitman shorthand (or, rather, he came up with a brilliant adaptation of the 1786 system invented by a Samuel Taylor), Isaac Pitman loved Bath but, a devout Swedenborgian New Church Christian and a workaholic, he would not have exactly been the life and soul of any party. In 1875 he helped set up a free library in Bath which collapsed six years later under the weight of debts when the council refused to back it. Busy and presumably happy to the end, shortly before he died he said: "To those who ask how Isaac Pitman passed, say 'peacefully', and with no more concern than in passing from one room to another to take up some further employment."

AMABEL WELLESLEY-COLLEY
22 ROYAL CRESCENT

In 1970, this descendent of the Duke of Wellington painted the door of No. 22 yellow. The city council took legal action against her for altering a Grade I listed building. She fought the much-publicised case all the way to Parliament and the then Minister of the Environment, Peter Walker. She eventually won on the grounds that she had repainted the door before the relevant Act had become law. To the council's continued irritation, she continued to repaint the door yellow until she left the house in 1984. Good for her! Maybe.

OLD BATHONIAN

JOHN WOOD THE YOUNGER

(1728-1801)

John Wood the Younger is the architect responsible for the Royal Crescent, the Assembly Rooms and many of the surrounding streets. More practical and less of a dreamer than his fellow-architect father John Wood the Elder (who designed the Circus, Queen Square and many other Bath landmarks), with his masterpiece the Crescent, famous the world over, he outshone even his old dad.

But before Wood built the Crescent he built the Circus. After his father's death in 1754 (he lived only long enough to lay the Circus' foundation stone) it was left to Wood the Younger to complete it, which he did in1768. What the older Wood had designed, the younger one turned into another of Bath's great architectural gems; it was even more of a triumph considering the poor state in which his father had left the business (indeed, the younger Wood too would die in debt).

As well as the Circus, Wood built Brock Street (1764), the restrained curtain raiser to his 1767 masterpiece the Crescent, which his father had only sketchily planned for. Wood's two other major contributions to Bath, the Assembly Rooms and new Hot Bath, were completed in 1771 and 1777 respectively.

An earnest man, alongside his grander schemes Wood took on housing projects for the poor. He built, for instance, a row of 16 cottages for the "impotent" of St Ives, saying: "For myself master of the subject, it was necessary for me to feel as the cottager himself." He also campaigned for more privvies for the poor – not a notion that would have greatly exercised his father.

Wood the Elder was not a handsome man, and neither was his son. In fact, the younger Wood, surely bemusedly, soon found himself voted in as a member of the celebrated "Ugly Face Club", a pocket book that described the features of the famous but aesthetically challenged. Amusingly, part of Wood's entry describes him as looking like one of his buildings: "Stone coloured complexion, a dimple in his attick story. The pillasters of his face fluted, tortoise-eyed, a prominent nose. Wild grin and face altogether resembling a badger."

The legacy that the younger Wood left behind is no less than his father's. In the space of a decade he raised the Royal Crescent, an Assembly Room, a Hot Bath and a fine grouping of streets, so he cannot be regarded as being merely the son of a genius. He was himself a genius. The great architectural critic Walter Ison went so far as to proclaim: "The finest achievements of the son surpass those of the father, both in breadth of conception and subtlety of realisation."

Wood lived at 41 Gay Street, a house that overlooks his father's Queen Square (see also Queen Square in Must-See Bath and Gay Street in A-Z section).

The Assembly Rooms are just part of John Wood The Younger's architectural legacy.

7 The Circus

It's big, it's circular, it's steeped in Masonic and druidic mysticism, it's a mini-Colosseum turned inside out...

■ The middle of the Circus was originally paved – and had a reservoir in the very centre where the trees now stand

You only have to look at the many rearing columns for a moment to realise that the Circus really does look like, as its designer John Wood intended, a mini-Colosseum turned inside out.

The first circular street in Britain, the 33 houses of the "King's Circus" (as it is was originally called) form a perfect 97-metre diameter ring. The Colosseum is actually elliptical, but, just like in the Roman amphitheatre, each ascending tier of the Circus has a different style of classical column – first "Doric", then "Ionic" and then "Corinthian".

Each segment faces an entrance, so whichever way you enter there is a magnificent façade confronting you. You can allegedly find the circle's true centre by clapping your hands and using the echoes to adjust your position.

Work on the Circus began in February 1754. Wood himself laying the foundation stone amid a blaze of publicity. But less than four months later, Wood died, leaving his son, John Wood the Younger, to complete an extraordinary scheme that would be as admired and as influential as the Royal Crescent.

Some people were determined to dislike the Circus, however. There was originally a raised cobbled bowl where the green and plane trees now stand, that formed a reservoir that gravity fed the basement kitchens – and for failed doctor and hilariously acidic writer Tobias Smollett, author of the 1777 acidic destruction of Bath that is *The Expedition of Humphrey Clinker*, this "open basin" was "liable to be defiled with dead dogs, cats, rats, and every species of nastiness, which the rascally populace may throw into it, from mere wantonness and brutality"... The Circus, he bitched, was merely a "pretty bauble, designed for show"

■ **Know your classical columns? The bottom ones are "Doric", the middle "Ionic", and the top "Corinthian"**

SPOOKY BATH
It's haunted! (allegedly...)

3 The Circus

The figure of a grey serving woman haunts this address, apparently. Other reported signs of haunting to out look for, should you be unlucky enough to visit this address are: objects moving about by themselves, a 'silent presence' moving around bedrooms at night and sudden bouts of wind... Happens to the best of us.

You Can't See The Wood For The Acorns

While planning his vision of a new Bath, John Wood was influenced not just by the Romans but also by an obsession with druidism and Freemasonry.

Bath's mythical founder, King Bladud, was, according to Wood, a druid, hence the Circus's crown of acorns (oaks were sacred to the druids)...

Meanwhile, the diameter of the Circus (318 foot or 97 metres) is roughly the same size as Wood's measurements of the nearby stone circles of Stonehenge and Stanton Drew – themselves, Wood maintained, the same size as the legendary Solomon's Temple in Jerusalem. And the 30 outer stones of Stonehenge match the number of doors of both the Circus and the Crescent...

Many of the Circus's 525 carved symbols are Masonic, while it is clearly no accident that when seen from the air the Crescent and Circus look like a huge sun and moon – two hugely important symbols for both druids and Masons.

Even more strange, the Circus together with Gay Street and Queen Square form the shape of a giant key, also a potent Masonic symbol...

which suffered from "childish and misplaced affected ornaments", iron railings "of very little use" and the lack of a colonnade to protect chairmen from the rain "which is here almost perpetual"...

Several houses were demolished during the Second Waorld War air raids of 1942 but the fate of the Circus would have been much worse if a high explosive bomb that dropped bang in the centre of the green had gone off.

Today the Circus is a peaceful place to visit even at the height of the tourist season. Where the cliff-like openness of the Crescent has something of the coast about it, the Circus, with its rearing columns, seems more like a clearing in some petrified forest.

The 525 carved symbols around the Circus reflect John Wood's preoccupation with Freemasonry

OLD BATHONIANS

SIR WILLIAM PARRY
(1790-1865)
27 THE CIRCUS

This rear-admiral and polar explorer was educated at King Edward's School in Bath. He didn't quite manage to discover the fabled Northwest Passage from the Atlantic to the Pacific, and in 1827 he attempted one of the earliest expeditions to the North Pole. An evangelical Christian and a pioneer of the use of food canning for his Arctic voyages, he was just as concerned for the moral as he was for the physical health of his seamen.

DR WILLIAM FALCONER
(1744-1824)
29 THE CIRCUS

Bath doctor and writer of a good many papers on subjects ranging from the use of the waters to the French Revolution.

The good doctor is responsible for the plane trees in the Circus – trees that not everyone approves of today, altering as they do the Circus's sense of space.

OLD BATHONIANS

JOHN WOOD THE ELDER
(1704-1754)

John Wood is the visionary behind Georgian Bath. He revolutionised town planning, using Bath Stone to create a city for the wealthy where they could stroll terraces and squares lined with grand houses that together looked like even grander palaces.

The son of local builder George Wood, John started off his career in Yorkshire before working in London, where he fell in love with the newly fashionable Palladian style of architecture. This style, based on a revival of the designs of the Renaissance Italian architect Andrea Palladio, was all about symmetry, balance, harmony and uniformity.

Aged just 20, in 1727 the ambitious John Wood returned to Bath with a grand Palladian blueprint of his own for the city that would turn it into a 'second Rome'. It was a plan of grand proportions, as his *Essay Towards a Description of Bath* shows:

I proposed to make a grand place of assembly, to be called the Royal Forum of Bath; another place, no less magnificent, for the exhibition of sports, to be called the Grand Circus; and a third place, of equal state with either of the former, for the practice of medicinal exercises, to be called the Imperial Gymnasium of the city…

The idea seemed far-fetched when it was confronted by a city corporation made up of men for whom corruption and foot-dragging were virtually bylaws – and Wood hardly helped his own interests by also propagating in his book sometimes bizarre and vague ideas about Bath's history, punctuating it with lurid tales of human sacrifices by druids on Solsbury Hill. At any rate, the self-interested corporation ridiculed his plans as "chimerical". But Wood had two important things going for him: his own certainty and Ralph Allen's Bath Stone quarry.

The Duke of Chandos championed the young architect at first by giving him, in 1727, his first job in Bath: rebuilding a group of lodging houses near the Cross Bath. Wood may also have designed Ralph Allen's "Town House" at this time, though it is not certain he was the architect.

The following year 1728, he began his "great design" with what turned out to be his crowning glory, Queen Square, finished in 1736. Gay Street followed, then came North (1740) and South Parades (1748). Ralph Allen's magnificent Prior Park mansion, intended to serve as an advert for Bath stone, was completed by Wood in 1741. The Circus was begun in 1754 but Wood never saw it finished. He died that year (he is buried at Swainswick Church, Bath) and the Circus would be built by his son, John Wood the Younger, who would go on to design and build the Crescent, which the older Wood had only vaguely sketched out.

Though he didn't achieve more in his 50-year life, which he would have no doubt liked, John Wood still did more than any other to make Bath a place of architectural pilgrimage. The city wouldn't be what it is without this great architect and great dreamer. John Wood the Elder died at 9 Queen Square, his other Bath masterpiece (See Queen Square in Must-See Bath).

WILLIAM PITT THE ELDER
(1708-1778)
7 THE CIRCUS

Prime Minister; great Whig, then Tory statesman; oversaw successful colonial campaigns against the French in Canada and India; MP for Bath and Freeman of the City; responsible for the phrase "an Englishman's home is his castle"; known as "The Great Commoner" because of his long-standing refusal to accept a title until 1766.

Later in his life, ill and crotchety with gout, Pitt stayed often at this address, once complaining, "I wish for nothing but a decent and innocent retreat, not to afford the world the ridiculous spectacle of being passed by every boat that navigates the river…"

But if he wanted peace and quiet,

OLD BATHONIANS

the chattering city of Bath may well have made a poor choice for a retirement retreat for him. Indeed, according to Thackeray's famous caricature of him, he made a sight round town that would have induced much pointing:

And if you and I had been alive then, and strolling down Milsom Street – hush! We should have taken our hats off, as an awful long, lean figure, swathed in flannels, passed by in its chair, and a livid face looked out from the window – great fierce eyes staring from under a bushy, powdered wig, a terrible frown, a terrible Roman nose – and we whisper, "There he is! There's the great commoner! There is Mr Pitt!"

DR DAVID LIVINGSTONE

(1813-1873)

13 THE CIRCUS

The British missionary and explorer, seeker of the source of the Nile and the first European to see the Victoria Falls. After surviving reports that he was dead, he was famously interviewed in Africa by the American reporter Henry M Stanley, their meeting immortalised by the words: "Dr Livingstone, I presume…" Livingstone died in Africa.

LORD ROBERT "CLIVE OF INDIA" CLIVE

(1725-1774)

14 THE CIRCUS

The military commander and administrator who effectively founded the honey pot that was British India. He didn't have much of a life by the time he tried to retire to Bath. Ill and addicted to opium, he found he was too sick to even take the waters (he used to live on Westgate Street). To make matters worse, his reputation had anyway been left in shreds by an ungrateful Parliament that had questioned the means by which he had gained his great wealth. He defended himself: "By God... I stand astonished at my own moderation." He returned to London to commit suicide, stabbing himself with a penknife.

THOMAS GAINSBOROUGH

(1727-1788)

17 THE CIRCUS

A young Gainsborough grew to fame living in Bath by painting all the local lights of the time, including Garrick, Sheridan, Quin, Nelson and the lovely Elizabeth Linley. He also may have completed his famous *The Blue Boy* during his stay. He eventually left for London after 14 years – one story goes, for falling over his friend the quarrelsome writer Phillip Thicknesse's portrait. Gainsborough had been slow to finish the picture, eventually angrily gave it to the bullying, complaining Thicknesse half done and promptly left town.

MAJOR JOHN ANDRE

(1751-1780)

22 THE CIRCUS

A dashing but unlucky British army intelligence officer during the American War of Independence. Denied the 'soldier's death' by firing squad, he was hanged as a spy by the Americans for his involvement in a plot to betray West Point to the British. His execution was greeted with outrage on this side of the Atlantic.

After telling himself that the noose would be "a momentary pang", his last words were reportedly: "I pray you to bear me witness that I meet my fate like a brave man."

8 Queen Square

John Wood the Elder's Palladian masterpiece was meant to look like a magnificent palace with wings...

■ Queen Square's obelisk was erected in 1732 in honour of the visit of Frederick, Prince of Wales. Alexander Pope penned the lukewarm inscription for it which can be seen on the plaque at the bottom corner of the garden nearest Wood Street

Hugely influential, Queen Square was the first speculative development by John Wood in Bath. The land was leased to Wood by a surgeon friend called Robert Gay (who gives his name to Gay Street). Wood then sub-let the site in small parcels to other builders who built the square for him. This arrangement led to endless battles with builders trying to make shortcuts and constant arguments with tenants trying to introduce their own ideas. Work started in 1729. Seven years later the Square was completed and named after George II's Queen, Caroline.

Adding magnificence to the whole square, the north

side, with its huge Corinthian columns, is intended to look like a single palace's front. The east and west sides were originally meant to be symmetrical wings. In the end, though, the west side was built with a large gap acting as a forecourt to a mansion further back. That mansion is now gone, the gap filled with John Pinch the Younger's 1830 building, which is in a completely different architectural style (neo-Grecian). The middle of the square, where the boules pitches are, was once a formal garden surrounded by a low stone balustrade.

Even the Georgian novelist and self-appointed scourge of the city Tobias Smollett was impressed…

The Square, though irregular, is, on the whole, pretty well laid out, spacious, open, and airy; and, in my opinion, by far the most wholesome and agreeable situation in Bath, especially the upper side of it.

Though Smollett did also complain that "the avenues to it are mean, dirty, dangerous, and indirect", new roads linking the upper parts of town to the old centre would soon be built. Today, to Bath's great shame, traffic has turned what could be a glorious space into a glorified roundabout. John Wood the Elder, who died at 9 Queen Square, would not be pleased. When something is done about this, Bath can have back one of its architectural gems.

The northern side of Queen Sqaure. As is intended, it looks like one big palace

SPOOKY BATH
It's haunted! (allegedly…)

9 Queen Square

'Bride of Death' story, anyone? And this one's true… partly. No 9, the house where John Wood died, is supposedly haunted by the spirit of his housekeeper, Sylvia Braddock. Wood was an upright, married man and when Sylvia realised he could never return her love for him she hanged herself, dressed in white.

Austen Watch

Jane Austen's family lived in Queen Square for a time and her writings reflect its changing status.

In 1799, Austen stayed at No 13 for several weeks and wrote admiringly to her sister: "It is far more cheerful than the Paragon, and the prospect from the drawing room, at which I now write, is rather picturesque, as it commands a prospective view of the left side of Brock Street, broken by three Lombardy poplars in the garden of the last house in Queen Square."

By 1801, when the family were house hunting before finally moving into No 4 Sydney Place, Jane wrote how her mother "hankers after the Square dreadfully".

In 1816, however, it's a different story – the square has gone out of fashion. In *Persuasion* Miss Musgrove says:

Remember, Papa, if we do go [to Bath] we must be in a good situation – none of your Queen Squares for us!"

HOW TO... PROMENADE GEORGIAN-STYLE

TAKE THE AIR AND SHOW OFF YOUR FINERY WITH A REFINED, GENTLE STROLL

People should never rush in Bath – it's not the sort of place that you make a good impression by looking overly busy – but they should certainly promenade. Why? Well for starters, during a good promenade (a kind of stately stroll with much greeting and bowing) you can take in the city's (cough) fresh air, its fine views and splendid buildings. But these are mere fringe benefits: for what promenading is really about is impressing people in a shallow and entirely superficial kind of way. And here's how it was done in Georgian times…

South Parade, built for promenading

Attire

Ladies: the good news is that you can accessorise. Fans, bags… if you can hold it, take it. The bad news is that while a wig the size of hayrick is optional you will still have to wear 15 layers of hooped skirt. Aprons, by the way, are so out.

A gentleman will require a three-vented coat, embroidered waistcoat, powdered wig, knee breeches, stockings and shoes (no riding boots – they're frightfully common). You'll also need a three-cornered hat, with a flat rim if you're searching for the 'country gent' look, that can be raised in salute to the lovely ladies and their daughters you'll encounter on your leisurely perambulation.

On a less savoury note, for both sexes, scratching sticks, used to deal with the Georgian city's burgeoning lice population, are highly recommended.

Company

An entourage of friends and family is absolutely essential for a successful promenade. The more numerous and more important you can make your company appear, the better. Grab a street urchin, pay him a farthing and make him a nephew for the day if you must; and if you yourself haven't got a real title, make one up. But don't be too ambitious. Claiming a knighthood could land you in trouble.

Location

After going to all that effort, it's no use promenading up and down the London Road. Instead use the North and South Parades, and Gravel Walk in Victoria Park. They were designed for it.

Conversation

Ladies, do say:

[Moving away to a safe distance] "Major, flattered though I am by your most generous offer (and I doubt not that it springs from intentions both wholesome and noble, for I hold you in the highest possible regard), and whilst I recognise that it is a truth universally acknowledged that a man with a good fortune must be in want of a game of whist, I would humbly beseech you on this occasion to also accept my sincerest apologies when I say I must decline, for admittedly I have little love for the card tables or indeed the people that populate them and it being such a fine day I should rather prefer to take a little more air. And besides, I haven't written a word of my next influential novel."

Whatever you do, don't say:
"Sod this for a game of soldiers, I'm off to the tavern. Anyone fancy a quick tankard? It's almost time for the bear baiting."

Gentlemen, do say:
[With a low bow including several flourishes and a series of subtly grave gestures]
"My dear Miss Elizabeth (if you can possibly find it within yourself to forgive my presumptuousness), may I be so bold as to condescend, on this afternoon so clement it invigorates the sprit to the uttermost degree, facilitating the kind of social intercourse that is so very agreeable indeed (to use the rather vulgar vernacular), to request the enchantment of escorting you – thrash me, for I am a cad and a scoundrel! – through these engaging, nay, charming, pleasure gardens (with all due respect, of course, and with the slightly haughty regards of my aunt, the 'estimable' Lady Catherine de Burger de Avery, who this very moment awaits anxiously news as to the status of my marital condition – a subject I also look forward to addressing in the near, or even – if I may be bolder yet – immediate future… And I have got loads of cash, by the way.)"

Whatever you do, don't say:
"Madam, would you permit me to rub pump water into your bodice?"

Or:
"It's about time they brought back the naked bathing if you ask me."

Poor Fred

The obelisk in Queen Square was put there by John Wood in 1732 for Beau Nash in honour of the visit of Frederick, Prince of Wales.

Frederick might have found this flattery refreshing, since his father George II detested him (once suggesting he was a "changeling"), and so did his mother Queen Caroline, who once famously complained: "Popularity always makes me sick, but Fretz's popularity makes me vomit." Hate-filled to the last, she even added on her deathbed: "I shall have one comfort in having my eyes eternally closed – I shall never have to see that monster again."

"Poor Fred", as a poem by William Makepeace Thackeray dubbed him, never became King. He died before his father and his son was crowned George III. But at least the snobbish Nash liked the prince, who had given him a gold snuffbox. Nash badgered Alexander Pope into writing an inscription for the obelisk – but when the poet finally relented and wrote one, its praise was so faint it was damning. Check out the copy of it on the plaque in the corner of the garden nearest Wood Street.

Once, Twice, Three Times Palladian

Bath is famed for its Palladian style of architecture. Indeed John Wood and others used to it such great effect in the city that it swiftly became the form for grand buildings all over the country. The style was developed by the great Italian designer Andrea Palladio (1508-1580), who came from Vicenza in Italy. His concepts were based on Greek and Roman architecture and paid detail to proportion and symmetry. For example, many Bath buildings have a central focal point, often the main doorway, with equal numbers of symmetrical windows or pillars arranged either side of it…

OLD BATHONIAN

RALPH ALLEN

(1693-1764)

Along with Richard 'Beau' Nash, John Wood and Dr William Oliver, Ralph Allen was part of the 'Gang of Four' that had such influence on the rise of Georgian Bath. A self-made businessman with an honourable reputation, he made his fortune reforming the postal system. It was Allen who really championed Bath stone – out of which the city was built.

The son of a Cornish innkeeper, Allen began his career as a boy working in his grandmother's post office in St Collumb near St Austell. There his skilled and diligent work was soon noticed by the local Post Office inspector and, at the relatively young age of 18, Allen was promoted to the position of deputy-postmaster in Bath (then in Bath Street). One famous story goes that the zealous young Allen's reputation was then quickly enhanced further when he passed on letters to the local militia leader General Wade that exposed a Jacobite plot to smuggle a shipment of arms into the West Country. The story, though nice, is probably dubious, but certainly the young Allen enjoyed the admiration and patronage of Wade (MP for Bath from 1722-1741), whose natural daughter Miss Earl he married and whose support was instrumental in securing him the job of chief postmaster – a position from where Allen would secure his fortune.

The Post Office system at the time was a corrupt and inefficient affair that was sub-contracted locally and then sub-contracted again. Everyone took their cut, many letters were robbed, precious few of them ever delivered and the government was being defrauded of tax left, right and centre. The alert Allen was appalled by what was going on and also quick to spot an opportunity for himself. With Wade's backing he bought the contacts to deliver mail off the main routes for himself and set up his network of postmasters. Despite initial opposition from them, the operation was a success and he soon made a fortune for himself (as well as the government).

Allen then turned his entrepreneurial skills to quarrying. Bath stone was not popular with the London architects, it being soft and easy to work but not durable enough in their opinion. Undeterred Allen bought land at Hampton and Combe Down and soon demand for the stuff (from Bath architects at least) was such that he had to invent a tramway system to get the stone to the river. The stone would never be universally used (though you'll see examples of it dotted throughout Europe) but in Bath it became famous, and Bath became famous for it.

In 1727 John Wood built Allen his Town House (see the York Street entry in Bath A-Z section) and in 1762 Richard Jones built his Sham Castle on the Bathwick hillside. But it was his Prior Mark mansion, began in 1735, that really showed off the Bath stone. Originally it was meant to possess all the architectural 'orders', though the plan changed as it progressed. Indeed, Allen fell out with Wood over the question of gables.

Allen was now rich and famous, and Prior Park enjoyed visits from the leading lights of the Georgian artistic world. The rarefied dinner parties there were frequented by the likes of Alexander Pope (a friend), Smollett, who wrote his famous satire of Bath, Gainsborough (who painted a celebrated picture of the actor David Garrick at Prior Park) and also Henry Fielding, who based his *Tom Jones* character Squire Allworthy on Allen. His life would never be blemished with scandal like so many others of the time were and, like his peers, he gave away at least some of his fortune (the stone for the new General Hospital was given free) for good causes.

Allen died in 1764, aged 71, having done as much as any single man to secure Georgian Bath's place in the world. He is buried in Claverton Churchyard with his second wife, Elizabeth Holder. This epitaph was penned by his friend Pope: "Let humble Allen, with an awkward shame, Do good by stealth, and blush to find it fame."

9 Assembly Rooms

Georgian Bath's swankiest party venue, the Assembly Rooms hosted huge balls – under the strictest of rules!

The Assembly Rooms was once *the* place be seen, the place where fashionable Bath came to gamble at cards, attend balls, concerts and plays and simply drink tea and gossip. For families visiting the city hoping to marry off daughters it was also the place in which to search for a suitable husband. Public balls attracting up to1,200 people were held at least twice a week, at which times the Rooms became a sort of posh cattle market.

■ Jane Austen certainly attended balls here at the Assembly Rooms, and it features in both of her Bath-set books

Built by John Wood the Younger, the Assembly Rooms opened in 1771 to serve the new upper parts of the city. It was known as the "New" or "Upper" Assembly Rooms to distinguish it from its rival, the older, smaller Lower Assembly Rooms (which burnt down in 1820) on Terrace Walk in the by then less fashionable lower part of the city.

Hidden behind the Circus and surrounded by streets, it seems an inauspicious location for such an important venue, but there are two reasons for this. First, there was once a plan for even larger Assembly Rooms on a site near Queen Square, but the money wasn't found for this. Second, the surrounding streets that hedge in the Assembly Rooms were not Wood's idea at all. Indeed, the building would have enjoyed both views and space in which to breathe but for the intervention of Wood's arch-rival, Thomas Warr Attwood. The east side, now blocked in by the Saville Row, was intended to be its front and look over lawns. However, after buying up the extensive grounds of a nearby inn, Attwood hemmed in the Rooms with a new street plan that took in Saville Row, Alfred Street, Bennett Street and Russell Street. Take away these streets and the building would have much more power.

The chandeliers, worth millions, were stored during the Second World War – which proved lucky for the place as it was gutted by fire in the air raids of 1942

Austen Watch

Jane herself went to one very poorly attended ball in May 1801, when the "Bath season" (winter) was nearing its end. "It was shockingly and inhumanly thin for this place," she wrote in a letter to her sister Cassandra – but she was at least able to report her amusement at seeing a Mrs B "run round the room after her drunken husband".

In *Northanger Abbey*, Catherine Morland goes to a much more crowded ball at the Upper Rooms…

The season was full, the room crowded, and the two ladies squeezed in as well as they could. As for Mr. Allen, he repaired directly to the card-room, and left them to enjoy a mob by themselves…

A new arrival in the city, Catherine failed to get a dance at the ball. This was because etiquette at public balls dictated that a lady couldn't dance with a partner who hadn't been formally introduced to her by the Master of Ceremonies. Catherine doesn't get to strut her stuff until another ball, at the Lower Assembly Rooms, where she is introduced to young Tilney.

In the time of *Persuasion*, boring, genteel entertaining at home (something Beau Nash had sought to discourage) was in vogue as by the end of the 18th century the Assembly Rooms had grown unfashionable. This is reflected in *Persuasion* in which, to Anne's displeasure, the Elliots spend their evenings "solely in the elegant stupidity of private parties". But the Octagon Room turns out to be the scene of great joy for Anne, for this is where Wentworth expresses his ardour for her. Indeed, she is so overcome that the grandeur of the Tea Room, which is the venue for Lady Dalrymple's concert, completely passes her by…

Anne saw nothing, thought nothing of the brilliancy of the room. Her happiness was from within. Her eyes were bright, and her cheeks glowed; but she knew nothing about it. She was thinking only of the last half hour.

The interior has four rooms: the Ballroom (the largest 18th century room in Bath), the Tea Room, the Octagon Room (originally known as the Card Room) and the Card Room itself (added in 1777). The Card Room was set up with tables for gaming. The Tea Room, where you took tea on ball nights, was also used for music nights and so was sometimes known as the Concert Room. The Octagon Room, which connects the Ballroom and Tea Room, must have been a place of much gossip on crowded ball nights.

The Assembly Room's nine huge chandeliers, made for the building when it was built in 1771, are some of finest surviving 18th century examples. An arm of one of the Ballroom's chandeliers once fell off, almost hitting Thomas Gainsborough. During WWII they were taken down and stored – which proved a very good idea, for the Rooms were gutted by fire in the air raids of 1942 (the restored Assembly Rooms didn't open until 1963). Today the chandeliers, which originally held candles, are insured for a cool £9 million.

Don't forget the excellent Fashion Museum in the basement [see listing in Attractions for more]. And don't take this badly, but those shoes you're wearing may have been fashionable in Austen's day…

You can find the Museum of Costume in the basement of the Assembly Rooms

The Assembly Rooms might not be quite so hemmed in by other buildings but for the schemes of John Wood the Younger's rival, Thomas Warr Attwood

"Sour Flatulences and Rank Armpits"

Georgian balls sound frightfully posh, but according to Tobias Smollett's novel *Humphry Clinker* the experience was a "horrid assault" of "putrid gums, imposthumated lungs, sour flatulencies, rank armpits, sweating feet, musk, hartshorn and sal volatile, beside a thousand frowzy steams, which I could not analyse." Nice…

HOW TO... HAVE A GEORGIAN BALL

THE MASTER OF CEREMONIES OVERSAW A STRICTLY REGIMENTED PROGRAMME OF EVENTS

Balls in Bath were strictly run under rules laid down by Bath's most famous Master of ceremonies, Richard 'Beau' Nash. Etiquette was everything. Long, extremely formal and appallingly tedious, even the most blue blooded of us today would run a mile rather an attend one. But if you're ever unfortunate enough to find yourself going to such a bash, you'll be needing this essential guide on what to expect and how to behave…

1 The wearing of swords, riding boots and aprons is prohibited at balls. Don all three and you will probably be escorted to the East Gate and asked to leave town.

2 Ladies dressed in their "full hoops", at 6pm the ball will open with a sublime series of subtly absurd "minuets" (stilted minces performed by single couples, noses in air) danced in a suitably restrained manner, beginning with the two persons of the highest distinction present. When the minuet is concluded the lady will return to her seat and the Master of Ceremonies will fetch the gentlemen a new partner. Each gentleman will also be expected to dance a minuet with at least two ladies. There will be no high kicking of heels. Expect the minuets to take a ludicrous two hours…

3 At 8pm, the at least slightly more jolly country dances begin. Ladies, according to their rank, standing up first, the men and women face each other in two rows and couples take turns to weave various patterns down the middle. Alas, we're not talking a hoedown here, with each successive couple trying to out do the last. It's all more of a stately prance, really, and while you wait your turn you stand around talking. Ladies will have their hoops removed to make room for all this, however the shedding of further garments is most certainly not permitted and could lead to ejection.

4 At 9pm there will be a short interval for tea (not to be sniffed at – it was very expensive in Georgian times). This over, the country dancing begins again.

5 A gentleman will not normally dance with any one lady more than twice during the night. If you break this rule it is a signal that you're *very* interested in her. Ladies, it is not seemly at all for you to go after a gentleman in the same way, though. As Tilney remarks to Catherine in *Northanger Abbey*, in dancing as in marriage, "man has the advantage of choice, woman only the power of refusal".

6 On the stroke of eleven, the MC would, with a single lift of his finger, silence the orchestra. After a polite period allowed for cooling off, the ladies will then be escorted to their sedan chairs.

7 That's your lot. Safe journey home. There will be no 'last orders'.

The regime was so strict that even the Royal Family was not powerful enough to sway Beau Nash from these rules. On one occasion, when Princess Amelia dared to ask for another dance after eleven, she was shortly informed by Nash that the rules of Bath would brook no alteration.

10 Pulteney Bridge

It's incredible to think that for nearly twenty years this world-famous bridge led nowhere...

■ Pulteney Bridge in the sunshine – a beautiful sight. The other side of the bridge is no longer quite so pretty though!

Built in 1773 by Robert Adam, Pulteney Bridge was meant to link the city to a grand new development on the estate of Bathwick, the other side of the river.

Wealthy businessman Sir William Pulteney – at the time reputed to be the richest man in England – wanted to build nothing less than a huge and grand neoclassical new town on an estate that had been inherited by his wife. However the American War of Independence knocked economic cofidence, investors failed to come forward and for years Pulteney Bridge ended in only meadows.

The bridge, like the Ponte Vecchio in Florence, is lined with shops on both sides – unique in Britain. The domed corner towers are little tollbooths. The decision to have shops on the bridge caused a confrontation between Sir William and the City Corporation, though he got his way. However, his plans to build a second bridge and road upriver at the village of Bathford was defeated by the Corporation, which had members who had interests in the Bath Turnpike Trust, which feared it would be robbed of tolls on its own roads.

Alterations made over the years – shop enlargements, extensions over the river and a redesign of the north side after flood damage in 1799 and 1800 – give the 'back' of today's bridge a dank and higgledy-piggledy look. Take a look from the back of the Podium shopping centre.

It wouldn't be until 1789 that Pulteney Bridge finally went somewhere – to the huge Great Pulteney Street. Robert Adam submitted a very grand design for the Great Pulteney Street development as well, but it would be William Baldwin who would build it, becoming bankrupt in the process.

■ It's the only bridgle lined with shops to be found in the country

The Roman Crossing

The Romans' Fosse Way, the great road stretching from Exeter in the south to Lincoln in the north, crossed the Avon at Bath. They probably built their ford between where Pulteney Bridge and Cleveland Bridge (a half mile or so up stream) stand today.

The Ferry and Ford

The shallowest point in the river near the city, in medieval times there was definitely a ford here where the bridge now stands. Then from the 17th century there was a ferry crossing here called Boatstall Quay. The ferry was pulled along a rope.

Today, on the riverbank opposite the balustrade of Grand Parade, you can take a boat trip up the river and back. Meanwhile, a pleasant walk along the river path down stream will take you to North Parade Bridge and John Wood's North and South Parades.

The Ducking Stool

In medieval times, just up river from where the bridge now stands, was the city's ducking stool, used for punishing "gossiping fishwives" and cheating traders. Ducking stools were first used towards the beginning of the 17th century. Basically waterboarding, they were chairs fastened to a long wooden beam fixed as a seesaw on the edge of a pond or river. Magistrates ordered the number of duckings the victim should have. Ducking died out, thankfully, in the early 19th century.

11 Great Pulteney Street

At over 1,000 feet long and 100 feet wide this is huge and grand, even for Bath...

■ **Great Pulteney Street, massive and magnificent – but it goes nowhere...**

By 1789 Pulteney Bridge finally went somewhere – to Great Pulteney Street. The street is all that was built of an idea dreamt up by the wealthy businessman Sir William Pulteney, who wanted to build a posh neo-classical new town on land inherited by his wife.

At 335 metres long and 31 metres wide this is by far the hugest street in Bath. In fact some architectural critics think it's built on a scale unfitting for Bath – and it does look like it should end with a Buckingham Palace or an Arc de Triomphe instead of the rather more modest (though lovely) Holburne Museum.

Robert Adam, commissioned by the wealthy Sir Pulteney to build Pulteney Bridge, was originally to build the street along with a great development of squares and circles. In the end, though, William Pulteney's daughter Henrietta Laura Pulteney, the heiress of the estate, wanted the cheaper but still very grand plans of William Baldwin.

William Pulteney's vision for a huge new town was left incomplete. A financial crisis bankrupted the builders and two of Bath's six banks, and construction was halted permanently. As a result, we are left with just the backbone of the project and, halfway down it, Sunderland Street, the shortest street in Bath with only one address.

Until the 1970s lime trees lined both sides of the road. The street lamps are actually 19th century gas lamp reproductions left to the city after the filming of the 2004 movie *Vanity Fair*. (William Makepeace Thackeray's novel, by the way, isn't set in Bath at all but London.) Numbers 39, 72 and 74 still have their original lamp holders or "throwovers".

Great Pulteney Street's rooms are large, with very high ceilings. This was a sign of changing times for the city, for instead of splendid public gatherings in assembly rooms, duller private parties in the home had become the done thing. Meanwhile, Bath as a whole was becoming a less colourful place. Society was deciding that holidaying at the seaside was better for its health than gambling and frivolity, and by the time Jane Austen arrived in 1801 the Georgian glitterati were replaced by mannered gentry who came to settle and retire rather than holiday and play cards. Bath's heyday was over.

At the far end of the street (as you leave town) is the entertaining and well worth a visit Holburne museum.

An original 18th century ironwork lampholder or "throwover"

Austen Watch

In *Persuasion* the snooty Lady Dalrymple and her daughter take rooms in Laura Place (the area that surrounds the fountain at the entrance to Great Pulteney Street), where they would be, according to the snobbish Sir Walter, "living in style"

Great Pulteney Street itself is where Catherine Morland stayed with the Allens in *Northanger Abbey*.

OLD BATHONIANS

LOUIS NAPOLEON BONAPARTE
(1808-1873)
55 GREAT PULTENEY STREET

Shortly before he became Emperor Napoleon III of France, Louis Napoleon, nephew of the other – slightly more famous – Napoleon, stayed here in 1846.

KING LOUIS XVIII
(1755-1824)
72 GREAT PULTENEY STREET

The French king stayed at No 72 in August 1813, towards the end of his 23 years in exile during the French Revolution. His brother, Louis XVI, was a customer of Madame Guillotine in 1793.

HANNAH MORE
(1745-1833)
76 GREAT PULTENEY STREET

During the 1790s, the 'social reformer' Hannah More's evangelical pamphlets, the *Cheap Repository Tracts,* were published by Samuel Hazard of Cheap Street. More's idea of social reform amounted to scalding the working classes for their wicked behaviour and telling them that the social order was ordained from On High – and that agitating for change invited only Divine Retribution. More, at that time, lived in this very nice house on Great Pulteney Street… The essayist Augustine Birrel buried 19 of her works in his garden complaining that she was "one of the most detestable writers that ever held a pen".

WILLIAM SMITH
(1769-1839)
29 GREAT PULTENEY STREET

One of the principle founders of geology because of his early work with fossils and rock strata. In Bath he worked on various canal and mining projects and in 1810 he was called in when the King's Spring failed, leaving the Great Bath and the Pump Room dry. Despite, inevitably, much opposition, he was eventually permitted to dig the Spring to the bottom, where he discovered the Spring had not failed but had found its way into a new channel. Smith returned the water to its original course and the bath filled even more rapidly than before. Hurrah!

WILLIAM WILBERFORCE
(1759-1833)
36 GREAT PULTENEY STREET

The MP, philanthropist, and campaigner for the abolition of the slave trade was married at Walcot Church in 1792 (the lady in question's parents lived on the Royal Crescent). He stayed at No 36 in 1802 and 1805. He also stayed at No 9 North Parade in 1831.

Boasting a splendid new extension at its rear, the Holburne Museum was originally the Sydney Hotel that stood at the entrance to the Sydney Pleasure Gardens. The hotel even had a pub in its basement that catered for servants, chairman and coachmen, who were not permitted to go into the pleasure gardens themselves. But as the Gardens waned, so did the hotel. After becoming Bath College for a while, in 1915 the building was bought by the Bath-based Holburne family, which left to the city its huge collection of silver, glass, porcelain, furniture and paintings. Treasures on show include works by Turner and Gainsborough. On the front edge of the grass forecourt of the museum is a watchman's box dating from about 1840 which would have sheltered constables of Bath's stave-armed City Watch.

■ The main, permanent exhibition at the Holburne Museum is free of charge

■ Rather than just cars, until the 1970s lime trees also lined either side of the road

SPOOKY BATH
It's haunted! (allegedly...)
71 Great Pulteney Street

Earl Admiral Richard Howe, who led a great victory against the French at the Third Battle of Ushant in 1794, haunts this address... Apparently.

Bath in pictures

From its stunning architecture to its glorious views, images of Bath will always lift the heart...

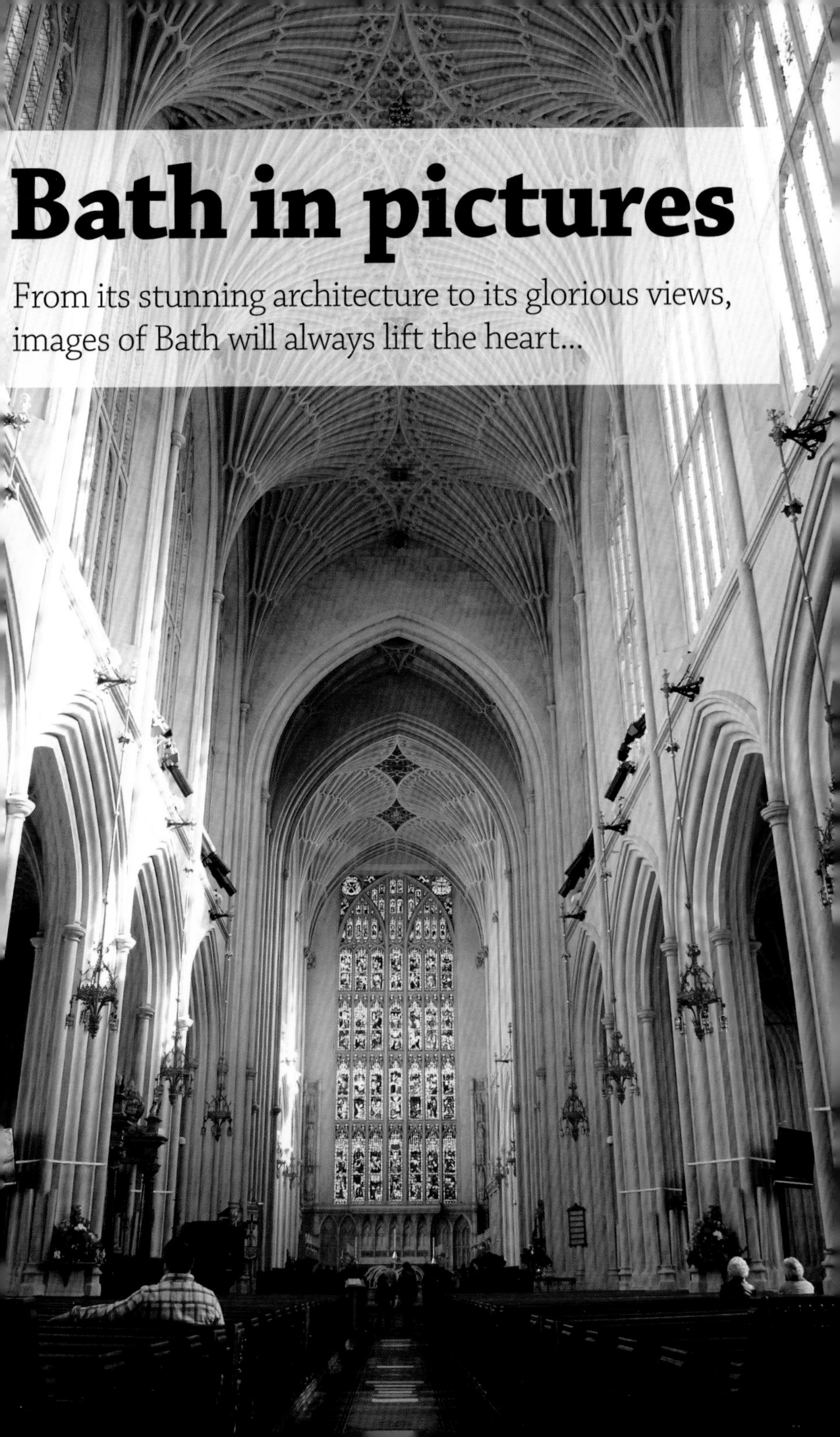

FRONT BATH ABBEY
The fan-vaulted ceiling of the Abbey is comparable to any in the world

← ROMAN BATHS
Hushed, hot, steaming, beautiful... the 2,000-year-old Great Bath

↑ THERMAE BATHS
Today you can still soak in the water of the city's fabled hot springs

↑ QUEEN SQUARE
The obelisk was erected to commerate the 1732 visit of Frederick, Prince of Wales

→ BOTANICAL GARDENS
A quiet oasis hidden in the heart of Victoria Park renowned for its plants that thrive on limestone

BOTANICAL GARDENS

← **PULTENEY BRIDGE**
Adam's masterpiece is lined with shops, like Florence's Ponte Vecchio

↑ **GREAT PULTENEY ST**
Huge and grand, part of a neoclassical new town that was never built

↑ **ASSEMBLY ROOMS**
A study in elegance and the scene of many a sumptuous ball

↑ **PUMP ROOM HALL**
Built in 1897, now the extremely posh entrance hall of the Roman Baths

↑ **PUMP ROOM**
Suffering from gout? This where you would come to "take the waters"

→ **PUMP ROOM INTERIOR**
Jane Austen visited the Pump Room during her stay in the city

KING'S AND QUEEN'S BATHS

← **BATHS & ABBEY**
The Queen's Bath was demolished in 1889, but the King's Bath survives

↑ **KING'S BATH**
Built around 1106 – on top of the Romans' long-forgotten Sacred Spring

↑ **KING'S BATH**
The facilities were slightly more rudimentary than Thermae Bath Spa's

Bath in pictures

↑ ROYAL CRESCENT
Massive, imposing, but built to blend harmoniously with the landscape

↑ THE CIRCUS
Designed by John Wood the Elder, the man who dreamt up Georgian Bath

→ ROYAL CRESCENT
Up close it looks like some beautifully carved limestone cliff…

HOLBURNE MUSEUM
Home to a collection of art including works by Turner and Gainsborough. The modern extension is by Eric Parry

↑ VICTORIA PARK
The park was just countryside and known as "Crescent Fields" in Jane Austen's time

↑ VICTORIA PARK
A lion guards the 1837 Victoria Majority Monument. At one time there were captured Russian guns from the Crimea too

HOW TO... BUY A HOUSE JANE AUSTEN STYLE

USE SOME OF THE GREAT LADY'S MORE ACID OBSERVATIONS – MAKE ESTATE AGENTS CRAWL

Jane Austen's family were singularly fussy when it came to choosing houses in Bath, a pastime they started in 1801. Mr Austen in particular – an increasingly infirm man who couldn't abide hills – was extraordinarily unimpressed by most of what he saw, even though he had a budget with little margin for fastidiousness.

House prices and rents in central Bath today are astronomically high. Historic terraced affairs go for the proverbial bomb and even those with work required on them – indeed, especially those with work required on them – are snapped up in short order. So problems like damp are considered no barrier at all; and you can be certain that if you don't buy it, someone else will.

But if you really would like your prospective Georgian home to be '"just so:" and have that "perfect aspect", here is a guide to those authentic Austen-esque complaints you'll need for the estate agent, as taken from our Jane's letters from Bath. They will, if you're persistent enough, surely have even the best agents eventually screaming for mercy and pulling their hair out...

Trim Street
She [Jane's mother] *shall do everything in her power to avoid Trim Street.*

Axford Buildings
We all unite in a particular dislike of that part of town.

Seymour Street
This house was not inviting; the largest room downstairs was not much more than fourteen feet, with a western aspect.

New King Street
One in particular of the two, was quite monstrously little... and the second room on every floor about capacious enough to admit a very small single bed.

Green Park Buildings
The only doubt is about the dampness of the offices, of which there were symptoms.

Green Park Buildings (second viewing)
We shall at least have the pleasure of examining some of these putrefying houses again... there is some satisfaction in spending ten minutes with them.

Green Park Buildings (final viewing)
Our views on G. P. Buildings seem all at an end; the observation of the damp still remaining in the offices of an house which has been only vacated a week, with reports of discontented families and putrid fevers, has given the coup de grace. We have now nothing in view.

Seymour Street (second viewing)
I have nothing more to say on the subject of houses; except that we were mistaken as to the aspect of the one on Seymour Street, which instead of being due west is north-west.

St James Square
We are disappointed in the lodgings of St James Square. We have looked at some other since but don't quite like the situation.

After finding fault with so many others, the Austens finally took a house at No 4 Sydney Place, on the right at the top of Great Pulteney Street, in October 1801. Little did they know that five years later they would wind up in hated Trim Street... Oh dear! No wonder they then left for Bristol.

12 Victoria Park & Gravel Walk

Lots to see and do here – splendid gardens, pitch & putt, romantic walks, and a curious Georgian lavatory

A manicured green mass in the heart of Bath and by far the biggest of its many fine parks, the 57-acre Royal Victoria Park was opened in 1830 and named after the then 11-year-old Princess Victoria. One of the earliest public parks in Britain, it was created out of the city common. The area right in front of the Royal Crescent was known as 'Crescent Fields' in Jane Austen's time.

At its eastern end, behind the Circus, is 'Gravel Walk'. This secluded path for sedan chairs was built to link the Crescent to the lower part of the city and the baths.

■ A beautiful open space in the heart of the city, Victoria Park is Bath's 'urban beach'

Off the Walk is the 'Georgian Garden' – the back garden of No 4 The Circus. Quite austere and exact to our eyes, it's a rare of example of the sort of garden many Georgian town houses would once have had.

Over the park's road from the garden, behind the cafe, is crazy golf – bedlam in high summer!

At the park's western end is the nine-acre Botanical Garden. Renowned for its collection of plants that love limestone, it's a peaceful place that transports you away from the bustle of the city.

In the summer months, early evenings see balloons take off from this end of the park – a sight well worth seeing. This area also has a small lake and an excellent children's play area, complete with a half-pipe for skateboarders and BMXers. Over the road from the play area, adults might like to refresh themselves at the Hop Pole, a pub with good ale, good food and a quiet beer garden at its rear.

The Victoria Majority Monument, built in 1837. Now gone, captured Russian cannons from the Crimean War stood near the obelisk from 1857

SPOOKY BATH
It's haunted! (allegedly...)

Gravel Walk, Victoria Park

A ghostly white-haired man with his hair tied back has been seen on this otherwise pleasant and scenic path. The phantom has been sighted by both a schoolboy and a Deputy Mayor of Miami, so it simply must be true!

Austen Watch

In the romantic climax to *Persuasion*, the main characters Anne Elliot and Captain Wentworth take the long way round to Sir Walter's home in Camden Crescent, along "the comparatively quiet and retired gravel walk", oblivious to everything around them…

And there, as they slowly paced the gradual ascent, heedless of every group around them, seeing neither sauntering politicians, bustling housekeepers, flirting girls, nor nursery-maids and children, they could indulge in those retrospections and acknowledgements, and especially in those explanations of what had directly preceded the present moment, which were so poignant and so ceaseless in interest.

Hanging Privvies

A parade along Victoria Park's Gravel Walk is very pleasant indeed – and it also affords you an excellent opportunity to discuss Georgian lavatory arrangements. On the right you'll see the back of part of the Circus and, tucked away on an upper storey of one of the houses, is what we call a 'hanging privy' – a box stuck on to the building where ladies and gentlemen did their business through a hole on to a waiting horse cart below. Efficient, perhaps, but also dangerous, if you believe the stories of people being killed when these privies fell crashing to the ground. What a way to go.

DUELLING: DOS & DON'TS

MANY DUELS WERE FOUGHT IN THE CRESCENT FIELDS. REDISCOVER THIS HARMLESS PASTIME...

■ No duel will be short of spectators in Victoria Park

The fields below the Royal Crescent saw duelling in Bath's heyday. During the reign of George III (1760-1820) there were 172 known duels in England (many more would have been kept secret), resulting in sixty-nine recorded deaths. Despite efforts to stamp out duelling by luminaries such as Beau Nash, many resorted to the duel to satisfy their honour including old Bathonians Edmund Burke, William Pitt the Younger, William Pulteney and Richard Brinsley Sheridan, while Samuel Johnson, another old Bathonian, defended the practice on the grounds that "a man may shoot the man who invades his character as he may shoot him who attempts to break into his house".

Duelling has long since fallen out of fashion in Bath, and the last known duel fought by Englishmen on English soil was in 1845. But should you during your time in the city feel impelled to rush off and demand 'satisfaction' from some impudent bounder, there are a few do's and don'ts on points of etiquette to remember – for above all duelling is very much a 'gentlemen's' way of settling matters...

✔ Do... challenge people to duels over bizarre "matters of honour"

You would think that only such things as cheating at cards or eloping with a lord's daughter after gleefully jumping on his roses would constitute a wrong serious enough for a duel challenge – but not a bit of it. In 1829 the Duke of Wellington challenged the Earl of Winchelsea to a duel after simply being accused of softness towards Catholics.

✖ Don't... admit to being of the lower classes

If your opponent gets wind of this he will refuse to demean himself by duelling with you and will instead merely beat you with his cane or set his servants on you.

✖ Don't... challenge your foe to a duel by slapping them in the face with a glove

That only happens in the movies. The correct way to issue a challenge is to *throw* a glove in their face – which, I'm sure you'll agree, is actually subtly more insulting. (Just be careful, though, not to accidentally miss your foppish target and hit a burly man-at-arms instead or you'll need running shoes rather than duelling pistols.) If a glove is thrown at *you, then* you may pick it up and slap them in the face with it. Incidentally, this practice of glove throwing originates from medieval times, when "throwing down the gauntlet" was a knight's method of choice for challenging another knight to a duel. Picking the gauntlet up was the signal that the challenge had been accepted. But enough of that. You yourself now have a duel to fight. Either that or it's time to get out of town – or say to your foe, "Here, you appear to have dropped one of your gloves..."

✔ Do... use your imagination when it comes to weapons

If you are given a choice of weapons,

remember that you don't have to go down the swords or pistols route. In 1843, for instance, two duellists settled their differences by aiming billiard balls at each other's heads. Other exotic weapons chosen for duelling have included howitzers, sledgehammers and forkfuls of pig dung (to show disdain for duelling). If you are invited to use handguns, do lay your hands on a finely-crafted set of duelling pistols. Remember at all times that you are a wealthy gentleman or nobleman.

If your opponent, to your horror, suggests swords, dismiss the idea with scorn, pointing out that blades are *so* pre-18th Century. Alternatively, demand swords *and* pistols. This occurred in a particularly bloodthirsty duel fought in 1778 on Bath's Claverton Down between one Count Rice and one Vicomte du Barri (it was over cheating at cards). Du Barri fired first, wounded Rice in the thigh. Rice then discharged, shooting Du Barri in the breast. Both men then rushed the other, discharging their second pistols and missing. According to witnesses, as the two prepared to finish things with swords du Barri suddenly grew pale and collapsed dead. Mmm. Howitzers it is then!

✔ Do... remember: location, location, location

It's no good having your formal set-to in the middle of town (the whole thing is technically illegal, remember). Victoria Park at dawn is a one traditional place and time, or, as we've already discovered, Claverton Down. In Jane Austen's time Gravel Walk at the back of the Circus was the field of choice. Alternatively – and perfect for Bath, where hot air balloons are a common sight in the skies – more daring duellists might consider copying the two Frenchmen who in 1808 fought in balloons over Paris. (For the record, one eventually did succeed in shooting the other down, killing him along with his second.)

✖ Don't... forget the rules of engagement

It's time for the fight. As well as a pair of brown trousers, 'seconds' are recommended. Your seconds will oversee fair play by checking that weapons are equal and that rules of engagement are adhered to. At the discretion of the wronged party, the duel can be fought to the death but it is acceptable to fight to "first blood", where the first person to draw claret is deemed the winner.

First blood is obviously the most sensible course – but tell that to Richard Brinsley Sheridan. The dashing playwright fought two very barbaric duels – one in London and one at Kingsdown in Bath – with a Major Mathews over the famously beautiful Elizabeth Linley. Sheridan was carried to a nearby inn after being seriously injured in the second contest, which was a particularly unpleasant affair devoid of all chivalry. It apparently ended with the two of them lying injured on the ground hacking at each with broken, bloodied swords. Nice.

✖ Don't... think you'll be able to cheat

Considering the possibility of getting in a sneaky early shot? Forget it. To negate cheating in pistol contests, instead of the romantic ideal of walking a set number of paces before turning and discharging, it became the custom to advance from fixed points, firing at will at each other.

✔ Do... try and get out of it with as much style as you can muster

Ask yourself: is this really worth it? Admit it – you're rubbish at cards, Miss Linley has bad breath and your views on the Catholic-Protestant struggle really aren't at all firm. It's time to do what both the Duke of Wellington the Earl of Winchelsea did in 1754 and aim wide... Now *that's* the gentlemen's way of settling things.

BATH A-Z

You've seen the best, now visit the rest! The city of Bath is crammed full of interesting places...

A

ABBEY GREEN

Part of the Abbey's grounds – which from the 9th century took up the entire south-eastern area of the city – the peaceful and secluded Abbey Green was once the monks' bowling green. King John (it is possible that the King's Bath is named after him) took a house on Abbey Green in 1201.

The site of the Crystal Palace pub has an interesting history. It started off life as a Roman villa (a Roman mosaic – and skeletons – were discovered in the pub's cellar in 1981). The Saxon church of St James later stood there, and when that was replaced by a new church by the South Gate in 1279 it became the Bishop's private chapel. By 1694 the site was occupied by a "Mr Webb's Lodgings", which provided extra rooms for the Three Tuns inn, then on Stall Street. The current building, built by Thomas Baldwin around 1780, was originally another storey high, which was taken off in 1933. Lord Nelson (though more associated with Pierrepont Street, where he lived for a time) is said to have stayed at the Crystal Place while recovering from wounds suffered during his victory over Napoleon in the Battle of the Nile.

The monks lost their grip on Abbey Green in 1543, when it was sold off as part of Henry VIII's Dissolution of the Monasteries. The Green was much larger before the three properties on the east side were built in 1698. The Georgians have remodelled the houses but they didn't quite manage to remove all traces of the original Stuart architecture. Mullioned windows and gables still survive, for instance, on the side and rear of No 2.

At the south end of the Green, towards Marks & Spencer, there stood until 1896 the National School, which was circular in shape and divided into wedge-shaped classrooms. It's nice to think that if you stood in the very centre of the building you could keep an eye on all the children at once...

Tranter's, on Church Street (between York Street and the Green), is Bath's legendary tobacconist and (cough) *the* place for an unusual blend of the evil stuff, be it a posh fag or a decent cigar. The Bath Festivals Box Office, where you can get tickets for all sorts of

Bath events, is almost opposite. Just over the road, on the right-hand side of the square (Kingston Parade, technically) is the Tourist Information Centre.

SPOOKY BATH It's haunted! (allegedly...)

A mysterious "transparent monk" has been sighted in the Crystal Palace. Could it be anything to do with the skeletons and Roman mosaic discovered in the cellar in 1981? Almost certainly not... Mind you, the plane tree in the middle of Abbey Green, planted around 1790, does have a sinister urban myth attached to it. It is supposed to be the "Hanging Tree", where executions took place... "Supposed to be", mark you. Could the absence of grass under the trees be the result of some sort of curse or other paranormal activity? No, it's the result of hordes of tourists traipsing all over it.

ABBEYGATE STREET

The arch between Abbey Green and Abbeygate Street marks the Abbey Gate, the main gateway of the walled Abbey grounds established in the 9th century.

On the other side of the street a lane called Leer Land ran south through what is now Marks & Spencer down to the city's "Ham Gate". The monks would drive their sheep along this lane to the "Ham", pastures outside the city walls [see New Orchard Street]. The word leer or "lear" comes from the Saxon for empty or hungry. The area got the name because here outside the Abbey Gate was where poor people waited for bread and alms from the monks.

Behind the row of shops on the right as you look up Abbeygate Street stood John de Villula's Bishop's Palace, built in the early 1090s, at the same time as he built the huge Norman cathedral to replace the Saxon abbey.

In 1749, John Wood described the gate has having a "triumphal arch". He was less enthusiastic about the "inferior" street, though, which by then was known as Abbey Lane. The Abbey Gate was taken down in the middle of the 18th century. The hinge, set there as a reminder, is all that is left of it.

A horrid tale to end with: After the end of Roman rule in Britain around AD 410 the people who remained in Bath were subject to Saxon raids. A Roman house of this period unearthed by archaeologists in Abbeygate Street contained the severed head of a young girl which had been thrust into an oven.

ALFRED STREET

John Wood was a big fan of Alfred, hence the name his son John Wood the Younger gave this street [see below].

Number 14 has a bust of King Alfred above its door. Just by the door is a rare surviving Georgian torch extinguisher (torches were lit by 'link boys' to illuminate the way for the sedan chairs coming from the Assembly Rooms). The house also still has its winch, once used to lower a sedan chair to the basement.

OLD BATHONIANS

CATHARINE MACAULAY *(1731-1791)* 2 ALFRED STREET

Influential historian, and notorious republican and feminist Catharine Macaulay lived at No 2 Alfred Street – shacked up with a 70-year-old vicar. Totally infatuated, Thomas Wilson, rector of St Stephen's, Walbrook in London, not only signed over the house to Macaulay but had a statue in her honour erected in his church. This met with such disapproval from his congregation that it was swiftly boarded up. Eventually, though, she married the younger brother of James Graham – a Scottish quack whose remedies included setting his patients on a magnetic throne and burying them naked up to their neck in earth. On hearing this the good Reverend Wilson, reputedly enraged, had the statue torn down.

WILLIAM HARBUTT *(1844-1921)* 15 ALFRED STREET

A painter and the inventor of Plasticine, William Harbutt was headmaster of the Bath School of Art and then the owner of an art school on The Paragon before he invented Plasticine around 1897 as a non-drying modelling clay for his students. In 1899 he was granted a trademark and in 1900 a factory was established at nearby Bathampton. For the rest of his life Harbutt travelled much to spread his ideas about teaching children art through free expression. The Harbutt family-owned company continued to make Plasticine in Bathampton until 1983. The brand then changed ownership several times and is now manufactured in Thailand for the UK company Flair.

Alfred: Bath's First Great King

Before the rule of Alfred the Great, King of Wessex, Bath was just a monastic settlement around the baths surrounded by fragments of the Roman wall. By his death in 899 Alfred had not only made Bath part of a network of fortified towns called burghs (from where we get the word borough) but he had also laid out the city's street plan, preparing the way for it to flourish as a market town.

A popular legend tells how Alfred, after being routed by the Danes in nearby Chippenham in Wiltshire, fled to the marshes of the Somerset Levels, where he was given shelter by a peasant woman. The story goes that the woman, unaware of his identity, left him to watch some cakes that were cooking on the fire. Fretting over the troubles besetting his kingdom, Alfred let the cakes burn. At the time Wessex alone of all the Saxon kingdoms still stood against the Danes. He would emerge, though, from the marshes to win a series of victories against the Danes in 878, including in the decisive Battle of Ethandun, fought near Westbury in Wiltshire. Alfred is the only English monarch still given the title "the Great".

ARGYLE STREET

Originally called Argyle Buildings, this street was built in 1789 by Thomas Baldwin to link Pulteney Bridge to his Laura Place and Great Pulteney Street, the centrepieces of the Bathwick estate project which would famously run out of cash, leaving short streets that lead nowhere.

The Rev. William Jay was minister at the Argyle Chapel (rebuilt in 1821) from January

1791 to January 1853. During this 62-year stint, Jay built a reputation as a great orator and many of the great and good went to hear him. Richard Sheridan declared him to be the most "manly orator" he had ever heard. Jay was not only manly but also prolific. Before he was even 21 the good Reverend had racked up an impressive 1,000 sermons.

Number 8 Argyle Street is a chemist with a great 19th-century shopfront – and it's worth a look inside too. Once featured on the BBC's *Antiques Roadshow*, hundreds of old medicine jars and bottles line its shelves.

OLD BATHONIANS

ADMIRAL JOHN JERVIS 8 ARGYLE STREET

Admiral John Jervis – best known for his 15-strong fleet's victory over a 27-strong Spanish fleet at the 1797 Battle of Cape Saint Vincent – lived at No 8, now a chemist's. A strict disciplinarian, Jervis dealt out often harsh punishment to those he felt deserved it. As First Lord of the Admiralty he introduced a series of unpopular reforms to root out corruption and inefficiency in a navy system he discovered to be full of "incapables, infirm boys, cripples, or idiots" and "every rogue and vagabond that could not obtain a meal by any other means".

AUSTEN WATCH

It is on Argyle Street that in *Northanger Abbey* the Tilneys see Catherine being driven off in a carriage against her will by the boastful and arrogant John Thorpe. At her frantic cries to stop Mr. Thorpe, the cad, "laughed, smacked his whip, encouraged his horse, made odd noises, and drove on"...

William Bowmen, the doctor who attended Jane Austen's father through his last illness in January 1805, worked from a practice at 1 Argyle Street. At the time the family lived at 3 Green Park Buildings East. Dr Bowman also attended Mrs Austen at 4 Sydney Place when she was taken ill in 1801. When she had recovered, Mrs Austen praised the "skill and attention of Bowen" in a poem.

AVON STREET & CORN STREET

This area just north of the river and east of Bath Spa Railway Station seems mostly devoid of culture now – bombing and tasteless redevelopment have seen to that. But the names Avon Street and Corn Street conjure up a dark and seamy side of Bath's history, one more doleful and brutal than that depicted in Jane Austen's books.

In the 1730s Avon Street was a fashionable area where the gentry lived, but by the 19th century it had become a poor slum district ridden with poverty, overcrowding, disease and crime. The area was particularly renowned as a red light district, the home of the "Nymphs of Avon Street". In those times, despite the low rents, desperately poor families would commonly have to do a 'moonlight flit' and move, their possessions in a cart, to even cheaper rooms in other slum districts. The distress and discontent all this brewed would boil over into rioting on the streets of 'respectable' Bath.

In the second half of the 18th century one house in every eight on Avon Street was licensed to serve alcohol. And by 1821, the population of Avon Street was 1,519. So five per cent of Bath's population was squashed into one short street. By then even the pubs were few and far between. And no wonder. The river regularly flooded the area, and sewage and even pigsty and slaughter house waste found its way into basements. In 1831 cholera was in city and more than half of those who died came from Avon Street.

In 1842 the clergyman and journalist the Reverend Whitwell Elwin savagely summed up the area...

Whatever contagious or epidemic disease prevailed, – fever, smallpox, influenza, Avon Street was the scene of the principal ravages... Everything vile and offensive is congregated there. All the scum of Bath – its low prostitutes, its thieves, its beggars – are piled up in the dens rather than the houses of which the street consists...

B

BATH SPA RAILWAY STATION

Bath's connection completed the sixth section of Isambard Kingdom Brunel's Great Western Railway from Paddington to Bristol to be built.

The city was stuck in a period of decline when the station opened in 1840. Visitor numbers, though, were not immediately boosted. It would take further improvements in the rail network and new bathing treatments to do that. That and the discovery in 1878 of the Roman's Great Bath.

Because the station is situated within a loop of the River Avon, Brunel had to build two bridges across the water. No contractor was prepared to commit to the building of the west viaduct because of the complexity of the work, so Brunel had to oversee its construction personally. The station was meant to open in the spring of 1838 but the engineering challenges present delayed this. The whole line to London was not opened until 30 June 1841, following completion of Box Tunnel [see below].

The station originally sported a huge glass roof, sidings and even a footbridge to the Royal Hotel opposite. The Italian leader Giuseppe Garibaldi – who led his country to unification in 1860 – was supposed to make a speech from the bridge in 1864. The idea was abandoned after he couldn't even get off the train to greet the mayor because of the massive crowds.

Tunnel Vision

Box Tunnel, between Bath and Chippenham, was the longest railway tunnel in the world when it was completed in 1841. Over 100 workers died building it. It is popularly believed that Brunel deliberately aligned the tunnel so that the rising sun shines through it on his birthday, 9 April, each year. Best not to test out the phenomenon yourself, though, as this would require you to stand right in the middle of a very busy high-speed railway line.

BATH STREET & ST MICHAEL'S PLACE

Originally named Cross Bath Street, city architect Thomas Baldwin's Bath Street was built in 1791 as part of the Bath Improvement Act redevelopment, which saw a great swathe of the crammed medieval city centre knocked down and rebuilt. Bath had finally decided that it was time it showed off its baths properly, and the new street's colonnades provided a grand covered walkway that allowed sick folk to be carried in sedan chairs between the Pump Room and the Hot and Cross baths in style.

At the entrance of Bath Street there used to be a steam-driven Hot Water Fountain. Erected in 1856, it was soon converted into a drinking fountain to replace the Pauper's Pump at the Hot bath. People did at first take water from it home with them but it was gradually used less and less. Its water was stopped in 1978 because of the meningitis scare and then it was moved to Terrace Walk, where it remains to this day.

Number 8, next to the entrance to the spa, was the city's Museum of Antiquities until 1800. The statue in the niche on the left is of the legendary Celtic king Old King Cole, the "merry old soul" of the nursery rhyme. Cole was, one legend has it, the first English king to reside in Bath. The figure on the right is King Edgar, crowned at the Abbey on 1 May 973 in a ceremony that still forms the basis of the present day British coronation. Believed to be 15th century, the statues themselves once adorned the town hall that stood on High Street.

In 1870, a "New Royal Bath & Physical Treatment Centre" was built along Bath Street, where BHS now stands. Stretching the whole length of Bath Street, one entrance faced what is now the Little Theatre Cinema and another was in the Grand Pump Room Hotel on Stall Street. It boasted the large New Royal Bath itself, six pools, thee reclining baths, enema baths, shower baths, vapour baths, the lot. The facility was closed down in 1976 when its NHS funding was withdrawn. After a fire in 1988, the site was turned into the Colonnades Shopping Centre development, which was a disastrous flop.

St Michael's Place, the passage connecting Bath Street and Westgate Street, was once called Nash Street, after Beau Nash. It was renamed after the only remaining Georgian chapel in Bath, the Chapel of St. Michael in nearby Chapel Court, which you can come to through the small gate behind the Cross Bath [see Westgate Buildings].

The Hospital Of The Baths

St John's Hospital, the "hospital of the baths", was founded around 1180 by Bishop Reginald Fitz Jocelyn, the fourth bishop of Bath. Built for the poor and infirm, it was the first hospital in the city and is one the oldest in England (though the building you see today dates back to 1716). The original building was laid out much like a modern open hospital ward, except it had a chapel at one end. The hospital today, which now also takes in Chapel Court [see Westgate Buildings], provides a home for 90 local elderly people and provides grants to people in hardship around Bath.

Little Theatre Cinema

St Michael's Place is home to the excellent Little Theatre Cinema – *the* place to go in Bath for proper films. The Little Theatre Cinema was built by community theatre pioneer Consuelo de Reyes and her husband in 1935, originally as a theatre and news cinema. The Little's first film programme was a newsreel plus a documentary on the Royal Academy and another on the life of the frog… The cinema itself features in the 2009 animated movie *Fantastic Mr. Fox*, and today you can even get married in it!

AUSTEN WATCH

Bath Street was one of the important shopping streets in Jane Austen's time, though it was not a particularly happy one for the Austens. It was in one of the shops at the entrance to Bath Street that in August 1799 Jane's aunt, Jane Leigh Perrot, was accused of stealing a card of white lace worth twenty shillings. She was arrested and forced to wait eight months at Ilchester jail until the trial. Because of her standing, she was able to 'do the time' in the jailer's family home. Yet as James Leigh Perrot, who stayed by his wife's side, wrote, the jailer's home was not salubrious accommodation:

Cleanliness has ever been his greatest delight, and yet he sees the greasy toast laid by the dirty children on his knees, and feels the small beer trickle down his sleeves on its way across the table unmoved...

Mrs Leigh Perrot's alleged crime was punishable by hanging or deportation to Australia. A jury took just moments to acquit her. Some still think she got off the hook because she was an important personage, but it is most likely that she was stitched up by the Miss Gregory who ran the shop. It emerged afterwards that Gregory had forced other women to pay for goods that she had planted in their parcels. Jane Leigh Perrot might well have been spared her ordeal had she agreed to pay up, but she was not that sort of person.

Jane had little love for her aunt but it seems the whole sorry affair may have coloured her view of Bath Street, for in the two Bath Street scenes in her novels disingenuous characters meddle with her heroines' happiness…

In *Northanger Abbey*, Catherine's rival in love Isabella Thorpe writes, pretending that she has given up on Fred Tilney: "The last time we met was in Bath Street, and I turned directly into a shop that he might not speak to me; I would not even look at him. He went into the pump-room afterwards; but I would not have followed him for all the world."

In *Persuasion*, the mischievous Mary Musgrove, sitting in the White Hart Hotel in Stall Street, spies Mrs Clay and Mr Elliot headed for Bath Street and says to Anne slyly: "There is Mrs. Clay, I am sure, standing under the colonnade, and a gentleman with her. I saw them turn the corner from Bath Street just now. They seem deep in talk. Who is it? Come, and tell me. Good heavens! I recollect. It is Mr. Elliot himself..."

Jane herself shopped in Bath Street. She wrote to her sister Cassandra in May 1799: "I saw some gauzes in a shop in Bath Street yesterday at only 4d. a yard, but they were not so good or so pretty as mine." Only three months later Mrs Leigh Perrot would find herself accused of theft – perhaps from the same shop.

BARTLETT STREET

Built in 1786 to link George Street to the Assembly Rooms, this small alley is by far the nicest route to take to the top end of town. Not only is it blessedly free of traffic, it's also the beginning of an area that's simply jammed with antique shops (indeed, you'd better have a fat wallet with you if you're visiting the area for that purpose).

There are some lovely Victorian shop fronts along here. In the early 1800s a Jacob Abraham, optician and telescope and microscope maker, had a shop at No 7 Bartlett Street. One of Abraham's customers was no less than Arthur Wellesley, the Duke of Wellington who defeated Napoleon at Waterloo in 1815. In 1830 the Duke built himself a very nice country house (now the Apsley House Hotel) on Newbridge Hill in western Bath. By this time Wellington was coming to the end of a two-year reign as an extremely unpopular anti-political reformist Tory prime minister. It was during this period that he earned himself the nickname the "Iron Duke" – and Apsley House was targeted by window-smashers, forcing him to install iron shutters. Welcome to Bath, Wellers!

BEAU STREET

Once called Bell Tree Lane after a now-gone secret lodging house used by monks after Henry VIII dissolved the Abbey in 1539, this was the only route from Stall Street to the Hot Bath until Bath Street was built in 1791.

The main point of interest on Beau Street is Bellott's Hospital. It was founded in 1609, just after the death of Elizabeth I. This was a period when the city was becoming famed for the healing power of its waters and several wealthy personages began giving money to spa projects for the poor. One benefactor was Elizabeth's chief advisor Lord Burghley, who had visited the city with the Queen in 1574. After Burghley's death in 1598, his steward Thomas Bellott invested money he left to charity in the building of Bellott's Hospital. Unlike nearby St John's and St Catherine's hospitals, Bellott's served not Bathionians but sick visitors to the city – "lame pilgrims". A forerunner of the modern hospital, its quadrangle boasted 14 rooms, 12 of which were for patients. Free medical advice (some of it quite probably bad!) could also be had from the hospital's physician.

The 17th-century building was replaced by the present one in 1859, making it a rare example of Victorian architecture in the heart of the city. Bellott had Burghley's coat of arms put up (it was over the door of the old building) to commemorate him. The Latin inscription translates: "Do not leave dormant in your store that which would relieve the poor. If the poor sleep soundly, so will you." This was meant as a reminder to the rich that giving to charity was one way of keeping the poor classes from rebelling. Today the building is a care home.

Looming above the west end of Beau Street is the Gainsborough Building. A hulking affair with imposing columns, it started off life as the United Hospital before being taken over by the City of Bath College. It is now to be turned into a luxury hotel and spa. Built by John Pinch the Elder in 1826, it had an extra storey added in the 1860s, though this didn't make John Betjeman like it any more – he called it "the terrible 'Tech' with its pointed behind". The remains of a Roman mosaic found in digs on the site are on display in the Roman Baths Museum.

BENNETT STREET

Named after Francis Bennett, mayor of Bath from 1773 to 1776, Bennett Street was completed in 1776. This street layout around the Assembly Rooms was begun by Thomas Atwood – it was not at all John Wood the Younger's wish to see the Assembly Rooms so hemmed in.

Number 19 still has its wrought-iron overthrow. You can see more overthrows in Great Pulteney Street. Before gas lamps superseded them in the early 19th century, they supported oil lanterns.

On the approach to the Circus is the small but beautiful Museum of East Asian Art. The only museum in Britain dedicated solely to the arts and cultures of East and Southeast Asia, some of the objects in its 2,000-strong collection of ceramics, jades, bronzes and bamboo carvings and more date back to 5000 BC.

OLD BATHONIANS

ADMIRAL ARTHUR PHILLIP *(1738-1814)* 19 BENNETT STREET

The first Governor of Sydney, Phillip led the first fleet of convicts to Botany Bay, the future city of Sydney. He retired to Bath where, after a stroke confined him to a Bath chair, he died in 1814. Some think Phillip committed suicide by throwing himself out of his window, though there is no evidence to support this. He *should* be buried in Bathampton churchyard. However, in 2007 an Australian lawyer alleged that his body had been lost after an extension of the church over the graveyard. During a campaign to have the remains exhumed and returned to Australia, Geoffrey Robertson claimed: "Arthur Phillip is not where the ledger stone says he is: it may be that he is buried somewhere outside, it may simply be that he is simply lost. But he is not where Australians have been led to believe that he now lies." Oops.

SPOOKY BATH It's haunted! (allegedly...)

Loads of people have got on the bandwagon since the "Man in the Black Hat" was first reported in the *Chronicle* in 1956 for haunting Bennett Street. Professedly he looks a bit like Guy Fawkes and has also made appearances in the nearby Assembly Rooms. It's supposed to be Admiral Arthur Phillip, naturally. Or unnaturally…

BILBURY LANE

An ancient Saxon lane (or *twichen*), this used to be called Binbury Lane. The whole area around the Cross and Hot baths, which lies just inside the medieval wall, used to be called Binbury, itself maybe a corruption of the Saxon word *Binnanburh*, meaning "in the fortified place".

The Mock Tudor St Catherine's Hospital, built in 1829, replaced a row of almshouses founded around 1435 by the Bath cloth magnate William Philips. Bath's first secular, city-ran centre for sick, the almshouses originally cared for eight people and boasted a "bedesman", whose duty it was to pray for the soul of their wealthy benefactor. It was named after St. Catherine, the patron saint of spinners, but soon became known as the "Black Almshouse". This sounds sinister but the name stuck simply because its patients were given black robes to wear. The inmates of nearby St. John's hospital wore blue.

BRIDEWELL LANE

This alley, which well could date from Saxon times, was in the 13th century known as Plumtreow strete or twichen. *Plumtreow* is Old English for plum tree, while *twichen* means where two roads meet, so it is nice to imagine a plum tree standing there all those years ago where the lane meets Westgate Street.

Walking the lane in medieval times, you would have seen small workshops, warehouses, maybe some vegetable and medicinal gardens and housing for poor families (evidence of which was found in excavations carried out in 1997).

The lane appears in John Speed's Map of the city of 1610 as Spurrier's Lane, a spurrier being a maker of spurs. However, in 1632 the city corporation, armed with the vicious Elizabethan Poor Law of 1601, built a House of Correction (or bridewell) on the north-western corner of the lane "to set the poor of this city to work". The word bridewell comes from Henry VIII's Bridewell Palace in London, which in 1553 was turned into a poorhouse and prison – hence the new, less pleasant name.

The bridewell eventually became the borough prison. Calling the lane one of the "inferior streets or ways of the town", John Wood's 1749 *Description of Bath* mentions the bridewell for "offenders against the law". A new prison, also now gone, was built in 1772 where Milsom Street now stands.

BROAD STREET

This narrow street was one of the first built outside the old city walls and dates back as far as the 13th century. Its name may be from the 'broadcloth' made in medieval times, when weavers lived on Broad Street and dried their wool on what is now Milsom Street.

Some very early, pre-Georgian buildings still stand on Broad Street, which used to boast a pub almost every other house. The Saracen's Head, where Charles Dickens stayed in 1835, has two gables that date back as far as 1713 (the final year of the Stuart age). A previous inn stood here before that. Once a major coaching inn, dive inside the Saracen's cavernous interior and you still get a sense of its age. Its rear entrance on Walcot Street – on the route from Bath to London – was the coach entrance and stables.

The Saracen's features in Dickens' *The Pickwick Papers*, and judging by his description of it in the novel it must have been a most convivial place to stay...

The candles were brought, the fire was stirred up, and a fresh log of wood thrown on. In ten minutes' time, a waiter was laying the cloth for dinner, the curtains were drawn, the fire was blazing brightly, and everything looked (as everything always does, in all decent

English inns) as if the travellers had been expected, and their comforts prepared, for days beforehand.

The smart building opposite the Saracen's is Thomas Jelly's 1752 free Grammar School (later King Edward's), which was built on the site of another inn, the Black Swan. The only other free public school at the time was the original Blue Coat School in Saw Close, now long demolished.

Number 6 was from 1821 until 1854 the Bath Post Office. The mail coaches left from the York House Hotel on the corner at the top of the street, behind which the old stables can still be seen. The Postal Museum is in the basement of today's somewhat less romantic Post Office at the bottom of the hill on the corner of Green Street. There you can find out about Thomas Moore Musgrave. Postmaster of Bath from 1833 until he died in 1854, he sent the world's first ever stamp – the legendary Penny Black. That first stamp was sold in 1990 for a cool £55,000.

Palmer's Magnificent Flying Machines

Confusingly, three John Palmers have become associated with Bath's history. One is the famous architect responsible for Lansdown Crescent; another is a rogue who ripped off hundreds of people in a timeshare scam in the early 1990s; the third is the man responsible for the first ever mail coaches, which ran from the Three Tuns Inn on Stall Street from 1784 and later from the York Hotel at the top of Broad Street.

This latter, 'Postie' Palmer, was the son of a wealthy brewer, also (annoyingly) called John Palmer. By 1755 he had already renovated (with the help of John Palmer the architect!) and made popular the old Theatre Royal on Old Orchard Street. A man of some vigour, he then followed in the footsteps of Ralph Allen as a Post Office reformer and introduced the 'flying machines' – relays of multi-horse carriages that revolutionised nationwide a postal service previously dependent on a single plodding horse and cart. The mail coach was also faster than the "stage coach", for the comfort of the passengers was secondary and they stopped only for deliveries. The industrious Mr Palmer went on to become Mayor and MP for Bath.

Bath's YMCA premises in Broad Street Place dates to 1888. A very upright institution, it then strove to offer help for "the spiritual, intellectual, social and physical welfare of young men" (in other words: bible classes, lectures, 'selected' books, board games and a gym). Today's YMCA still has a gym but the rest of its offerings are a bit less Victorian!

Bath Chairs

At the bottom of Broad Street, at No 4, was James Heath's Bath Chair Works. Invented by Heath around 1750 as a means of getting invalids to and from the baths and the Pump Room, Bath chairs were, basically, scarily massive prams. A light carriage on three or four wheels that could be drawn or pushed by one person, they sported folding hoods and even glass fronts. By 1830 they had seen to the demise of the more stylish but less comfy and more labour-intensive sedan chair.

BROCK STREET

The idea behind John Wood the Younger's restrained Brock Street, completed in 1766, is that after the magnificence of the Circus you are given a little breather before you are suddenly and completely bowled over by the huge Crescent. Brock Street is named after Thomas Brock, the town clerk of Chester and John Wood's brother-in-law. Brock was the first leaseholder of No. 1 Royal Crescent.

Numbers 20-21 Brock Street used to lead to Margaret's Chapel, which stood behind Brock Street and nearby Margaret's Buildings. The chapel was destroyed in the 'Blitz of Bath' – the air raids of 1942.

OLD BATHONIANS

BENJAMIN DISRAELI *(1804-1881)* 8 BROCK STREET

Benjamin Disraeli, who climbed what he famously termed the "greasy pole" of politics to become one of the great British prime ministers, bought 8 Brock Street in 1861, seven years before he became PM. He had stayed in Bath before – in 1833, in an "unfashionable part of town", with his writer friend Lord Lytton – but he would never find the time to retire to his Brock Street address.

JOHN CHRISTOPHER SMITH *(1712-1795)* 18 BROCK STREET

Handel's copyist and manager John Christopher Smith retired to 18 Brock Street in the 1770s. Smith would write down Handel's scores and even conducted for him after the composer became blind in 1752. Handel himself would stay in Bath with the actor James Quin at 3 Pierrepont Street when he was taking the waters for his rheumatism. In 1759, the *Whitehall Evening Post* announced that the composer was to visit the city once again to "try the benefit of the waters, having been for some time past in a bad state of health", but he died before he could make the trip, leaving Smith a fortune, his manuscripts and his precious harpsichord.

CHARLOTTE STREET

You can reach Victoria Park and the Royal Crescent through the top of Charlotte Street car park. The rather grand building guarding the left side of the entrance, originally Bath Savings Bank, is a Bath rarity: a smart building that isn't part of a terrace. Built in 1841 by George Alexander, it's inspired by Sangallo's Palazzo Farnese in Rome (also the inspiration for London's famous gentlemen's club, the Reform Club). Next door is the Moravian Chapel, built for the Moravian free church in 1845 by James Wilson. Opposite, the Elim Pentecostal Church faces west rather than east…

Queen Charlotte's Face Lift

Charlotte Street is not named after Queen Charlotte, King George III's wife, but after Lady Charlotte Rivers, wife of the Lord of the Manor of Walcot. But Queen Charlotte did stay in Bath, in 1817, a year before she died. She was known for being a somewhat plain woman and Bath's waters apparently did her no harm in that regard. On it being remarked that the Queen was looking better, her chamberlain, Colonel Edward Disbrowe, famously replied: "Yes, I do think the bloom of her ugliness is going off."

CHEAP STREET

One of Bath's oldest streets, in medieval times this was a narrow (just 13-foot-wide) bustling thoroughfare which fed into the main open-air market in High Street. It was once known as Sutor Street, or Shoemaker's Street, but in 1339, by which time shops with accommodation above and behind them lined the street, it was decided that shoemaking was such a lowly profession that a name change was called for. In the end the city elders went for "Cheap". This comes from the Saxon word *ceap* or market, which became a common name for streets that thronged with travelling merchants.

At the junction of Stall Street and Union Street and Westgate Street you are standing at the heart of the medieval city and can see as far as where the old walls once stood (though the view north was hidden until Union Street was built in 1810). The "Bear Conduit" or "Stall's Conduit", one of the city's many public drinking fountains, stood here.

Also on this central junction, where Prêt-a-Manger now is, stood the church of St. Mary of Stalls. It had a chapel dedicated to St. Catherine, the protector of spinners – a patron saint ideal for Bath when it was a woollen town. It was demolished in 1659.

On the other side of the road, in 1694, stood the Turk's Head. The city's first coffee house (which were already fashionable in London by this time), it moved here from its original site at the market.

In his 1742 *Description of Bath*, John Wood called Cheap Street a "narrow inconvenient way, being only 13 feet broad". But with Westgate Street, which was also only a few paces across, it was widened and rebuilt around 1790 as part of the Bath Improvement Act redevelopment.

AUSTEN WATCH

In *Northanger Abbey* Jane describes how busy and crowded Cheap Street was...

Everybody acquainted with Bath may remember the difficulties of crossing Cheap Street at this point; it is indeed a street of so impertinent a nature, so unfortunately connected with the great London and Oxford roads, and the principal inn of the city, that a day never passes in which parties of ladies, however important their business, whether in quest of pastry, millinery, or even (as in the present case) of young men, are not detained on one side or other by carriages, horsemen, or carts. This evil had been felt and lamented, at least three times a day, by Isabella since her residence in Bath...

THE CORRIDOR

Linking Union Passage and High Street, this is one of the world's earliest shopping arcades. Designed by local Henry Edmund Goodridge – the architect also responsible for Beckford's Tower, just north of Bath – it was opened to great fanfare in front of a large crowd in 1825.

After Goodridge's death in 1864, The Corridor was given the columns and glazed roof it has today. Goodridge's wife died a few years later, triggering a family dispute over her will that ended in the sale of the site in 1877.

The Corridor needed a further refurbishment in 1974, when an IRA bomb caused extensive damage. Fortunately a coded telephone warning ensured that no one was killed or injured.

Until 1965 a familiar sight here would be a red-uniformed "Corridor Constable" whose job it was greet shoppers and to open and shut the gates each day. Meanwhile, a band, perched in the roof, would also play.

Let's hear it for a return of the Corridor Constable! It would smarten up the place no end. And while they're about it they should bring back the band too.

OLD BATHONIANS

WILLIAM FRIESE-GREENE *(1855-1921)* 9 THE CORRIDOR

A photographer and inventor, with his friend and fellow old Bathonian John Arthur Roebuck Rudge, Friese-Greene helped pioneer modern cinematography. With Rudge he created a "Biophantic Lantern", a camera that displayed moving pictures by revolving slides on a drum. Friese-Greene then took the idea a step further when he invented the first celluloid motion picture cameras. So Hollywood has its roots, of all places, here. However Friese-Greene never made any money or received any recognition for his pioneering work while he was alive. There is, though, now a bronze statue of him at Pinewood Studios, and in London's Highgate Cemetery his tomb describes him as "The inventor of Kinematography". One of his patents would also influence the first X-ray machine in Britain.

GAY STREET

Part of John Wood's scheme for a swish new upper town, Gay Street links his Queen Square to the Circus. Wood completed the lower section in 1740; his son, John Wood the Younger, completed the section leading to the Circus in 1760.

The street is named after the London surgeon and Bath landowner Dr Robert Gay, who leased the land on which both Gay Street and Queen Square were subsequsently built. John Wood the Younger lived at 41 Gay Street, which overlooks his father's Square. If you're not exactly bowled over by Gay Street, well you're in good company. In Tobias Smollett's 1771 satire *The Expedition of Humphry Clinker*, Mathew Bramble is most unimpressed by it…

Gay-street, is so difficult, steep, and slippery, that in wet weather, it must be exceedingly dangerous, both for those that ride in carriages, and those that walk a-foot; and when the street is covered with snow, as it was for fifteen days successively this very winter, I don't see how any individual could go either up or down, without the most imminent hazard of broken bones. In blowing weather, I am told, most of the houses in this hill are smothered with smoke, forced down the chimneys, by the gusts of wind reverberated from the hill behind, which (I apprehend likewise) must render the atmosphere here more humid and unwholesome than it is in the square below.

A harsh review, maybe, but it really is quite steep. But then, as the writer and politician Horace Walpole observed about Bath, "One cannot stir out of the town without clambering…"

AUSTEN WATCH

At 40 Gay Street, on the right leaving Queen Square, is the Jane Austen Centre. It's a fascinating place if you're interested in the writer and her time in the city.

Though they would one day live there the Austens were at first disinclined towards the idea of a home in Gay Street, considering it too hilly for Mr Austen's health. Jane wrote to her sister Cassandra in 1801: "Gay Street would be too high, except only the lower house on the left-hand side as you ascend. Towards *that* my mother has no disinclination; it used to be lower rented than any other house in the row, from some inferiority in the apartments…"

Despite this the family did end up in the street, and in sad circumstances. In January 1805 Mr Austen died, depriving the family of his vicar's income and leaving them in a worrying financial position. In March that year they moved from the (now demolished) Green Park Buildings East to 25 Gay Street. It would have been busy with carriages and chairs but it was a pleasant enough Bath address – for the Austens certainly more so than their next one.

Money a pressure, the family left the city towards the end of 1805. When they returned in 1806 they took a house on Trim Street, the very place that – Jane wrote in 1801 – her mother had promised to "do everything in her power to avoid".

Gay Street plays an interesting role in *Persuasion*. The arch-snob Sir Walter is extremely concerned that the Admiral and Mrs Croft's lodgings should be lower in the city than his Camden Place address in the posh, new, upper end of town – but not so much lower that he wouldn't dare be seen visiting there. The Crofts eventually plump for Gay Street, which is "perfectly to Sir Walter's satisfaction." (Hooray for him.)

OLD BATHONIANS

HESTER THRALE (or "MRS POIZZI") *(1741-1821)* 8 GAY STREET

Wealthy Welsh widow Hester Thrale was a key member of the Georgian literati and her diaries and letters, only published in 1949, shed new light on the life and character of her friend Dr Samuel Johnson (he of dictionary fame). A self-declared "Bath cat", Mrs Thrale scandalised polite society by running off and marrying the Italian music teacher Gabriel Poizzi just after she had buried her young daughter. After Piozzi died from gout, "Mrs Poizzi" came to live at this address in 1814 and proceeded to embark on a series of intimate intrigues with a naval surgeon, an actor and a would-be baron. The rivals reduced her to comparative poverty – though this didn't stop her from completely bankrupting herself by throwing a famously lavish 79th birthday bash at the Lower Assembly Rooms. Seven hundred guests attended the concert, ball and supper, and according to one observer she danced with "astonishing elasticity". She died in Clifton, Bristol and is buried at Corpus Christi Church, Tremeirchion in Wales. A plaque inside the church reads: "Dr. Johnson's Mrs. Thrale. Witty, Vivacious and Charming, in an age of Genius She held ever a foremost Place."

SPOOKY BATH It's haunted! (allegedly...)

Number 8 Gay Street: Mrs Thrale no longer entertains at this address, yet now – when it's empty – it is said that voices can be heard conversing in the drawing room. Could the voice of Mrs Thrale be among them? As her friend Dr Johnson once said: "No man will be found in whose mind airy notions do not sometimes tyrannize him and thus force him to hope or fear beyond the limits of sober probability." In other words: No.

GEORGE STREET

Built along a medieval route through farmland known as the Town Acre, George Street was by begun by John Wood the Younger in 1762. It stretches across the top of Milsom Street from Gay Street to the Paragon and Broad Street. Like Milsom Street it started off life as a residential area but became fashionable for shopping, hence the nice shopfronts.

On the corner where George Street meets Broad Street is York Buildings. Completed by Wood in 1769, it was once a great coaching inn called the York House Hotel. This establishment when it opened made great play of the fact that its stable yard to the rear, now a car park, couldn't be smelled by its patrons! Very nice. It became known as Royal York Hotel after a 10-year-old Princess Victoria stayed there in 1830 on her visit to open Royal Victoria Park. She never returned to the city and no one knows quite why. One theory is that the Prince Consort was given a grand reception on his visit, an honour not bestowed on the young Princess. Another, much better, theory is that she overheard someone calling her ankles fat… Oops.

Fittingly for Bath, the birthplace of the first mail coach service, at 13 George Street, past the Porter bar at the Gay Street end of the street, lived the pioneer of philately,

Henry Stafford Smith. With his brother William Smith he published *The Stamp Collector's Magazine* from 1863. Perhaps not Bath's most exciting claim to fame!

The formidable Selina Countess of Huntington stayed at No 4 [see The Paragon].

AUSTEN WATCH

In *Northanger Abbey*, the Thorpes stay in "Edgar's Buildings", above the raised pavement opposite Milsom Street. Edgar Buildings is named after King Edgar, "the first king of all England", crowned in Bath in 973.

GRAND PARADE

A lean over the stone balustrade gives you a fine view of Pulteney Bridge. In medieval times, when there was no bridge, there used to be a ford here (the shallowest point in the river near the city), and after that a ferry. Both were reached via the walled city's East Gate – the remains of which you can still see today if you head down tiny Boat Stall Lane, which runs along the side of Joya restaurant. Today, sadly, the East Gate stays firmly shut. The sooner Bath opens up this magical, secret way the better, for this is the only one of its ancient gates that survives [see below].

The row of houses overlooking the river – New Market Row – was built around 1786 over the site of a riverside market place. At the end of the 19th century, Bath's city architect, Major Charles Davis, widened the road to create Grand Parade, which is raised on a colonnade of 13 Tuscan-pillared bays running from the entrance to Parade Gardens to Pulteney Bridge. The base of the Parade's pillars marks the level of the medieval city.

If you cross Pulteney Bridge and descend the steps at its right-hand end you are rewarded with a fine view across the river of Grand Parade. Behind the pillars, under the road, are vaults. These vaults were once part of the market that disappeared with the expansion of the Guildhall in the 1890s. (The car park behind Boat Stall Lane was also once a market, and Boat Stall Lane is lined with doors to the vaults.)

The weir once stretched in a straight line diagonally across the river. It ran from Bathwick Mill (a corn mill that stood by the trees shadowing the Boater beer garden) to the priory-owned Monks Mill (a fulling mill, where wool was cleaned before being turned into cloth, situated at the edge of what is now Parade Gardens). The V-shaped weir you see today was built in 1972.

Victoria Art Gallery, on the corner of Bridge Street and Grand Parade, is well worth a visit, especially if it's raining. Completely free, downstairs there is always a decent visiting exhibition and the upstairs gallery is rammed full of great oil paintings, including works by Gainsborough and Turner.

The East Gate

On the left as you enter Boat Stall Lane, far below today's street level, the city's East Gate still guards a centuries-old route down to the river. An even earlier East Gate once stood near the steps down to Parade Gardens. The gate was shifted to its current spot around the beginning of the 12th century, when Bishop John de Villula was building the Norman cathedral and the King's Bath.

The East Gate used to be known as the "Lot" or "Lud" Gate, a derivative of the Old English word *ludgeat* or postern gate. A postern was a small secondary gate in a city wall – and such was Bath's East Gate. The East Gate, like the nearby Ham Gate [see New Orchard Street] and several other very small doors, was for foot traffic only. The grander, larger main entrances to the medieval city (the North, South, and West gates) and the small doors were shut at night and those people left outside would be forced to use one of the two smaller gates (though these, too, would be shut in times of war).

In medieval times, Boat Stall Lane took you the city's Market Place on High Street. The lane was then known as "Fish Cross Lane" because the gate opened onto the Fish Cross – a priory-owned fish market on a quay with a cross at one end. The Fish Cross stood at the southern end of what is now New Market Row. Beyond that, where Pulteney Bridge now stands, was Boatstall Quay, the ferry crossing

The Fish Cross and Boatstall Quay could also be reached via Slippery Lane, a narrow path that led from the North Gate along the outer face of the city wall. Most of Slippery Lane is gone but the beginning of it still leads off Northgate Street today. The lane carried on past the East Gate to Monks Mill, of which a fragment yet survives under some shrubbery on the northern edge of what is today Parade Gardens.

Empire Hotel

Bath has modern-day monstrosities aplenty – like the vast blocks of 1970s packing case architecture built with no rhyme nor reason and with scant regard for the lines and theme of the city. But the Empire Hotel, on the corner of Grand Parade and Orange Grove, is one of the earliest examples of duff post-Georgian planning and not the least controversial. Designed by Major Charles Davis, this pseudo-Jacobean monster caused a storm when it was completed in 1901 and it has remained disliked by many ever since. Certainly it manages to dominate just about everything about it – even the Abbey. Coming down Bathwick Hill into Bath from the east today, the Empire's form looms very large next to the fabled 'Lantern of the West'. But the building has survived for over a hundred years, despite many calls for its demolition, and it is still impressively ostentatious. Take a look at its roofline and you'll see that it is designed to reflect the three levels of English society, depicting cottages (representing the working class), gables (the middle class) and a castle tower (the aristocracy). After stints as a hotel and then a Government building, it has now been converted into prestigious retirement flats replete with a roof garden, library and card room.

GREEN STREET

In medieval times, the city boasted two bowling greens. One of these, the "New Bowling Green", stood here on drained land just outside the old city walls, hence the name.

Built between 1715 and 1720, Green Street, like Broad Street, has some of the few surviving buildings that were erected before John Wood's arrival in Bath. Shopfronts have been added since and, untouched by the Georgian redevelopment of the city, today Green Street provides a quaint breather from the austere grandeur of the surrounding streets.

Talking of a quaint breather, the Old Green Tree, a pub that dates back to the 1770s, has to be visited for its rare beef lunches, fine ales and hushed, oak-panelled rooms.

On the corner of Green Street, opposite the Bath Belushi's bar, in the basement of the Post Office, is the Postal Museum. Here you can find out how the first ever stamp was posted in Bath and about how Bath's John Palmer introduced the revolutionary mail coach system [see Broad Street].

Eagle-eyed

Ace Cameras at 16 Green Street has planted a fake eagle owl in the spire of St Michael's church at the end of the street so customers can test out their binoculars and telescopes. In 2002 headlines were written when a local woman called the RSPCA, fearing a bird could be trapped. "When they got to the church saying they were coming to rescue a bird they were told it was far beyond help," Ace Camera's Robin Gower told Reuters, adding: "It's a stuffed eagle owl named Ollie. Whoever spotted it must have good eyesight."

Dr Oliver Takes The Biscuit

A Dr William Oliver once lived at 9 Green Street, now a Belushi's bar. Who was he? Well, if the social scene of Georgian Bath was the realm of Beau Nash, its architecture the realm of John Wood and its stone Ralph Allen, then the leading light of its medical scene was Dr William Oliver. A Cornishman, Oliver was intensely interested in the medical properties of the Waters and in 1738 with Wood, Nash and Allen he saw to the building of a Mineral Water Hospital for the 'deserving poor', which still stands on Upper Borough Walls. In 1751 Oliver wrote his famous and splendidly named *Practical Essay on the Use and Abuse of Warm Bathing in Gouty Cases*. He also invented the "Bath Oliver" biscuit, a savoury cracker designed as part of a regime for obesity that included drinking Bath's waters all year round (an idea that was popular with many in the city as it suggested Bath could be turned into something more than just a winter resort).

Oliver died in 1764, shortly after inventing the biscuit, but he left the recipe to his coachman, a Mr Atkins, along with £100 and one hundred sacks of flour. Atkins made his fortune selling Bath Olivers from 13 Green Street (now the art shop F. J. Harris & Son). The last Bath factory making Oliver biscuits closed in 1963 and now they are only made in Reading, of all places. Even more shocking, the Huntley and Palmers factory makes sweet *chocolate* Olivers, not exactly a diet biscuit! Dr Oliver – who is also reputed to have invented the Bath Bun before deciding it was too fattening – is buried at nearby Weston Church.

Meanwhile, here is a highly amusing caption from a late 19th century *Punch* cartoon: – Dingy Bohemian: "I want a Bath Oliver." Immaculate Servitor: "My name is not Oliver."

Ah! That's funny.

GREEN PARK

This little triangle of green was once a communal garden for two Georgian terraces built around 1799 – Green Park Buildings East and Green Park Buildings West. The western side was demolished because of severe bomb damage, leaving just the row we see today, now known simply as Green Park. The 1942 air raids also accounted for a terrace that once stood on the other side of what is now Green Park Road. At the end of the park you can get down to the riverside path along the Avon.

AUSTEN WATCH

Unable to afford to renew lease of 4 Sydney Place, the Austen family lived at 3 Green Park Buildings East from the end of 1804 to early 1805.

Jane had been disparaging of the address during the family's house hunt of 1801, when she reported to her sister Cassandra:

Our views on G. P. Buildings seem all at an end; the observation of the damps still remaining in the offices of an house which has been only vacated a week, with reports of discontented families and putrid fevers, has given the coup de grace. We have now nothing in view. When you arrive, we will at least have the pleasure of examining some of these putrefying houses again; they are so very desirable in size and situation, that there is some satisfaction in spending ten minutes within them.

As it turned out it was even more of an unhappy address for Jane than she had feared, for her father, George Austen, died there in January 1805. Jane herself wrote the letter to her brother to tell him how "an Illness of only eight and forty hours carried him off yesterday morning between ten and eleven".

Mr Austen was buried in Walcot Church [see Walcot Street]. His death was a severe financial blow for Jane and her mother. Their next move in Bath would be to Gay Street.

GREEN PARK STATION

Operating from 1896-1966, Green Park Station – originally called Queen Square Station – was built as a stop on the Midland Railway's Bristol to Birmingham line. The station was restored in the 1980s and is now home to the famous Green Park Market as well as shops, a café-bar and office space for local charities and social enterprises.

Bath Farmers' Market

Farmers' markets now happen all over Britain, but established in September 1997 to help local producers gain a fair price for their goods, Bath Farmers' Market was the first in the country. Nowadays on Saturday mornings every week thousands of people pass through it, browsing dozens of stalls selling everything from enormous mushrooms to gamey pheasants to tasty cheddars and a hundred and other fine things besides. If you want to take a bit of local produce home with you this is the place to come.

HAY HILL

At the town end of the Paragon is a short rising passageway, Hay Hill, that cuts through to Lansdown Road. At the top of the little rise once Stood St Werburgh's Chapel. One of the earliest medieval buildings outside the city's walls, it was built in 1170 and housed a cistern supplying water to the upper parts of Bath. Revered after her life (she died in 699), Werburgh was a nun and convent reformer who is today the patron saint of Chester, where her remains were later transferred.

By Georgian times the site was just an alehouse. John Wood, who had a vivid imagination, decided erroneously that the chapel had been an ancient "place of sanctuary to murderer's fled", reasoning that such sites were once called *wera*.

On the junction of the Paragon and Lansdown Road, Fountain Buildings (built around 1745) is named after the cistern. A drinking fountain was erected in 1860.

HENRIETTA PARK

With its little Scent Garden, designed for blind people, and lovely trees Henrietta Park is a beautifully secluded spot to take a rest on a fine day. However, it was only opened (on Queen Victoria's Diamond Jubilee in 1897) to fill in the space left when the Bathwick development ground to a halt.

HIGH STREET, GUILDHALL & GUILDHALL MARKET

In medieval times you would not have been able to see the Abbey from High Street – amazingly, the view would have been blocked by houses stuck to the Abbey's sides. In the middle of the street, at least as early as the 1600s, stood St Mary's Conduit. One of the city's grand drinking fountains, it featured five spires tipped with globes. It was filled with claret for the coronation of Charles II in 1661.

The city has been presided over by a mayor and a "corporation" from roughly 1220. The city's first civic hall stood a little north of where today's Guildhall is. Markets have been held in High Street from Saxon times. If you had the money, you would have been able to buy all manner of livestock and seasonal produce. By 1551 a "Market House" had been built in High Street, and in 1569 a town hall was built. The first administration-centre-and-market-building-in-one was built around 1625 alongside a great big coaching inn, the White Lion, which stood on what is now Bridge Street.

The main Guildhall building we see today is one of the typically corrupt but handsome schemes of Thomas Atwood (who also built Paragon Buildings). Atwood was a very talented architect but he also used his position as City Architect for his own ends. He made very sure, for instance, that it was he who got the contract for building the Guildhall – despite the fact that in the original scrum for the work the just as talented John Palmer had offered his services for nothing (with a few provisos attached, admittedly). In the event, though, Atwood was killed falling through a floor on Market Street and it was his apprentice Thomas Baldwin who inherited the job.

After adding a few ideas of his own, Baldwin completed the Guildhall in 1776. Originally it had wings but these were replaced in 1891 by the buildings now seen on either side by the Irishman John McKean Brydon, who then in 1898 completed the block with what is now the Victoria Art Gallery on Bridge Street.

Council offices occupy large sections of the Guildhall, and locals pay their Council Tax and all sorts of other monies here. You can also get married here (as well as at the Roman baths, Assembly Rooms and even the Little Theatre Cinema). The very grand banqueting hall is free and open to the public during office hours. Worth a quick look.

Stocks Market!

By 1551 a "Market House" stood in the middle of High Street – and just behind it was the pillory. The pillory's victims were petty criminals whose heads were locked in holes in hinged wooden boards. If you were unfortunate enough to be sentenced to a stint in the pillory the ordeal would not normally last more than a few hours. But it would still have been painfully uncomfortable, and you would have had to endure all sorts of unpleasant things being thrown at you – insults, rotten food, excrement, the lot. Meanwhile, market waste, including meat not thrown at the poor occupants of the pillory, was often dumped in the river. Fish, anyone?

Guildhall Market

Today's Guildhall Market is marvellous. Not only can you stock up on Bath chaps, cheese, cider and fine blended tea but you can also grab a second-hand book, eat a hearty breakfast and read chapter two of your book while you're waiting for your haircut. By the time you've walked out you're well groomed, you've got a full belly and you're hooked on a science fiction novel. And it's stopped raining. Just inside the High Street entrance to the Market is a small pillar supporting a flat tabletop. As the inscription details, this the 'nail' where business was done. It dates from about 1768 and it is from such tables we get the term 'cash on the nail'.

HOT BATH STREET

The original route to the Hot Bath, which ran to the left of the current one, had the much prettier moniker Nowhere Lane. Hot Bath Street, built by Thomas Baldwin, was a result of the 1789 Bath Improvement Act redevelopment to open up the city centre.

J

JOHN STREET & OLD KING STREET

John Street and Old King Street were designed by John Wood as part of his Queen Square development. His son John Wood the Younger finally built them in the 1770s – on land belonging to the Barton House estate.

Barton House, which still stands at the corner where the two streets meet, was the heart of an estate that once surrounded the west of Bath, from the parish of Walcot in the north to Widcombe in the south. The estate was created by Edward VI in 1547. Today's house, though, which was taken over by Jolly's department store in 1867, is 17th century. Barton Buildings, off Old King Street – also built by the younger Wood – was the location of Barton House farmyard.

An earlier Barton House was the home of William Sherston, Bath's first mayor under the city charter created by Elizabeth I in 1590. Tradition has it that Elizabeth honoured the mayor by staying at the house on her way to see her godson, John Harrington, at the nearby village of Kelston, but we have no evidence of this.

The entrance into Jolly's serves as a handy shortcut through to Milsom Street, if you can find your way past the labyrinthine lingerie department.

JULIAN ROAD

This inauspicious-looking road behind the Crescent is actually an historic Roman junction. It was the point where the Roman's Fosse Way – the great, straight road linking Exeter, Cirencester, Leicester and Lincoln – met another road, the Julian Way, which stretched from Bath across the Severn to Carmarthen in south-west Wales. The temple and bathing complex of Aquae Sulis was extremely well linked to the rest of Roman Britain. Bath was not only a great holiday camp but it was also easy to get to.

In Victorian times a Roman sarcophagus was discovered here – it was common practice for the Romans to bury their dead along roads outside towns. By the time of the Georgian building explosion the area was farmland and the once-famous road was just a track.

As you're standing behind the Crescent, over the roundabout is the marvellously secret and sleepy St James Square [see The Bath Perambulator]. If you turn right and head up Julian Road to the Museum of Bath at Work you can find out about Bath's industrial past (Bath's not all wearing stockings and smoking pipes, you know…).

K

KINGSMEAD SQUARE

Another victim of the 1942 bombings and now towered over by the hideous Rosewell Court block of flats, Kingsmead Square can nowadays hardly be called a Square at all, such are the gaps in it.

The scene of the comic duel in Sheridan's *The Rivals*, this was once an area known as Kings Mead – meadows lying beyond the West Gate of the city where citizens grazed cattle. In 1698, Celia Fiennes described it as "a pleasant green meadow with walks round and cross it and no place for coaches". She also tells us that there were "several little cake houses selling fruit syllabubs and summer liqueurs to entertain the company that walk there". Sounds rather nice.

The first planned Bath development, and the first outside the city walls, Kingsmead Square's construction was overseen by the architect John Strahan from about 1727. Largely forgotten these days, Strahan was also responsible for Beauford Square (by the Theatre Royal) and the road that became Bath's infamous poor district, the original Avon Street (now long gone). On the west side of Kingsmead Square, by the Jazz Café, Rosewell House is notable because it is built in a decorative Baroque style rather than the orderly Palladian style like the rest of the Georgian city.

John Wood's description of Bath when he first arrived in the city carefully ignores the Square. Bitchy, but Wood would go on to become the victim of jealous rival architects himself.

Cross over James Street West to Kingsmead Terrace and you'll see 1942 bombing shrapnel scars on the left-hand wall. Also close at hand is the towering cinema multiplex and the King of Wessex, a Wetherspoons chain pub that serves remarkably cheap beer.

AUSTEN WATCH

When the Austens were house hunting in 1801, the countryside-loving Jane wrote to her sister Cassandra declaring that living close to "Kingsmead Fields" would be "a pleasant circumstance". They never did live in this part of town though.

LOWER BOROUGH WALLS

This street does indeed follow the line of the old city wall. Indeed, in medieval times it was a thoroughfare with the wall and a small door on one side of it and houses on the other.

According to one of Bath's most splendid urban myths, the tiny green where college students lounge and smoke was where the city buried witches. The truth is a little more prosaic. It was merely the cemetery of St James Church (demolished in 1957 after being bombed during the War) and now has the rather charming name Pigeon Park.

On the left-hand side of the green as you face it is the Chapel Arts Centre, which hosts all sorts of entertainment and which was once the church hall.

The pub, the Lamb and Lion, was the site of Bath's last blacksmiths (it shut in 1937).

MARGARET'S BUILDINGS

The pretty Margaret's Buildings was named after Margaret Garrard, the niece and heir of Dr Robert Gay (on whose land the street was built).

Behind the buildings on the west of Margaret Buildings – that is, on the left as you look up from Brock Street – used to stand Margaret's Chapel. Destroyed in the air raids of 1942, you actually reached it though the columned front door of 20-21 Brock Street.

MILSOM STREET

Bath's most famous shopping street was in medieval times an area outside the city walls where the weavers living on Broad Street dried their wool.

Roll on a few hundred years and it was just a garden and five small houses in 1735, when a poor house was built by John Wood where Somersetshire Buildings stands – now the NatWest Bank.

Then, to make use of this last bit of space in the centre of the growing Georgian city, in 1761 the corporation and landowner Charles Milsom announced plans for a grand street "fifty-three feet wide from house to house". Because of the poor house, though, Somersetshire Buildings would not be completed until 1782.

Milsom Street was designed as a street of houses with huge pavements for parading. Its position linking the north and south parts of town meant that shops and other businesses were soon attracted there.

On the front of 43 Milsom Street, opposite Waterstones, you can see painted on the wall the sign "Circulating Library and Reading Room". In Austen's day there were as many as ten such libraries in Bath, to which you would subscribe. In Bath you would retire there after your morning trip to the Pump Room.

In 1819 the early journalist Pierce Egan wrote this marvellous description of the street, then at the height of its popularity...

Milsom and Bond Streets afford to the utmost extent every thing towards supplying the real or imaginary wants of the visitors: containing libraries to improve the mind, musical repositories to enrich their taste and science; confectioners to invite the most fastidious appetite, tailors, milliners of the highest eminence in the fashionable world.

He goes on: *All is bustle and gaiety: numerous dashing equipages passing and re-passing, others gracing the doors of the tradesmen; sprinkled here and there with the invalids in the comfortable sedans and easy two-wheeled carriages, all anxious to participate in this active part of Bath, giving a sort of finish to the scene.*

Built in 1767, the Octagon Chapel, now incorporated into the Milsom Place shopping mall, was one of *the* places to worship in Jane Austen's time. Pews were rented out to keep the rabble from the Abbey away. Diarist, author, and Bath socialite Hester Thrale wrote of one memorable occasion there: "You will rejoice to hear that I came out alive from the Octagon Chapel, where Rider, Bishop of Gloucester, preached on behalf of the missionaries to a crowd, such as in my long life I never witnessed. We were packed like seeds in a sunflower."

William Herschel, the Bath astronomer and the discover of Uranus, played the organ at the Octagon. You can see some of the keyboards and pipes at the Herschel Museum on New King Street, where he lived. Nowadays the Octagon is worth keeping an eye on for the occasional intriguing art exhibition it hosts, including the annual Bath Prize, which celebrates only pictures of the city.

Opened in 1831, Jolly's is one of the oldest department stores in the country. Today Milsom Street has been boosted by the opening of Milsom Place. In the 2010 "Google Street View Best Streets Awards", Milsom Street was voted "Britain's Best Fashion Street".

Water Water Everywhere...

In his 1771 satire *The Expedition of Humphry Clinker* Tobias Smollett has great fun denouncing Milsom Street's water supply...

Here, in Milsham-street, we have a precarious and scanty supply from the hill; which is collected in an open basin in the Circus, liable to be defiled with dead dogs, cats, rats, and every species of nastiness, which the rascally populace may throw into it, from mere wantonness and brutality... Lovely.

AUSTEN WATCH

Though it was already filled with shops, Milsom Street was still a fashionable place to stay in Austen's day. In *Northanger Abbey* it is a clearly impressed Mrs Allen who describes General Tilney's lodgings as being in "Milsom-street you know". And it is in Milsom Street that Isabella Thorpe sees "the prettiest hat", and in *Persuasion* it is where Admiral Croft sees the picture painted by such apparently "queer fellows".

Also in *Persuasion* Austen chooses to have a go at the local weather by having Captain Wentworth flourish an umbrella in Milsom Street, declaring: "I have equipped myself properly for Bath, you see."

MONMOUTH STREET

Home of the Ustinov Theatre, Monmouth Street is named after James Scott, the 1st Duke of Monmouth and the illegitimate (and Protestant) son of Charles II who tried to seize the throne from the Catholic King James II. The Monmouth Rebellion of 1685 is known as the "Pitchfork Rebellion" because it was joined by poor artisans and farm workers, many of whom were armed with nothing but the tools of their trade.

Six Somerset men were arrested for their part in the uprising and sentenced to be hung, drawn and quartered by the infamous "Hanging" Judge Jeffreys. On 16 November 1685 the County Sheriff ordered Bath's corporation:

I require you immediately on sight hereof to erect a gallows in the most public place of your said city to hang the said traitors on, and that you provide halters to hang them with, a sufficient number of faggots to burn the bowels of four traitors and a furnace or cauldron to boil their head and quarters, and salt to boil therewith, half a bushel to each traitor, and tar to tar them with and a sufficient number of spears and poles to fix and place their heads and quarters, and that you warn the owners of four oxen to be ready with a dray or wain... You are also to provide an axe and a cleaver for the quartering of the said rebels.

The men were possibly executed near the George Inn, in the nearby village of Norton St Phillip. Despite begging for mercy, Monmouth himself was beheaded at the Tower of London. It is said that it took five blows of the axe by James's notorious executioner Jack Ketch to sever his neck.

OLD BATHONIANS

CLAIRE CLAIRMONT & MARY SHELLEY *(1798-1879 & 1797-1851)*

12 NEW BOND STREET

Claire Clairmont, the stepsister of Mary Shelley, gave birth to Lord Byron's daughter Allegra here in January 1817. Claire, who was estranged from Byron, would give the child into Byron's care. Allegra's seemingly unfeeling upbringing by Byron culminated with her death at the age of five from a fever. Claire blamed Byron entirely and hated him for the rest of her life.

A bit more happily, in December 1816 Mary Shelley wrote to Percy Shelley from New Bond Street: "I was awakened this morning by my pretty babe and was dressed in time enough to take my lesson from Mr West and (thank God) finished that tedious ugly picture I have been so long about. I have also finished the 4 Chap. of Frankenstein which is a very long one and I think you would like it."

The lessons were drawing lessons from the miniature painter John West. Chapter 4 of Frankenstein includes the famous portrait of the Creature...

His yellow skin scarcely covered the work of muscles and arteries beneath: his hair was of a lustrous black, and flowing; his teeth of a pearly whiteness; but these luxuriences only formed a more horrid contrast with his watery eyes, that seemed almost of the same colour as the dun white sockets in which they were set, his shrivelled complexion and straight black lips.

JOHN ARTHUR ROEBUCK RUDGE *(1837-1903)*

1 NEW BOND STREET PLACE

On the corner of this alleyway just off New Bond Street lived John Arthur Roebuck Rudge. Rudge was an inventor who, with his friend and fellow old Bathonian William Friese-Green, helped give birth to modern cinematography. An instrument maker by trade, he gave the world the "Biophantic Lantern", a camera that displayed moving pictures by revolving slides on a drum. Friese-Green would take the idea a step further when he invented the first celluloid motion picture camera. Rudge, meanwhile, who became known as the 'Wizard of the Magic Lantern', also created a quick-firing gun and a self-inflating lifebelt.

NEW BOND STREET

New Bond Street had the much better name of Frog Lane in medieval times, when it was a narrow street that ran along the outside of city wall from the North Gate. It was given the Frog moniker because of its somewhat boggy nature. (The area was once drained, along with the Green Street area, to make way for the New Bowling Green for the monks, and in his 1749 description of the city John Wood described a "spring of cold water" here.)

In 1552, a house in Frog Lane became the first site of King Edward's School, which was founded under measures passed by Henry VIII to replace the monastic schools that disappeared with the Dissolution.

Soon after the Catholic James II's 1687 "Declaration of Indulgence", granting rights to Protestant nonconformists and Roman Catholics, Bath's first Presbyterian Meeting House was established in Frog Lane and would remain in use until it was demolished in 1805.

Day in the Life

Bath-based Photoshop artist Tim Daddio creates a 24-hour view of a Georgian city.

→ http://timdaddio.blogspot.com/

Virgin

A Summer Day

NEXT WEEK
MONROE
COTTEN
PETERS
Niagara

The Royal

Aió

That year the ancient route was flattened to make way for the modern and wide New Bond Street. Design by John Palmer, it was meant to be a posh shopping zone, so much so that in 1830 the corporation refused permission for the establishment of a butcher's.

NEW ORCHARD STREET

A stretch of Bath's medieval city wall still stood here until the building of Marks & Spencer in 1959. A tiny section of the wall, marked by a plaque, survives yet in the loading bay behind Marks & Spencer.

Close to the rear entrance to Marks & Spencer was one of the city's two smaller gates, the priory-built Ham Gate [see below]. The Ham Gate opened onto part of the Abbey Orchard to the east of the city.

To the south-east and south was the "Ham", grazing land that John Leland described in 1530 as "fair meadows". Just inside the wall was the priory stable area, the "Shoe-ery". In the 17th century an ornamental garden known as the Shury Garden was laid out here that would have enjoyed lovely views across the fields.

By the beginning of the 18th century John Wood was complaining that the drainage from the baths had deteriorated so badly that the Ham – on which he built his North and South Parades – was covered in "old moats and ponds" and had become "little better than an unfathomable bog".

The Ham Gate

The Ham Gate, like the East Gate and several other very small doors in the city wall, was for foot traffic only. The North, South and West gates and other portals were shut at night, leaving just the Ham Gate and the East Gate as a way in. The Ham Gate was set in a many-gabled building and was similar in size to the East Gate, which still survives [see Grand Parade]. In medieval times the Ham Gate led to Stall Street. It also took you, via a lane called Leer Lands, to the Abbey Gate. From the Abbey the monks would drive their sheep along Leer Lands and out to pastures outside the city walls.

In 1643, during the Civil War, the Ham Gate was filled in. It remained shut ever afterwards so that the corporation could exact tolls at the four main gates.

The Bull Garden

Among the many dubious entertainments that Bathonions delighted in was the deeply unpleasant 'sport' of bull and bear baiting, which took place where Marks & Spencers now stands. Bear or "bull gardens", which featured a "pit" and raised seating for spectators, would see dogs set on the unfortunate animals, the dogs being replaced as they tired or were killed or wounded. Despite the corporation's efforts (animal baiting was banned in 1603), the practice continued outside the city limits and it remained popular in England until the 19th century.

The Bum Ditch

John Speed's famous map of the city of 1610 shows Bath's "Bum Ditch", a dyke that carried water from the King's Bath out through the Ham gate and behind the east side of Southgate Street and then down to the river. From the 13th century this stream turned a mill known as Isabelle Mill. The mill may have fallen into disuse with the building of the Queen's Bath in 1576. It was certainly gone by 1641 – which is just as well, for the water powering it would have become steadily more unpleasant. Some houses on Southgate Street had privies that emptied into the ditch, and from 1623 a row of privies for the public – the "Hame Privye" – stood over it as well. Elsewhere in Bath human waste was disposed of everywhere; in the street, out of windows, over the city walls and into the river. Some houses even stored it in their basements. In 1613 the corporation decreed that it be collected in carts, but as this was then dumped outside the city near the gates the city still reeked something awful in the summer.

The Horse Bath

A "Horse Bath", a rectangular pool for the bathing of horses that was apparently fed by the Bum Ditch, is shown on John Speed's famous map of the city of 1610. Little is known about the bath, though, and it wasn't in existence for long. We do know that Dr William Turner, the writer of the 1562 treatise on the benefits of the waters, suggested that baths might be good for animals too. It is possible that the old pool of Isabelle Mill became the Horse Bath for just a short time. Certainly it seems unlikely that after 1623 people would have led their horses into a bath fed by the Bum Ditch, which by that time had become a public latrine.

NORTH & SOUTH PARADES

North and South Parades were built in the 1740s on what used to be the Abbey Orchard and pastures. By John Wood's time it had turned into a boggy marsh.

Wood's second great building project in Bath, after Queen Square, these two terraces – along with Pierrepont Street and Duke Street – are all that he managed to complete of his plan for a huge "Royal Forum" and "Place of Public Assembly", a huge square stretching south that would echo Rome. The scheme was never finished because of a lack of money and the risk of flooding.

To deal with the slope towards the river, Wood built the terraces on huge vaults (like those you can see at the back of the Paragon on Walcot Street). As a result, the houses closest to the river have extra floors below street level.

The sunnier and more protected South Parade, which was to form the north side of the Forum, is designed to be enjoyed during autumn and winter. Shady North Parade, which had steps leading down to what is now Parade Gardens, was designed for use in the summer.

North Parade features in a beautifully bleak description by acid-tongued novelist Tobias Smollet (who himself lived in 7 South Parade) of Bath when its winter social season was over.

OLD BATHONIANS

WILLIAM WORDSWORTH *(1770-1850)* 9 NORTH PARADE

The plaque proudly pronounces that the romantic poet stayed here, though the letters he sent from Bath are addressed 12 North Parade.

EDMUND BURKE *(1729-1797)* 11 NORTH PARADE

An Irish, mostly liberal and reformist political philosopher and statesmen who was MP for Bristol for six years from 1774. Friends with William Wilberforce, whose anti-slavery views he shared, Burke fell out with Sheridan, whose revolutionary views he didn't. He came to Bath, like so may others, on medical advice and stayed at No. 11, the same address as fellow Irishman Oliver Goldsmith.

OLIVER GOLDSMITH *(1728-1774)* 11 NORTH PARADE

This Irish poet, playwright and biographer of Beau Nash famously concluded that "Scandal must have fixed her throne in Bath". Goldsmith wrote the brilliant and influential comedy of manners *She Stoops to Conquer*. His *Life of Richard Nash*, which illuminates fabulously not just Beau himself, but the Bath of his time, is still very funny and readable.

ELIZABETH CHUDLEIGH, DUCHESS OF KINGSTON *(1720-1788)* 5 SOUTH PARADE

This rather naughty duchess secretly married Augustus John Hervey, the 3rd Earl of Bristol, and then got a court to declare that the marriage didn't take place. She then proceeded to marry Evelyn Pierrepont, the 2nd Duke of Kingston. After Pierrepont promptly died his family investigated and Lizzy was subsequently convicted of bigamy. In disgrace she fled to Europe where, using large sums of money from her second marriage (which his relatives never recovered), she lived the high life. She died in France.

SIR WALTER SCOTT *(1771-1835)* 6 SOUTH PARADE

Scottish writer, author of *Ivanhoe*, 'father' of the regional historical novel.

The music and entertainments of Bath are over for this season; and all our gay birds of passage have taken their flight to Bristolwell, Tunbridge, Brighthelmstone, Scarborough, Harrowgate. Not a soul is seen in this place, but a few broken-winded parsons, waddling like so many crows along the North Parade.

And it is from the two Parades that Jack Absolute and Sir Lucius O'Trigger plot their next moves in Sheridan's great play *The Rivals*.

Fifty feet-wide Duke Street, which links the North and South Parades, is the widest pavement in Bath. The Gothic church of St John's Church by South Parade was built by Charles Francis Hansom, brother of Joseph Hansom the creator of the Hansom cab.

OLD BATHONIANS

TOBIAS SMOLLET *(1721-1777)* 7 SOUTH PARADE

Having failed to establish a medical practice in the city Tobias Smollet vented his spleen on its medical community with his novel *Peregrine Pickle*, labelling Bath doctors "ravens hovering round a carcass". The marvellous *Humphrey Clinker* followed – a fabulously scornful account of Bath in general through the eyes of a cantankerous old bachelor called Mathew Bramble. Nothing escapes Bramble's grumbles. Bath's supposedly posh population was made up of "clerks and factors from the East Indies", its stone was "soft and crumbling" and its waters filled with "abominable discharges of various kinds". Even the innocent sedan chairs he described as "soaking in the open street, till they become so many boxes of wet leather". Smollet died the year it was published, but his daughter carried on the good work, claiming that the Pump Room was "crowded like a Welsh fair".

FANNY BURNEY *(1752-1840)* 14 SOUTH PARADE

Diarist; author of a series of novels about young girls entering 'society'; housemate of Mrs Thrale's and also a member of Mrs Montagu's Bluestocking Circle. Burney's letters and diaries shed much light on the posh side of 18th century Georgian life and a vivid account of the – terrifying from her point of view – anti-Catholic Gordon Riots in Bath. She describes an angry mob "pausing only to consume all the wines and other liquors" and a great burning that cast "a lurid light over the whole city". She is buried at St Swithin's church, Walcot, where she also has a plaque [see Walcot Street].

NORTH PARADE BRIDGE & DELIA'S GROTTO

North Parade Bridge was built in 1836 by William Tierney Clark, designer of Hammersmith Bridge in London, the first suspension bridge to span the Thames. The bridge is in fact made of iron and it was only encased in stone 100 years later, in 1936.

If you look into the garden at the end house of North Parade you can see a little stone structure called "Delia's Grotto". Tradition has it that dashing playwright Richard Brinsley Sheridan left love poems here to Elizabeth Linley, including one that begins:

Uncouth is this moss-covered grotto of stone,
And damp is the shade of this dew-dripping tree;
Yet I this rude grotto with rapture will own;
And willow, thy damps are refreshing to me.

The words may have actually been written in a grotto in "Spring Gardens", a large pleasure garden that existed on the other side of the river from 1735. Inspired by London's Vauxhall Pleasure Gardens, Spring Garden's paying guests would enjoy concerts (London musicians were introduced both here and in the baths by Beau Nash), teas, hot breakfasts and fireworks.

Until the completion of Pulteney Bridge in 1774 the pleasure gardens were reached by boats caught at the bottom of some steps leading from South Parade. A gravel path called Harrison's Walk also ran along the riverside from the Parades, round St James's Triangle (now Parade Gardens) and to the now demolished Harrison's Assembly Rooms on Terrace Walk.

NORTH PARADE PASSAGE

Sally Lunn's restaurant is the main reason visitors venture down this charming little lane, once called Lilliput Alley.

Sally Lunn was supposedly a young French Protestant refugee who around 1680 arrived in Bath, where she found employment in a bakery known as "Sally Lunn's House" and invented the Sally Lunn bun – a bun that did indeed become popular throughout Georgian England.

You can certainly try a bun at today's Sally Lunn's (they enjoy a mixed reputation), though it is probably not the original Sally Lunn's House. Exactly where that stood in the alley is unknown. The current building is still very old – perhaps as old as 1620 – with an 18th-century frontage. If you do go in for a bun don't forget to check out the Kitchen Museum downstairs, where they have original faggot ovens.

A lovely little side street, Thomas Jelly's North Parade Buildings was built around 1750. Once called "Galloway Buildings" after the house of local apothecary William Galloway that stood here, it was designed for wealthy people but became tenements when the new upper parts of town became more fashionable. The inventor of the mail coach, John Palmer, lived at No 1 [see Broad Street].

The Bath Bun

A sweeter alternative to the Sally Lunn, the origin of the "Bath bun" is even more shrouded in mystery than the Sally Lunn bun. The popular story is that it was invented by the creator of the Oliver biscuit, Bath doctor William Oliver, who apparently developed the bun as part of his dietary regime for his patients before realising it was too fattening. Others have it that it was invented in 1756 by Bath resident and cook Martha Bradley as "Bath seed cake". Whatever the truth of its origins, according to Nigel Slater, "the true Bath bun is soft, like a marriage between a brioche and a hot cross bun, but encrusted with currants and gritty nubs of sugar…" Hungry yet?

NORTHGATE STREET

Northgate Street was the main road into the city and also its poorest quarter in medieval times. The line of the city wall cut along what is now Upper Borough Walls and Bridge Street. The North Gate stood where High Street meets Upper Borough Walls.

Demolished in 1755, the North Gate was most traveller's first experience of the city and important visitors including royalty would be greeted there. A fifteen-foot high, ten-foot wide arch, complete with side gates and rooms for arms and soldiers, it was adorned with a large statue of King Bladud, Bath's mythical founder. Walking straight on through the North Gate towards the Abbey would have taken you to the market and stocks on High Street.

Just inside the gate stood St Mary's Church. After the church fell into disuse its tower was used as a prison whose inmates would hurl abuse at those passing through the gate. Welcome to Bath!

Outside the North Gate – roughly where the traffic island in front of the Podium shopping centre is – stood St Michael's conduit, one of the city's grand drinking fountains fed by spring water piped from the hills. The narrow alley beside the barber's is all that remains of what was once known as Alford or Slippery Lane, now called Northgate Lane. Blocked off today, it was a medieval route that led along the outer face of the city wall to the ferry, fish market and East Gate [see Grand Parade].

The Victorian church you see today – called "St Michael's Without" because it stands outside the walls – is actually the fourth church on this site. The first existed in 1180 and possibly much earlier than that. Saint Michael, the leader of the forces of Heaven, was a suitable guardian for a gate. A second church was built around 1400, and another in 1743. Today's church was consecrated in 1837. Unusually, because it is squeezed between two roads, its altar faces north rather than east.

NORTHUMBERLAND PLACE

Formerly known as Marchant's Passage or Court, Northumberland Place was built in 1729 on land owned by the Duke of Northumberland by the bath banker and property developer Richard Marchant. Marchant made a killing leasing a small parcel of land that John Wood badly needed to build his North and South Parades. Marchant also loaned John Wood the Younger the then tidy sum of £4,000 to help him build the Circus.

The famous Bath bookbinder George Bayntun started his business in Northumberland Place in 1894. According to the American writer and collector Wilmarth Lewis, "He wore a smock in the shop and after selling a certain number of books took snuff. The sneeze released fresh energies." Bayntun adhered to traditional book binding techniques and when once asked why is quoted as replying: "We work in the old way. Machine binding? Ah yes… but not for us."

OLD BOND STREET

Aided by the closeness of the port of Bristol, Bath became an important shopping centre in the 18th century and so the city felt no embarrassment in borrowing the name of London's famous shopping street. The West side was built between 1760 and 1769; the east in 1780.

The cherub looking up Milsom Street from the niche above No. 5 (Mallory the jewellers) once decorated the Cross Bath. It was made to commemorate the apparently miraculous visit of James II's wife Mary of Modena in 1687. Unable to conceive a male heir, the waters of the Cross Bath were recommended to Mary by her physician. And the next year a son was indeed born. But James II would be deposed in the Glorious Revolution for being too Catholic and his son James Stuart would spend his life in exile in France as the "The Old Pretender". The royal coat-of-arms commemorates 11-year-old Princess Victoria's visit to the city in 1830, when she bought jewellery from the shop, which was then called Payne & Sons.

AUSTEN WATCH

This is the "Bond Street" referred to in Jane Austen's *Persuasion* (nearby New Bond Street was built later). As you might expect. Jane uses the street to have a good bitch about Bath folk. She has Sir Walter Elliot complain:

The worst of Bath was the number of its plain women... He had frequently observed, as he walked, that one handsome face would be followed by thirty, or five-and-thirty frights; and once, as he had stood in a shop on Bond Street, he had counted eighty-seven women go by, one after another, without there being a tolerable face among them…

The men of Bath though also wither under Austen's fire. Sir Walter goes on:

And as for the men! They were infinitely worse. Such scarecrows as the streets were full of!

Anyone would think she hated the place.

OLD ORCHARD STREET

This quiet little cobbled street is worth a detour to see the old Theatre Royal, which then became a Roman Catholic Church and later a Masonic Hall.

In 1705 a converted stables in Parsonage Lane, off Upper Borough Walls where the Mineral Water Hospital now stands, became Bath's first permanent theatre. In 1723 another theatre opened in the now mostly demolished Kingsmead Street off Kingsmead Square. The Parsonage Lane theatre remained open until 1730, when it was knocked down to make way for the Mineral Water Hospital.

The Kingsmead Street theatre operated until 1751, when John Wood decided that this site, on what was the Abbey Orchard, was ideal for a smart new theatre.

Under the management of John Palmer, Bath's inventor of the mail coach system, it opened on 27 October with a performance of Shakespeare's *Henry IV, Part 2*, and obtained a royal patent in 1768, making it the first Theatre Royal outside London.

The great Sarah Siddons was just one of many leading actors of the day who trod the boards at the theatre, and Richard Sheridan's Bath-set play *The Rivals* was a hit here after flopping in London.

The theatre remained here until 1805, when the present Theatre Royal opened in Sawclose. Deemed too cramped and out of the way, it closed with a performance of Thomas Otway's *Venice Preserv'd.*

In 1809 it was consecrated as a Roman Catholic chapel. The vaults once used to store scenery were used instead as tombs for 286 bodies. The church closed in 1863 and was unused, until in 1866 it became one of England's oldest provincial Masonic Halls.

Today there are guided tours of the building on Tuesdays, Wednesdays and Thursdays at 11am and 2.30pm, and at 2.30pm on Saturdays. The tour finishes in the vaults, where there is now a Masonic Museum stuffed with rare artefacts.

At the Pierrepont Street end of Old Orchard Street is Linley House, once a home of Elizabeth Linley [See Royal Crescent].

AUSTEN WATCH

In Northanger Abbey Henry Tilney very studiously ignores Catherine's attempts to catch his eye at a performance at the old Theatre Royal:

No longer could he be suspected of indifference for a play; his notice was never withdrawn from the stage during two whole scenes. At length, however, he did look towards her, and he bowed – but such a bow! No smile, no continued observance attended it; his eyes were immediately returned to their former direction.

Jane herself could have seen Elizabeth Inchbald's *Lovers Vows* (which influences *Mansfield Park*) in Bath, and it is known that she saw Thomas Dibdin's comedy *The Birthday* at the old Theatre Royal in June 1799.

SPOOKY BATH It's haunted! (allegedly...)

LINLEY HOUSE, PIERREPONT PLACE, OLD ORCHARD STREET Once the home of the Bath Festivals Box Office, the footsteps of an invisible caller have been heard here. Paranormal investigators have so far only been able to establish that the story must have been good for ticket sales.

ORANGE GROVE

This was once the priory "litten", or graveyard, an open area by the city wall. Soon after the Dissolution of the Monasteries in 1536 the space was given to the city and it was used for a time as a bowling green. Then in 1674 it was laid out as the "Grove", a promenade with gravelled walks through rows of sycamore trees bounded by shops and lodging houses. Nice? MP and barrister Spencer Cowper, a son of the 2nd Earl Cowper, described the view from his house: "The river is generally intolerably foul and yellow, but is a great addition to the prospect." Er, yes, *quite* nice then...

Fashionable and popular, by the 1720s the Grove had become enclosed, with houses on the north and also the east side by the city wall. Then in 1734 it became known as "Orange Grove" after Beau Nash erected the obelisk to commemorate the visit of William, Prince of Orange.

After 1834, when the road linking it to Terrace Walk was put through, the Grove went into decline and houses were gradually demolished to make way for Grand Parade and the Empire Hotel [see Grand Parade].

Until 1966 Browns Bar & Brasserie was Bath Police Station (now on Manvers Street). The huge doors allowed horse drawn vehicles through. The cells are now the loos...

"Rebecca Fountain", the statue by the Abbey of a female figure pouring water into a basin, bears the inscription "Water is best". It was given to the city in 1861 by the Bath Temperance Society.

P

PARADE GARDENS

A very pleasant spot indeed in which to laze (it has a café and you can hire deckchairs too), in the 7th century it was the site of the Abbey Orchard. The vast Cathedral that John de Villula built in the 11th century stretched, staggeringly, all the way from today's Abbey to the balustrades overlooking the Gardens. From Saxon times the priory operated a water mill known as Monk's Mill at the north end of the park. A few shattered remains can still be seen underneath some bushes by the wall.

John Wood intended this area to be a green jewel in his "Royal Forum" development taking in North and South Parades. Thwarted by cash flow and flooding issues, the scheme was never finished, but its pleasure gardens – in Georgian times called "St James's Triangle" – did make it off the drawing board. Laid out in 1737, the gardens boasted a gravelled riverside path known as Harrison's Walk because it led from the now demolished Harrison's Assembly Rooms in nearby Terrace Walk.

The colonnade bordering the park was built, along with Grand Parade, in 1901. Now known as Parade Gardens, the park you see today, complete with its balustrades, stone urns and ironwork, was laid out in 1933. From the riverside path you get a fantastic view of Pulteney Bridge.

Bath In Bloom

The floral displays in Parade Gardens (they have a different theme each summer) has helped Bath scoop the national "Britain In Bloom" title 13 times. In 1964 the city became the first ever national winner of the competition.

PARSONAGE LANE

Laid out in Saxon times, the earliest name for this narrow route is "Culverhouse" Lane, deriving from the Old English for the keeper of a dove or pigeon house. It then became known as Vicarage Lane, after the house and lands that from 1322 were provided for the vicar of the church St Mary de Stall on the corner of Cheap Street and Stall Street.

At the junction of Parsonage Lane with Upper Borough Walls, where the Mineral Water Hospital now stands, stood Bath's first permanent theatre. It was built in 1705 on the site of an old stable block by George Trim, wealthy clothier, member of the Bath corporation and the builder of Trim Street. The theatre was a cramped and rude affair, though, with seats that rose within a few feet of the ceiling. Having grown too small, and a rival theatre on Kingsmead Street having opened, in 1730 it was demolished to make way for the Mineral Water Hospital.

The filled-in arch at the Westgate end of Parsonage Lane was the dray entrance of an 1810 brewery.

PARAGON

Now known simply as the Paragon, this great curving row of houses is actually three distinct terraces – Axford Buildings, Paragon Buildings and Bladud Buildings. Bath's terraces are normally higgledy-piggledy at the rear (look at the back of the Crescent), but not on the Paragon – they have smooth backsides. Again, unlike other Georgian terraces, their principle rooms face the rear too, all the better to take in the pleasantly verdant views. Their cliff-like backs can be viewed from Walcot Street. From here you can also see that the houses have more floors and great vaults to the rear because of the steeply sloping ground.

Bladud Buildings – situated at the city centre end of the row – is the earliest of the three terraces. It was complete by Thomas Atwood in 1755. The ambitious Atwood was John Wood the Younger's arch-rival architect and very much the wily politician. (He would be killed in the collapse of a derelict building while inspecting the site the new Guildhall.) Paragon Buildings, in the middle and the longest of the three terraces at 350 metres, was completed by Atwood in 1771. Axford buildings – opposite the wonderful Star Inn at the London Road end – was completed by the local stonemason Joseph Axford in 1775.

The line of houses on the other side of the road is The Vineyards, where there were indeed vineyards until the 1730s. It is also known as Harlequins Row because of its multi-coloured frontage, which hides not Bath Stone but common brick (splutter!).

Halfway along The Vineyards is the Countess of Huntingdon's Chapel, which now houses the Buildings of Bath Museum. Well worth a look, the museum reveals how Georgian Bath was developed and examines Georgian homes from their cellars to their rafters. It has an amazing model of the city in miniature as its highlight. [See "The Countess of Huntingdon"]

The oak-lined Star Inn, which has been in business since 1760 and which retains 19th century fittings, is a must-visit for anyone interested in English pub culture (as is the Old Green Tree, in Green Street). A fine pint of ale they serve too.

OLD BATHONIANS

SELINA, THE COUNTESS OF HUNTINGDON
(1707-1791) VINEYARDS, THE PARAGON

Filthy rich, radically Methodist and friends with the famous preachers George Whitefield and John Wesley, Selina, Countess of Huntingdon was a formidable woman. Determinedly appalled at all the goings-on in Bath, she had no time for pleasure and even less for Beau Nash who, she declared, was "a monument of irreligion, folly and vice". She believed it her duty to put a stop to Bath's gambling, drinking and womanising and to this end she had a chapel built opposite Paragon Buildings, from where she would wage her war against sin. Even if Beau Nash, Bath's distinctly liberal Master of Ceremonies, wouldn't have anything to do with her low-church Christianity, she was determined to bring her message to the rest of the city. And she made a pretty good go of it, too. Wesley preached there several times, "attacking the devil in his own headquarters". It all came to a head one day when Nash had a particularly unpleasant confrontation with the Countess. Anxious to appease her, he reluctantly agreed to go and hear the extremely zealous Whitefield speak. It proved to be Nash's first and last flirtation with Methodism.

SARAH SIDDONS *(1755-1831)* 33 THE PARAGON

A celebrated actress and West Country girl made good, after a initial flop in London, where she was savaged by the critics, Siddons relaunched her career in Bath and, after scintillating performances in *The School for Scandal* and *Macbeth* at the Theatre Royal in Old Orchard Street, she was catapulted to fame and fortune. Towards the end of her long, successful career Siddons grew so large that she had to be helped to rise from her seat. To prevent this from becoming embarrassing on stage it became the convention for other actresses appearing with her to also be helped to rise. Her friends used to tease Siddons at the dinner table because she couldn't help but make conversation in blank verse.

AUSTEN WATCH

Jane Austen's aunt and uncle the Leigh Perrots lived at No.1 Paragon Buildings each winter Season until 1810 (when they bought a house in Great Pulteney Street). The Austen family were guests there while they were house-hunting in 1801. Jane was not enchanted to be there. The decision to move from the Steventon countryside to Bath was not to her liking as it was, and she did not much love her aunt. Her letters written from there leave us in no doubt that she disliked the address (the road, London-bound, would have been busy with traffic as it is indeed today). She wrote to her sister Cassandra in January 1801: "We know that Mrs Perrot will want to get us into Axford Buildings, but we all unite in particular dislike of that part of the town, and therefore hope to escape."

Happily for Jane, the Austens eschewed the Paragon and instead moved into Sydney Place, by the countryside on the edge of the city.

PIERREPONT STREET & MANVERS STREET

Because of money problems and the danger of flooding, Pierrepont Street together with Duke Street and the North and South Parades is all that John Wood managed to build of a huge Roman-esque "Royal Forum" development. Pierrepont Street and South Parade, both built in the 1740s, were to form one side of a great square.

As you go towards the station Pierrepont Street becomes Manvers Street. On the left is the Police Station – where a few years ago the boys in blue were confounded to find a marijuana plant growing on the wall in front of the building.

OLD BATHONIANS

LORD HORATIO NELSON *(1758-1805)* 2 PIERREPONT STREET

Nelson visited Bath often to recuperate during his arduous career – and sometimes to completely refit after losing some part or other of his body, when he would lodge with his doctor at No 2 Pierrepont Street. Clearly appreciating the place, he described Bath as "more like Jamaica than to any other part of England". His parents also lived in the city for a time (his father ran a school in New King Street), as did his wife and indeed his mistress, Lady Hamilton, who very much enjoyed the gambling, to her great cost. After Nelson's death at Trafalgar, Hamilton spent 13 months in a debtors prison before, stricken by poverty, she died of amoebic dysentery in Calais in 1815.

ISAMBARD KINGDOM BRUNEL *(1806-1859)* 14 MANVERS STREET

The great civil engineer stayed here during the building of his Great Western Railway.

Q

QUEEN STREET & HARINGTON PLACE

Lovely little cobbled Queen Street was built around 1760. The Raven here is one of Bath's best pubs, serving as it always does an excellent selection of perfectly kept ales.

The Harington Hotel and Harington Place (which is just off Queen Street) get their names from the family that once owned the land here, the Haringtons.

Sir John Harington, 1561-1612, was one of Elizabeth I's many (she had over a hundred) godchildren and had his seat in the nearby village of Kelston. Not only a poet and a benefactor of the Henry VIII-ravaged Abbey, Sir John is famed as the inventor of the very first water closet. It was just like a modern flush loo, complete with a cistern, a bowl of water and a handle-operated flush. Sir John had one installed at his (now demolished) Kelston manor house and Elizabeth had one installed at Richmond Palace.

However, the invention didn't catch on, for Elizabethans were apparently impervious to filth and smells. Indeed, eyebrows were raised at the queen for having a bath once a month "whether she need it or no". And Sir John himself was positively weird for bathing once a day.

At the time of the Civil War his grandson Captain John Harington (1627-1700) is thought to have stabled his horses on the site of what is now the Harington Club in Harington Place.

Dr Henry Harington (1728-1816), a well-known Bath doctor, was the city's mayor in 1793 [see Wood Street].

The historic, oak-panelled Harington's gentlemen's club (it now welcomes both sexes of course), which styles itself as a "safe haven from the rigours and stresses of 21st century life", boasts two very fine snooker tables.

SPOOKY BATH It's haunted! (allegedly...)

The Raven: A pale and wan spectral figure carrying its head under its arm has been sighted staring through the windows onto Queen Street. The apparition, though essentially benign, waves its free arm at those who glimpse it, seemingly trying to scare them away. But from what?

QUEENS PARADE PLACE

Possibly the only examples left in the country, the two odd little symmetrical buildings behind No 24 Queen Square were built for sedan chair carriers to wait in while their charges visited the house.

S

ST JAMES'S PARADE

Initially called Thomas Street, St James's Parade was began in 1760 and completed in 1785. It was once completely paved and closed off at both ends. It was designed to give the gentry a lovely big and private parading space, but as the new upper parts of the city became fashionable St James's Parade along with the surrounding streets in the southern part of town quickly became less salubrious.

The area was the epicentre in Bath of the anti-Catholic Gordon riots that swept the country in 1780. The rioters, led by John Butler, a Bath footman working in Royal Crescent, ransacked a newly built Roman Catholic chapel between St James's Parade and Lower Borough Walls. When the Bath Volunteers opened fire, killing one of the crowd, the mob turned really angry and burned the chapel and also several new Catholic-owned houses to the ground.

Edmund Rack, founder of the Royal Bath and West Society of Employers (made famous by the annual agricultural show at Shepton Mallet) lived at No 5. The show was held at Widcombe Lock in 1877, when the pedestrian Widcombe Bridge collapsed.

Twelve people died and over fifty were injured.

The imposing art deco building at the southern end of the street is "The Forum". Built in 1934, it was until 1969 Bath's 2,000-seater cinema. Today it is a concert venue and the home of Bath City Church.

SOUTHGATE STREET

Today part of a bright new shopping zone, Southgate Street is named after the old city walls' South Gate, which stood at the junction of Stall Street, Lower Borough Walls and New Orchard Street.

In 1132 the South Gate was rebuilt as an impressive arch 11 foot wide and 15 foot high and incorporated into a building decorated with three statues (including one of Edward III). Southgate Street ran from the gate into meadows south of the city known as "The Ham". In the 14th century the end of the street nearest the gate was lined with workshops. From documents of the time we know that dyers, fullers, spinners, fletchers and blacksmiths plied their trade here. A tanner – a smelly business – worked in a spot well away from the gate. A lead conduit known as the Magdalen Conduit and then St James's Conduit brought spring water from the southern hills.

In Saxon times Southgate Street took you over the River Avon at the bridge of St Lawrence. Built in 1332, at the same time as the new gate, the bridge had five arches and a chapel attached to it. On his visit to Bath in 1536, John Leland approached the city over the bridge, noting "fair meadows on either hand". The bridge of St Lawrence was demolished and replaced by another in 1754. The current bridge, Churchill Bridge, was built in 1966.

For a short time around the beginning of the 17th century the Horse Bath stood to the east of Southgate Street, which was for a time renamed Horse Street. In 1825 the residents campaigned successfully to have the original name reinstated.

By the 19th century Southgate Street was a commercial area packed with shops, pubs, eateries and hotels, and because it was the place the working classes from the Avon Street district flocked to at night for entertainment it was also filled with brothels. In the 1880s the Rev JW Bolton of the now demolished St James's Church campaigned against vice in the area. He was particularly exercised by activity at the Bell, a pub that stood opposite what is now Lloyds Bank:

By day, even on Sundays, and within a stone's throw of St. James's Church, dissolute women, half-dressed, would stand in groups, soliciting passers-by. At night, riots, fighting and piano playing disturbed the whole neighbourhood. Respectable people were ashamed to live in or pass through such a district.

The Southgate Street area was bombed badly in the Second World War and then turned into a simply dreadful shopping precinct in the 1960s and 1970s. Today's development opened in 2009 and has brought established high-street brands flocking to Bath. The suspicion among many locals is that it will soon seem as outdated and ugly as the concrete block architecture it has replaced.

STALL STREET

Stall Street, which led down to the South Gate of the medieval city, was built around 1091 when work began on the huge Norman cathedral and priory. Little did they know that they were building over part of the Roman baths.

Named after the ancient church of St Mary of Stalls, like Bath's other old streets (Northgate Street, Westgate Street, Cheap Street and Binbury – now Bilbury – Lane), Stall Street was once a narrow way hemmed by houses, inns and, from the 14th century, shops. In 1765 John Wood described "82 houses, some of which have the aspect of as much magnificence as one would expect to meet within a King's Palace". However these fine houses completely hid the baths, which visitors could reach only via narrow lanes and passageways, jolted there by sedan chair.

Stall Street was rebuilt as part of the 1789 Bath Improvement Act development aimed at smartening and opening up the city centre. On one side the colonnade was built to introduce the main baths and new Pump Room. The new Bath Street took you to the smaller baths.

On the right of the entrance of Bath Street stood the great White Hart Inn. In its heyday in the 18th and early 19th century, the White Hart was one of the most famous inns in the country and the most illustrious in the city. Many important new arrivals in the city would lodge there.

Charles Dickens gave the name of the inn's famous portly landlord Eleazer Pickwick to the equally portly main protagonist of the *Pickwick Papers*. Eleazer Pickwick had made a fortune running a stage coach service to London that Dickens himself used. In the book the name Pickwick is emblazoned on the coach that takes Sam and his master to Bath and Sam is concerned that the "properiator" is playing some "imperence" by daring to go by the name Pickwick.

Dickens has little to say in the novel about the hotel except to note that its waiters (who were paid only by tip) "from their costume, might be mistaken for Westminster boys, only they destroy the illusion by behaving themselves much better".

Writing in 1810, the American travel writer Louis Simond gives us a more detailed account of the hotel's splendour:

We arrived at Bath last night. Two well-dressed footmen were ready to help us alight, presenting an arm on each side. Then a loud bell on the stairs, and lights carried before us to an elegantly furnished sitting-room where the fire was already blazing. In a few minutes a neat looking chamber maid with an ample white apron pinned behind, came to offer her services to the Ladies and shew the Bed-rooms. In less than half an hour five powdered gentlemen burst into the room with three dishes etc and two remained to wait. I gave this as a sample of the best or rather of the finest inns.

The Grand Pump Room Hotel, which had lifts and baths of its own, replaced the White Hart Inn after it was demolished in 1867. It was the Victorian area, the age of the train, and visitors demanded not stables but luxury. The hotel was not thought an overnight success.

In 1909, the city council proposed to extend the hotel to take in the columns but the idea was abandoned after a public outcry. The Grand Pump Room Hotel was itself pulled down in 1959.

Today the White Hart Inn in Widcombe, in the south of the city, bears the original carving of a white hart that once adorned the front of its great namesake.

As you walk down Stall Street from the baths, on the left, just past the junction with York Street, stood the Three Tuns. In 1784, John Palmer's first mail coach service to London started from The Three Tuns, many coaches horsed from its stables [see Broad Street]. The Three Tuns' stable yards ran to the rear of many Stall Street houses and the inn itself boasted 33 fireplaces in 1654.

Inns that were found to be operating without a licence could be fined and have their signs removed. In 1622, bailiffs looking for the landlord of the Three Tuns, Phil Sherwoodson, were seen off by a crowd led by Sherwoodson's son armed with a gun. Later that same night the bailiffs returned and removed the sign – only to find a new one up the next morning.

AUSTEN WATCH

The White Hart Inn's huge size (which makes its reputation for fine service all the more impressive) meant that it was an extremely busy place. Indeed, in a letter to her sister Cassandra in September 1813 Jane describes the racket from the place as "terrible". Bus this doesn't prevent Austen from staging the climax from *Persuasion* – one of the great scenes in literature – in the Musgrove's rooms at the White Hart. There Anne Elliot, debating with Captain Harville the nature of love to men and women, concludes: "All the privilege I claim for my own sex (it is not a very enviable one, you need not covet it) is that of loving longest, when existence or when hope is gone." Gloomy words that mirror the writer's own feelings, but Captain Wentworth overhears them and is inspired to write a letter declaring his own, very dependable love for Anne. Cue happy ending.

SWALLOW STREET

Built by the Corporation in 1808 (at the same time as York Street), the east side of Swallow Street lies over John de Villula's Norman Bishop's Palace. A series of excavations have unearthed parts of the large late 11th or early 12th century rectangular building.

The street is named after a William Swallow, a wealthy tallow candle maker who dug here in an effort to discover new thermal springs. He dug to some depth too but his path was eventually blocked by the huge millstone of an old mill. The mill was possibly once driven by outflow from the nearby King's Bath.

At the top of Swallow Street, its hot water piped from the Queen's Bath through the 'bridge' spanning York Street, is the old Bath City Laundry. Built in 1888, it was converted from a chapel. It was definitely one posh laundry.

SYDNEY GARDENS

Originally meant to be part of the aborted Great Pulteney Street development, Sydney Gardens is what remains of Bath's only surviving Georgian pleasure garden.

Opened in 1795, at the same time as the Sydney Tavern (now the Holburne Museum), it was much bigger and more outlandish than Bath's earlier pleasure garden, Spring Gardens, over the river from the North and South Parades. Here, for a subscription or an entrance fee, you could marvel at, among many other things, the ruins of a castle (complete with cannons) and a labyrinth so perplexing that you could buy a plan at the centre to get you out again. In the middle of the maze was a "Merlin swing". Merlin swings were the creation of Belgian-born John Joseph Merlin, who in the 1760s is also said to have invented the rollerskate. At the time it was thought that swinging was good for people suffering from TB. It is not known if Bath's example really was a genuine Merlin swing or if it was just labelled so to grab tourists.

By around 1840 the Great Western Railway cut through the gardens. The line lies in a deep cut so as not to spoil the landscape, but half the gardens were nevertheless destroyed and the labyrinth and castle lost.

The mock temple halfway up the gardens – modelled on the temple that stood by the Roman baths – was put here to commemorate the 1909 "Bath Pageant", a six-day celebration in which over 3,000 performers revived great celebrities from the city's past and re-enacted historic moments ranging from the curing of King Bladud's pigs to the visit of Queen Charlotte in 1817.

AUSTEN WATCH

For countryside-loving Jane, moving to Bath from Steventon in Hampshire was a wrench. While the Austens were house hunting in the city Jane dared hope in a letter to her sister Cassandra Austen dated 21st January 1801 that "it would be very pleasant to be near Sydney Gardens – we might go into the labyrinth every day..." Happily for Jane this was one dream that would come true in a city in which she endured many sad times. In October 1801 the family moved into their first home in the city – 4 Sydney Place, just across the road from the gardens.

The Austens stayed at the house for three years, during which time Jane often walked the gardens, and the canal path too (the canal was built while the Austens were at No 4, her uncle James Leigh Perrot was impressed by the locks). She also attended public breakfasts there, and concerts followed by firework displays. She noted in one letter how "there is a public breakfast in Sydney Gardens every morning, so that we shall not be wholly starved". Another letter reveals her apparent dislike of the music of the time and her relief that "the gardens are large enough for me to get pretty well beyond the reach of its sound".

SYDNEY PLACE

Sydney Place was to be part of a hexagon of streets surrounding the Pleasure Gardens, but like most of the Great Pulteney Street development, the plan was never finished. The northern side of Sydney Place (on the left at the top of Great Pultneney Street) is the famous one because this is where from October 1801 to September 1804 Jane Austen and her family lived.

The terrace would have enjoyed greenery front and back when the Austens moved into No 4. The front overlooked the Pleasure Gardens and the rear meadows (Daniel Street, behind the house, was not built until 1810).

The advert for the house in the *Bath Chronicle* in May 1801 read: "The situation is desirable, the rent very low and the landlord is bound by covenant to paint the two first floors this summer."

AUSTEN WATCH

Number 4 Sydney Place was the Austen's first proper home in Bath after almost a year's search. It was their nicest home in the city, but it stretched their budget to breaking point. In September 1804 the lease was up and they moved to Green Park Buildings East, which Jane had previously described as "putrefying", "damp" and suffering from "reports of discontented families and putrid fevers". Worse, a sad blow would strike the family there.

Austen wrote *Northanger Abbey* based on previous visits to Bath and put the finishing touches to it at Sydney Place. In 1803 she offered the book to the London publisher Crosby, who bought the copyright for £10 but never published it. Around 1816 Jane's brother Henry bought it back for £10 – and only then revealed to Crosby that it was by the author of the massive hit *Pride and Prejudice*. The novel was published bound with *Persuasion*, her other Bath-set story, after Jane's death in 1817.

T

TERRACE WALK

Once the old Abbey cloister, this area became a public bowling green after the Dissolution of the Monasteries. According to John Wood, it also became used for "smock-racing, playing at football and running with feet in bags".

By the early 1700s the area also boasted "Terrace Walk", a parade for gentry lined with shops. Then in 1709 Bath's first assembly rooms – the Lower Assembly Rooms or "Harrison's Rooms" – were built where the central pavement is today. Presided over by Beau Nash, until then Bath had nowhere where people could gather to meet, gossip eat, dance or play cards. To cope with the number of visitors flocking to the city, in 1730 John Wood then built the Wiltshire Rooms where Terrace Walk now meets York Street.

The Wiltshire Rooms were demolished in 1796 to make way for York Street. Harrison's Rooms were gutted by fire in 1820 and replaced in 1825 by the hulking Greek temple-style Royal Literary and Scientific Institution. The Institution was thought by many people of the time to be somewhat austere and ugly and it was demolished in 1932 and the road and balustrades to Orange Grove put through. Some called this vandalism, though the *Bath Chronicle* report of the time thought it "a very striking improvement".

The title of only surviving 18th century shopfront in Bath belongs to No 1 Terrace Walk. Built in 1750, perhaps by John Wood, it is now the Huntsman public house. Number 2, Bridgwater House, opened the same year as the Parade Coffee House. It was from here in 1772 that Richard Sheridan wrote a letter to the *Bath Chronicle* denouncing Captain Thomas Mathews as a liar after their second – and almost fatal for Sheridan – duel over Elizabeth Linley. Sheridan also claimed in the letter that he won the duel.

Today the area is known as Bog Island on account of the old Victorian toilets that used to lie under the island (which became a cavernous nightclub for a time). Before it was moved here in 1978 from opposite the King's and Queen's Baths on Stall Street, the fountain used to gush hot spring water.

AUSTEN WATCH

In *Northanger Abbey* a frustrated Catherine Morland has to sit out her first dance in Bath, which takes place at the newer (and rival) Upper Assembly Rooms (today's Assembly Rooms). This was because as a new arrival in the city she hadn't been, as etiquette demanded, formally introduced to a dancer by the Master of Ceremonies.

But she has better luck at her next dance at the Lower Assembly Rooms on Terrace Walk, where she is introduced to young Tilney:

They made their appearance in the Lower Rooms; and here fortune was more favourable to our heroine. The master of the ceremonies introduced to her a very gentlemanlike young man as a partner; his name was Tilney. He seemed to be about four or five and twenty, was rather tall, had a pleasing countenance, a very intelligent and lively eye, and, if not quite handsome, was very near it. His address was good, and Catherine felt herself in high luck.

THEATRE ROYAL, SAWCLOSE & BEAUFORD SQUARE

This area used to be known as "Timber Green". As the name suggests, it was a timber yard until the medieval city wall here was demolished in the 1770s. Stretching from the bottom of Sawclose (and the West Gate) to the junction with Upper Borough Walls, this section of wall was called "Gascoyne's Rampire". It was named so after a tower that stood at the end of Upper Borough Walls called Gascoyne's Tower. According to 1530s visitor John Leland, Gascoyne was a Bathonian who had built the tower in payment of a fine for an unspecified "fault he had committed in the city". During the Civil War this section bristled with artillery. At the bottom of Sawclose, by Schwartz Brothers burger bar, was the Cock Pit, used for cock fighting. (Don't be put off the chicken burgers!)

Built in 1720, what is now the Garrick's Head pub and the Theatre Royal foyer was Beau Nash's very fine house when he was at the height of his powers as Bath's Master of Ceremonies. When he later fell on hard times he would move into more modest accommodation next door up the hill (now Strada restaurant).

Replacing the by then too small Old Orchard Street Theatre, the Theatre Royal itself was built in 1805 and opened with a performance of Shakespeare's *Richard III*. The front entrance only opened onto Sawclose after 1862, when the theatre was rebuilt following a fire. Before the fire the main doors were around the corner in Beauford Square (well worth a look, not least because you can sometimes see actors changing in the windows).

The inside of the theatre, with its sumptuous chandelier high in the auditorium, is considered by many to be one of the most beautiful in the country – a fact lampooned by Les Dawson when he once cried on stage: "Look about you at the magnificence of it all. What a job it must be for the cleaners! No wonder they don't bother."

Before 1862 the Garrick's Head was a pub called the Deed O'The Day – the title of the last play performed at the theatre before it burned down. In those days the theatre was struggling as a quality attraction. Sawclose was by then an open area in the Avon Street slum district, which stretched from Southgate Street though Lower Borough Walls and Westgate Buildings. Sawclose at night was a crowded and rowdy market place with much drinking and brawling, and the Lyric Music Hall, opposite the theatre, offered more lowbrow entertainment.

SPOOKY BATH It's haunted! (allegedly...)

Sawclose is literally infested with ghosts. In the Garrick's Head, a misty shape wearing the scent of jasmine apparently rubs shoulders with the clientele of this pub – the same ghost that has allegedly been seen hanging out in the Theatre Royal next door. Some have it as the ghost of a woman who hanged herself from a door there after her lover was killed in a duel, though it's probably just a marvellous tale made up by some half-cut actor. What is clear, however, is that she can walk through walls.

Strada, or "Beau Nash House", where Beau Nash lived out his last days, is allegedly haunted by his mistress, Juliana Popjoy. Unlikely, perhaps, but then she did die living as a hermit in the bole of a tree in Wiltshire.

The Theatre Royal. Where does one start? With half-cut actors again, one suspects, but anyway, the theatre is supposedly riddled with spectres. Not only has the Garricks Head's Grey Lady appeared 'live' on stage beside Dame Anna Neagle but stage clocks with no mechanisms have also chimed... Then there's the little girl who appears at the window, even though she's obviously far too small to reach over the sill (the tale is obviously rather taller than she is). Even less convincing is the story of a tortoiseshell butterfly flitting about the auditorium during (winter!) pantomimes since 1948. In 1979, during an *Aladdin* season, Leslie Crowther (Wishee Washee) claimed to the crowd after a performance that it had landed on his shoulder. (Oh no it didn't!) An even more splendidly dubious ghost is the Phantom Doorman, who is dressed in Georgian attire – and "only cast members have ever seen him"...

TRIM STREET

Built in 1707 by wealthy clothier and corporation member George Trim, Trim Street was the first development outside the medieval city walls. You might say that Bath's Georgian house building explosion started here. The arch, called St John's Gate but now known as Trim Bridge, was built in 1728 by John Wood as a route for carriages through to Queen Square and the new upper town. In 1969 the council knocked down many of the older houses and built the ugly Trimbridge House.

AUSTEN WATCH

During the Austen's great house hunt of 1801 Jane wrote how her mother had determined to "do everything in her power to avoid Trim Street". In early 1806 it was in a house in poor, noisy, busy and viewless Trim Street (we don't know the exact location) that the Austens ended up. Mr Austen was dead and the family, under financial pressure, had been living at 25 Gay Street. Unable to afford anywhere nicer, the family quickly moved first to Clifton in Bristol and then, in autumn 1806, to Southampton. Two years later,Jane remembered in a letter to Cassandra, "what happy feelings of escape!"

The Bath of *Persuasion*, completed in 1816, paints a more sombre picture of city than the Bath of *Northanger Abbey*, finished in Sydney Place, that's perhaps not surprising given the unhappy times that marked the Austen's last years in the city.

Jane did start another novel during her stay in the city, *The Watsons*, but it was never completed.

OLD BATHONIANS

GENERAL JAMES WOLFE 5 TRIM STREET

This military commander, noted firstly for his great victory over the French in Canada, once wrote to a friend: "My health is mightily impaired by the long confinement at sea. I am going to Bath to refit for another campaign." Wolfe died at the age of 32 after being wounded three times in the Battle in the Heights of Abraham in Quebec.

U

UNION PASSAGE

Developed as you see it today after the Bath Improvement Act of 1789, this ancient route possibly existed in Saxon times and has variously been called Slaughterhouse Lane, Cock's Lane, Cox Lane and Lock's Lane. The upper windows used to jut out so far that burgling the neighbours opposite would have been a synch.

UNION STREET

What is now Union Street was once the yard of the famous Bear Inn. In the City Corporation's Survey of Bath of 1641 the Bear is recorded as one of 18 inns in the city. Together with the White Hart on Stall Street and the York Hotel at the top of Broad Street it was the first port of call for many important visitors to Bath. It is celebrated in Christopher Anstey's satirical *New Bath Guide* of 1767. On his arrival, Simpkin

Blunderhead writes to his mother: "And sure you'll rejoice, my dear mother, to hear we are safely arrived at the sign of the Bear."

By the end of the 18th century, though, the huge inn was seen as blocking the way to the baths and new upper parts of town, as Tobias Smollett gleefully points out in *The Expedition of Humphry Clinker:*

Communication with the baths, is through the yard of an inn, where the poor trembling valetudinarian is carried in a chair, betwixt the heels of a double row of horses, wincing under the curry-combs of grooms and postilions, over and above the hazard of being obstructed, or overturned by the carriages which are continually making their exit or their entrance. I suppose after some chairmen shall have been maimed, and a few lives lost by those accidents, the corporation will think, in earnest, about providing a more safe and commodious passage.

The inn was demolished in 1807 as part of the Bath Improvement Act development and Union Street was built in its place. They named it Union Street simply because it unites Milsom Street to the North and Stall Street to the South.

AUSTEN WATCH

It is in Union Street that, after Anne's climatic chat with Captain Harville at the White Hart Inn, Captain Wentworth catches up with Anne. The reunited lovebirds decide to take the scenic (and long) route back to Camden Place, along the "comparatively quiet and retired gravel-walk, where the power of conversation would make the present hour a blessing indeed, and prepare it for all the immortality which the happiest recollections of their own future lives could bestow". All together now: Ahh…

UPPER BOROUGH WALLS

A part of the ancient town, many Roman finds have been made around the area of the Mineral Water Hospital. The rough wall opposite the hospital marks the northern section of the old, roughly pentagonal, medieval city wall. It once looked over greenery – today's Milsom Street area. The rough wall you can see is not medieval, though its foundations are. It is actually a Victorian copy, but the original wall did have crenellations – gaps in the walls through which you could fire.

Completed in 1738 by John Wood, the Mineral Water Hospital was – like Bellott's Hospital in Beau Street – built not for Bathonians but to cope with the large numbers of poor sick from outside Bath who came for treatment. All four of Bath's leading lights of the time – John Wood, Beau Nash, Dr William Oliver and Ralph Allen – got behind the hospital scheme, which was paid for through donations. Beau Nash charmed much of the cash from female aristocrats, Ralph Allen provided the Bath stone for free, and Wood's services as architect and builder were also given for free. William Oliver (the inventor of the Oliver biscuit) was appointed the first physician to the hospital. Initially the hospital had room for 110 patients, who were, according to Beau Nash's biographer Oliver Goldsmith, mostly "the paralytic and the leprous".

The courtyard below the city wall is the site of the hospital's cemetery, as a plaque explains…

This piece of ground was in the year 1736 set apart for the burial of patients dying in the Bath General Hospital and after receiving 238 bodies was closed by the governors of that charity in the year 1849, from regard to the health of the living.

In 1835 the rules were relaxed and Bathonians began being admitted for treatment as well. The western end of the hospital, which was added in 1860, has a carving depicting the story of the Good Samaritan with the message: "Go thou and do likewise."

Now called the Royal National Hospital for Rheumatic Diseases, hot water spa treatment here continued up until 1976. Today it specialises in rheumatic disease and brain injury rehabilitation.

SPOOKY BATH It's haunted! (allegedly…)

Upper Borough Walls: Hospital patients buried in the cemetery by the wall still linger in this area, so if you hear any "wailing and groaning" you shouldn't mistake this for the Theatre Royal audience. There was also once a pub on Upper Borough Walls called the Seven Stars. Reported manifestations at that establishment over the years have included "shaking tea cups", "cold spots in the cellar" and disconcerting "grabbing sensations" in the lavatory.

W

WALCOT STREET

There has been a settlement outside the old city walls around Walcot Street since Roman times. In fact in those days the area was something of a major junction. Walcot Street itself was the final approach to Bath of the Roman's Fosse Way from Lincoln to Exeter, while other roads left the area for London, Poole and for Avonmouth and South Wales. Villas, farmsteads and lots of burial sites have been found here and it is thought that a fort was close by too.

After the Romans abandoned Bath at the end of the 4th century Walcot remained inhabited. When the Saxons arrived they named the area "Wealas", meaning foreigner, after the local Romano-British. Medieval Walcot Street was a farming and weaving community and in 1317 Edward III granted charter for a market in Bath here. Elizabeth's 1590 charter established Walcot within the city's boundary.

In the 18th century, when the area was quite a well-to-do suburb, Dr Johnson stayed at the Pelican Inn here. By the 19th century it was an industrial area and its traders included gun makers, printers, tailors, bookbinders, cobblers and wheelwrights, to name just a few.

In the 1970s the area survived – though not entirely intact – a plan to drive a road tunnel beneath it. Walking from Northgate Street, where the open car park is on the right, old pubs and houses thrived, all sadly bulldozed in the 1970s. The site today is home to a Saturday flea market.

Up the street on the right is the old 1855 corn market, cattle market and slaughterhouse. In the 1960s a bull escaped from the market and went on the rampage before being shot in the Circus. Next door was the city tramshed. Bath's first horse-drawn tram service ran from here in 1880; electric ones then operated from the turn of the century to 1939. This is Beehive Yard, a name that comes from the honey-laden wild bees that were discovered in cellars here in the 18th century.

There is no path at all on the other side of the road for a short walk from here, but notice the steps cut into the dark wall opposite. They lead up to the Paragon – houses that were built on huge vaults backing onto Walcot Street. Just to the right of these steps is a decrepit little drinking fountain, put here in 1860 for horses.

On the right just before you get to the Bell Inn is Ladymead House, parts of which date back well into medieval times. From 1816 it was a penitentiary for the "reform" of prostitutes (or "fallen women"). The adjoining houses were used as venereal disease isolation wards. Next door is Cornwell Buildings with its rare and beautiful concave shop front that once allowed carts to turn.

Opposite the Bell public house is Chatham Row. The end house at the bottom, No 12, was in 1967 deliberately set ablaze by the Bath Fire Department in an experiment to test the mettle of Bath stone and Georgian architecture. The building was gutted but as you can see it survived to be refurbished.

Turn right at the top of the street and you come to Walcot Village Hall, built in 1842 as St Swithin's Cemetery Chapel. On the other side of the road is St Swithin's Church itself, built in 1790 by John Palmer (who's also buried inside). This is the likely site of an earlier pagan temple. The first St Swithin's Church was built here in 971. Very tiny, the remains of it can still be seen in today's crypt.

Whacky Walcot

Now styled by the city's council as Bath's "artisan quarter", Walcot remains very much independently-minded part of the city. In the 1970s the area spawned the Bath Arts Workshop, whose members went on to establish such local institutions as the Natural Theatre Company, the Bath Fringe Festival and the Bath Festival of Blues and Progressive Music (a 1970 event that inspired Michael Eavis to hold the first ever Glastonbury festival). Established in 1970, the now world-famous Natural Theatre Company are a company of actors who perform as comic and surreal characters at events, festival and parties. Among their most famous creations are the "Naked People", who wander around chatting, happily dressed in nothing but pink body stockings. Keep your eyes peeled about Bath – not everything is always as it should be. A very very popular street festival, Walcot Nation Day, was held once a year in Walcot Street From 1997 until 2007.

AUSTEN WATCH

Jane's father, the Rev George Austen, and his wife Cassandra were married at St Swithin's Church in 1764. George Austen, who died at Green Park Buildings East, is also buried here. His tomb and an accompanying plaque are in the graveyard by the roadside. Alongside it is a memorial to the novelist and diarist Fanny Burney [see North & South Parades] who lies buried somewhere here in a now-unknown grave.

WESTGATE BUILDINGS & CHAPEL COURT

St James's Rampire, a section of wall stretching from the South Gate to the West Gate, once stood here. Then on the green edge of the city, it was a very fashionable area until the wall was torn down and Westgate Buildings was built in the 1760s. By the 1830s the street had become part of the Avon Street slum district.

Chapel Court, a grouping of lovely buildings surrounding a hushed courtyard, stands between Westgate Buildings and the Cross Bath. It is an extension of St John's Hospital, the "hospital of the Baths", established by the nearby Cross Bath in 1180. By Elizabeth I's visit to the city in 1574 the hospital was housing wealthy visitors rather than poor ones and in 1716 the Corporation decided it was time to give the place a Georgian facelift. The 12th century St Michael's Chapel was rebuilt in 1723 by William Killigrew. The rest of Chapel Court was begun in 1726 by a 22-year-old Wood. It was his first major job in the city and it displeased the landowner James Bridges, the Duke of Chandos. After his tenants complained of thin walls and stinking drains in Chandos House and Chandos Buildings the Duke wrote to the man who would go on to design North and South Parades, Queen Square and the Circus: "No two houses have been worse finished and in a less workmanlike manner by anyone who pretended to be an architect."

Further down the road, formerly known as Hetling House and then Skrine House, is the ancient Abbey Church House. From 1138 it was the site of the small Leper's Hospital. Today's building was built in 1570 for the Bath MP John Clerke, and from 1590 it was Dr Robert Baker's practice, from where he took rich clients, including the likes of Sir Walter Raleigh, to the nearby baths. John Wood described it as the "second best house in the City" and in 1740 it was considered one of the few important enough to accommodate Princess Mary, daughter of George II, during her stay. German bombers all but destroyed it in 1942 but, as the plaque by its doors tells, it was rebuilt and reopened in the 1950s.

AUSTEN WATCH

In *Persuasion* the impoverished Mrs Smith lived in Westgate Buildings, close to the baths where she was being treated for her arthritis. Supper-snobbish Sir Walter is appalled that Anne could consider visiting anyone here:

Westgate Buildings! And whom, pray, is Miss Anne Elliot to be visiting in Westgate Buildings? A mere Mrs Smith, an everyday Mrs Smith? Upon my word, you have the most extraordinary taste!

WESTGATE STREET

A main Saxon thoroughfare through the city this street led to the West Gate as its name implies. The way into the city for journeyers from Bristol and the west, the West Gate was the only one of Bath's main gates that looked out over greenery. In fact, it had fine views over lovely meadows known as the Kingsmead [see Kingsmead Square].

Enjoying the fine views above the gate were a set of VIP apartments known as Westgate House. Queen Elizabeth and Ann of Denmark probably stayed in the rooms there during their visits of 1574 and 1616 respectively. The rooms, renovated for Elizabeth's visit and enlarged twice after that, were leased as private dwellings by the time they and the gate were demolished in the 1770s to ease the flow of traffic.

Just outside the gate, from 1692 until 1723, there was a fives court. Played against a wall, fives was a handball game a bit like today's game of squash.

In medieval times Westgate Street, like Cheap Street, was much narrower – just 13 foot wide. Bridewell and Parsonage Lanes, like nearby Union Passage, were lined with workshops and housing for the poor but by the 1600s Westgate Street itself was lined with fine houses and inns. The Grapes dates back to 1620, its frontage added a hundred years later. Conveniently close to the baths, in the middle of the 17th century a Dr Ostendorph lived here. It was a wine merchants by 1728 and a pub by 1800 – by which time the faces of the houses on the north side had been cut back to widen the street.

The Westgate was once a coaching inn called the Angel Hotel that serviced traffic coming through the West Gate. William 'Lord Haw-Haw' Joyce, who radioed Nazi propaganda to Britain during WWII, once stayed here.

WOOD STREET & QUIET STREET

John Wood laid out Wood Street as part of his Queen Square development. He finished the, very restrained in design, north side around 1730.

The south side of the street – the more ornate Northumberland Buildings – was not built until 50 years later. The architect was Thomas Baldwin. As city architect at the time the streets were being reordered under the Bath Improvement Act of 1789, Baldwin was also responsible for the Pump Room's colonnade, Bath Street, Great Pulteney Street, the Guildhall and a great many other of the city's streets and buildings. The land was leased to Baldwin by a Dr Henry Harington, a descendant of Sir John Harington, godson of Elizabeth I.

A local doctor and landowner who would go on to become a mayor or the city, Harington was a champion of the Mineral Water Hospital and worked hard for the poor as well as for his wealthy clients. Also something of a wit, the good doctor, noticing so many tombs in the Abbey, penned this famous, humorous (apparently) epigram:

These walls, adorned with monument and bust, Show how Bath waters serve to lay the dust.

The humour hasn't survived the years.

According to John Wood, Quiet Street was "so named from the meek temper of a washerwoman espoused to one of the builders". Its two major buildings are after Wood's time. The two figures on the bank building – which dates from 1824 and was originally an "Auction Mart and Bazaar" – are worth a look. The statuette on the left represents "Commerce"; the one with wings is "Genius". It was built by Henry Goodridge, the man responsible for the Corridor. The façade opposite, now Kitchens, is an 1871 work by Major Charles Davis, who also built the Empire Hotel on Grand Parade.

Y

YORK STREET

The Roman Great Bath complex covered much of what is now York Street. Built in 1808 (at the same time as Swallow Street), York Street opened a route for carriages from Stall Street to the Parades. Previously you were forced to go on foot through Lilliput Alley, Abbey Green, and Abbeygate Street.

The 'bridge' over York Street piped hot water from the Queen's Bath to the Bath City Laundry (previously a chapel). The slightly scary-looking Quaker Friends Meeting House at the other end of York Street was built as a Masonic Hall in 1842 (the year 5819 by the Freemasons' calendar).

Next door is Bath stone quarrier Ralph Allen's Town House, the hidden Georgian gem here. Now surrounded by other buildings, which have over the years sprung up around it like nettles, when it was originally built Allen could see from the garden his Sham Castle on the eastern hillside (erected there to show off Allen's Bath stone). The house can be glimpsed from the (often locked) path to the right of the Friends Meeting House. The estate agents Crisp Cowley, on the corner of York Street and Church Street, have a key to the gate. There is also a passage running to the back of the Huntsman at the end of the street, which, technically, is private.

The Kingston Baths

The benched space by the Abbey is Kingston Parade, the home of Bath Tourist Information Centre. Where the Parade opens on York Street stood the Kingston Baths. To build these baths in 1755 the Duke of Kingston pulled down Abbey House, the last surviving bit of monastery after the Dissolution and possibly the place Queen Elizabeth stayed during her famous visit of 1574.

The digging for the baths also unearthed a Saxon cemetery and, even more importantly, the eastern part of Roman bath complex. It was the first bit of the Roman baths discovered, but the remains were reburied and in 1766 the new baths were completed.

The men-only Kingston Baths drew water from the King's Spring and offered such delights as Turkish baths and "vapour" treatments. But not everyone was impressed.

In Tobias Smollett's satire *The Expedition of Humphry Clinker*, Mathew Bramble visits the Kingston Bath to purify himself of the "contamination" of the King's Bath:

I went to the Duke of Kingston's private bath, and there I was almost suffocated for want of free air; the place was so small, and the steam so stifling…

The Kingston Baths were demolished in 1923 to dig out the Roman Baths.

The Bath Perambulator

A scenic tour route around Bath, featuring a heady combination of Crescents, Parades and sheer drops...

The Bath Perambulator takes you in a snail-shell figure around Bath. You will be able to parade all seven Crescents and you will also see the views from Beechen Cliff and Sham Castle. All this finery, however, involves some serious perambulation, so although there are plenty of pubs along the way, Gentlemen and Ladies wishing to complete the Perambulator in one day, with full view admiring rights included, will rise above the temptations of most of these hostelries. (Indeed, you should know that the so-called 'Bath Perambulator Pub Crawl Challenge' – see panel opposite – is aptly named.)

If you want to use a map to help you follow the detail of the route, be sure that it is not one that only covers the centre of Bath.

Bennett Street: the start of your perambulation. Good luck!

THE CIRCUS TO THE ROYAL CRESCENT AND THEN DOWN TO THE RIVER

Present yourself in the King's Circus at 12.50pm sharp. You will have brunched heartily and will have brought additional food and water. You will be wearing comfortable footwear: shoes that will enable you to parade for between four and five hours, should you wish to totter the lot. Your pockets or purse will contain Her Majesty's coinage.

After limbering up, parade directly into Bennett Street, past the Assembly Rooms, and take a left up Lansdown

Road, past the Grappa Bar and past the Belvedere public house. Shortly you will be greeted by the Farmhouse Tavern. The door may be open. Do not go in if you intend to complete your perambulation. Head instead right into Camden Crescent. Admire it. Take in the view. Parade. At the very end of the Crescent, go up St Stephen's Road and trip left up the shadowy steps. At the top, turn right – back onto St Stephen's Road. After some 200 yards you'll reach two modernist pillars that advertise 'The Towers'. Walk between them and up the road and then take the path on the right at the end of the road.

Presently, you'll see a Victorian terrace. But before you reach it, a bestepped path will reveal itself on the left. Take it: it winds up to Summerfield Road. At the top, turn around and gape at the splendid (winter only) view. You should be able to see Sham Castle. Your armpits will gently perspire when you realise that this is on your route. Later. Much later.

At the brow of the hill, turn left up Summerfield Road. You will soon come to a high Common with some swings and things on it. That's the hard work done, for a while; Gentlemen and Ladies might avail themselves of the Common for some light parading and a sandwich but those wishing to complete their perambulation would not at this point remove themselves to the Richmond Arms (300 yards on the right up Richmond Place).

To continue, cross the Common on the lower side and walk down Mount Beacon, where more splendid (winter only) views of the City are to be had to your left through the trees. Go straight on down the path on the

DARE YOU?

The Bath Perambulator Pub Crawl Challenge

This now world famous scenic drinking tour (people do it for charity these days!) is a challenge thirsty walkers will want to take on. Have a pint in each of these hostelries: **Assembly Inn, Grappa Bar, Old Farmhouse, Richmond, St James Wine Vaults, New Inn, White Hart, Pulteney Arms, Boater...**

Camden Crescent

Originally known as Upper Camden Place, John Eveleigh's 1788 Camden Crescent more than holds its own in the League of Crescents. Boasting a sumptuous sweep and splendid views, it even has a characterful off-centre aspect due to a landslip in 1889 that demolished the nice houses of its eastern end. The remains of the houses were demolished and Hedgemead Park built. The rather nice elephant heads above the doors (each pulls its own peculiar face) are based on the family crest of Charles Pratt, 'Recorder of Bath' and Marquis of Camden, after whom the Crescent is named (a portrait of Pratt by the Bath painter Hoare hangs in the Guildhall). As well as Camden Crescent and Somerset Place, Eveleigh also built Grosvenor Place near Larkhall – the last great town house terrace as you leave the city by the London Road, and part of a building project that collapsed through lack of money (like the Great Pulteney Street scheme).
The view from this marvellous crescent is spectacular at any time of day, but in the early morning and at dusk the city takes on a positively ethereal aspect.

Lansdown Crescent

Twenty huge houses long and with a radius of 100-odd metres, Lansdown Crescent is arguably Bath's second crescent. Built by John Pinch around 1790, imperious, it sits regally on its hillside so comfortably you might think that beneath it there are huge silk cushions. Even more romantic perambulators might consider the fabulously restored ironwork to be like a necklace about a throat! (Or maybe not.) The field before it is too steep for a conventional lawn, which is why sheep – Jacob's Sheep, to be precise – still graze there today. The building of Lansdown Crescent is largely due to the finance of Charles Spackman, a coach builder and patron of Thomas Marker of Doric House.

Somerset Place

Began by John Eveleigh in 1790, the lovely Somerset Place is not at all, as you might think, part of the design that saw the development of Lansdown Crescent and its wings, though they were built during the same period. The two central houses were built first as a grand, semi-detached pair (and these two are in fact much less curved than the houses that make up the rest of the Crescent) and the remainder was not completed until 1820 because of the economic difficulties of the 1790s. Somerset Place was badly bombed during the Second World War.

St James Square

Inspired by Queen Square, John Palmer's 1794 Square is unusual in that it sits very definitely on a slope. "Boo! Hiss!" some pedantic architects might object, but though, overall, it doesn't quite achieve the grand, palatial effect of Wood's masterpiece (which also sits on at least a slight slope) it does benefit from that kind of peace granted by a complete lack of through traffic – unlike noisy Queen Square.

St James Square was built on a site used as gardens by the tenants of the Royal Crescent. One of those evicted from his garden was Christoper Anstey, author of the 1766 *New Bath Guide*. Miffed at having to transplant his beech trees, he famously complained in this epitaph:

Ye men of Bath, who stately mansions rear
To wait for tenants from Lord knows where,
Would you pursue a plan that cannot fail,
Erect a mad house and enlarge your goal.

Don't bother trying to examine the words too closely just now. Simply parade and take in the fine, quiet environs, occasionally nodding stiffly to passers-by, perhaps even glancing suspiciously at the odd parked car, daring it to suddenly spring into life and shatter the place's sublime tranquillity.

Doric House

Built by J M Gandy in 1805, the extraordinary Doric House was the house and public gallery of the celebrated Bath painter Thomas Barker, known at the time as 'Barker of Bath'. Of the Gainsborough school, Barker was from Pontypool in Wales and came to Bath when he was 13. Under the patronage of the prosperous Bath coach builder Charles Spackman, who set him to study in Rome, his star rose until his most famous painting *The Woodman* was sold for the then very princely sum of 500 guineas. At the height of his fame he even advised on the redecoration of Parliament in 1841. In later years his popularity faded, though, and he died in poverty. Today you can see his pictures upstairs in the Victoria Art Gallery and at the Tate in London. The building is perhaps a little scary-looking, considering it was once a home. It gets its name from its imperious array of Doric columns. Inside, painted on the walls, is Thomas's huge 1825 fresco *Massacre of the Inhabitants of Scio by the Turks*.

left and at the fork take the path on your right through to St Stephen's Road. (What a cunning short cut this is.) Turn right towards St Stephen's Church. It should be no later than half-past two. On the left is a smashing row of church cottages: St Stephen's Place.

At the end of the road take a sharp left and double back past the cottages onto Lansdown Road. Follow down past Doric House and turn right into Lansdown Crescent, after Upper Lansdown Mews. Parade the Crescent into Somerset Place, which also looks very much like a Crescent but isn't called one.

At the end of Somerset Place walk down the steps and turn left into Cavendish Road. Shortly, Cavendish Crescent curls into view. Walk around it. Please. When you come back onto Cavendish Road, go down and take your next left into Cavendish Place, which leads to Park Place. Turn right into Park Street and you'll stand in the regal St James's Square. It is now three o'clock. The St James Wine Vaults public house is on the south east of the Square; the Mangia Bene deli is over the road from there. The deli's closed on Sunday, but that's the day when the Chequers conveniently does a hearty roast lunch till 4.45pm. The hungry and thirsty may decide to duck out here, though Gentlemen and Ladies intending to complete the Perambulator will be brave to adjust their schedule by more than a swift half this early in their perambulation.

Leave the Square by the south west, cross over Crescent Lane, walk down Marlborough Buildings and take your first left into the Royal Crescent. Parade it. Now head down the gravel walk at the end and take a left into Queen's Parade Place, and then a right into Queen Square.

Turn right into Charlotte Street and, opposite the public toilets, turn left into Palace Yard Mews. Cross over the road at Monmouth Place into Cumberland Row and continue to New King Street. Turn right and continue

■ Shoot up this flight of steps. It's pleasantly shady and cool

■ The Richmond Arms. Everyone deserves a short break at this point. Pray they're still in business

Cavendish Place

One of the later Crescents, the John Pinch-designed Cavendish Place was begun in 1817 by the builder Willam Broom. He went bankrupt in 1825 but the development was completed by 1830. A gentle parade reveals this minor Crescent to be an elegant address that catches the light just so and which has a handsome aspect overlooking the golf course (properly, the High Common). The area was once known as St Winifred's Dale and the Crescent as St Winifred's Crescent, after an ancient stream that springs from St Winifred's Well in the hills of Bathwick near the University.

to Norfolk Crescent on your left. Parade the Crescent informally and stumble onto the river path (there's a kissing gate in the fence, though solitary perambulators might prefer to traverse the gap to its right). Turn left and walk along the river path until you arrive at the Churchill Bridge at Broad Quay. It's about half a mile.

If you see this sign you're on the right track and headed for some lovely Crescents. Parade at will!

A DIGNIFIED CANAL-SIDE SHORTCUT

Should any perambulators at this point wish to truncate their parade (thereby avoiding two arduous accents but missing out on some breathtaking views, a hidden Crescent and a sham castle), this gentle constitutional along the River and the Canal will bring your journey to a sedate, if foreshortened, end and deposit you in the pleasant surroundings of Sydney Gardens, which is at the top of Great Pulteney Street and a mere moment's walk

OLD BATHONIAN

WALTER SAVAGE LANDOR
(1775-1864) 35 ST JAMES SQUARE

This quarrelsome and extravagant poet, writer and friend of Dickens was famed for his series of dramatic dialogues entitled *Imaginary Conversations of Literary Men and Statesmen*.

A hasty character (he once admitted of himself: "I neither can nor ever shall be popular"), after collecting debts and firing a gun at a fellow student's window at Oxford, for which he was thrown out, Landor set himself up in some style in Bath with monies advanced from his mother's estate.

Here, where he afforded himself a fine carriage, three horses and two manservants, he quickly gained a reputation for lavishness. Extremely impulsive, after fighting for a time with the rebels against Napoleon in Spain (and giving them large sums of cash) he asked a girl at a Bath ball to marry him as soon as he clapped eyes on her.

The marriage was an argumentative and expensive one. The two first went to live in Florence, where the theft of some silver saw Landor branded a "dangerous man", and then Tuscany, where he proceeded to fall out with his neighbours over water rights. Their stormy relationship eventually saw him return to Bath alone and in reduced circumstances.

Back in Bath, with his dog Pomero, he would do tricks to entertain children on the High Common, and he once again became a famous fixture; but quarrels, libels, law suits and debts eventually drove him away and he spent the last six years of his life in Italy. He was the type of character who, according to his friend Sydney Colvin, was given to "tempests of hilarity" almost as formidable as his tempests of anger at the "suspicion of a contradiction or slight" and the kind of man "who would put his spectacles up over his forehead, and after oversetting everything in the wildest search for them, submit himself with desperate resignation to their loss".

A few days before his death he told his landlady: "I shall never write again. Put out the lights and draw the curtains."

from the town centre.

(The more stout among you intending to press on with the 'Main Stroll' to its rubber-legged end will want to skip on ahead to the next section of the Perambulator: "Up and Down Beechen Cliff".)

Shortcutters: Emerge from the river path. Turn right onto the pavement. At the road bridge cross over onto the pavement opposite and keep walking: you're headed for the footbridge. Parade the footbridge, then turn left onto the river path.

Stroll serenely. Bar falling in, nothing possibly can go wrong now. Pass under a bridge. Under a second bridge, lean on the railings and observe the markings on the wall (see "The Tides of Time"). Onwards. At the bend in the river, see where the canal starts. You're headed for the canal.

Take the path that climbs upwards; pass over onto the towpath. Admire the lock; there are more ahead. Pass under a road bridge, then another, then up the steps. Issue, blinking, into the light; cross the lock to your left. Turn right onto the towpath. What a lovely spot this is. Parade it. Pass a pretty white bridge, another lock, some

Shortcutters, head for the far bridge. A delightful waterside walk awaits you

OLD BATHONIAN

CHARLES DICKENS
(1812-1870) 35 ST JAMES' SQUARE

Dickens stayed often in the Square with his friend Walter Savage Landor; before that he had lodged regularly at the Saracen's Head inn (still on Broad Street). He knew Bath well and two chapters of his *Pickwick Papers* poke delicious fun at Bath society. Even the water is not sacred, Sam Weller declaring it to taste of "warm flat irons".

Dickens fell out of love with Bath, though, when a production of the comedy *Not So Bad As We Seem* at the Guildhall bombed and got panned in the local papers. Dickens had advised on the project and, despite being warned of its terrible acoustics, had insisted that the play be staged in the Large Room. The author Robert Peach, who was at the show, wrote that the audience "could not detect one clear syllable".

He took all the criticism very personally indeed and never excused the city for its rudeness. Afterwards his affectionate portraits of Bath were replaced with altogether less pleasant ones. Bath had become, he wrote in a letter, "a mouldy old roosting place", adding: "I hate the sight of the bygone old Assembly Rooms and the Bath chairs trundling the dowagers about the streets..." Pure vitriol, and shortly before his own death he penned this even more famous obituary for the city:

Landor's ghost goes along the silent streets here before me... The place looks to me like a cemetery which the Dead have succeeded in rising and taking. Having built streets of their old gravestones, they wander about scantly trying to 'look alive'. A dead failure.

benches (have a break; think of the brave hearts climbing Beechen Cliff). Ahead there is a bridge; cross over the road and continue your parading. Before you is another lock. Some refreshments can be obtained from the 'Pump Shed'. When it's open.

More locks; another pretty white bridge; adequate (it's not as if you've ascended Beechen Cliff) views to your left. At the road bridge, up the steps with you and onto Bathwick Hill. Don't worry, you're not climbing it. Cross over; the towpath continues. Parade at will, past the narrow boat station. Cross the bridge over the water with the house on it. Down the steps and into the tunnel. Shout: it's echoey. Pass under the white bridge (this really is delightful, isn't it?), but before you reach the next bridge, take a left through the small set of white gates.

You're in Sydney Gardens. Parade. The Gardens were made for it. Literally. You've had enough now. Exit the Gardens at its bottom-left entrance (which is the least fraught with traffic). Turn left and the City is again before you. Avail yourselves of its many houses of refreshment.

This is exciting isn't it, shortcutters? Proceed at a moderately sedate rate

UP AND DOWN BEECHEN CLIFF

Perambulators who did not take the dignified canal-side shortcut will now emerge from the river path. Things are about to get tricky. Turn right onto Churchill Bridge, then turn right again and cross the Lower Bristol Road at the traffic lights. Walk through the little subway tunnel by the road under the railway bridge arches and turn right onto the Wells Road.

Cross the Wells Road at the traffic lights, then come back down to the thin line of old steps by the 'private road', opposite a redundant letter box. Walk up the steps to Crescent View; then take your first left up Magdelen

Shortcutters, if you see this lock you're all ship-shape and, erm, Bath fashion

Widcombe Crescent

This tucked away but simply awesome Crescent by Charles Harcourt Masters (1805) seems to rear like a cliff as you approach its behind from Beechen Cliff, and it reflects the sunlight on a pleasant day in a breathtaking manner. Its chief living rooms are placed to the rear, where they catch both the light and the remarkable views.

Widcombe Terrace, with its south-facing raised terrace and gardens that emerge from beneath it, is built on a far less grand scale but is inordinately cute. A little peek is all you should give it, though: the space is small, private and not meant for hordes of perambulators (even if they are made up of Ladies and Gentlemen).

Road to Holloway. You will see a small church on your left. Cross over the road and take the adjacent thick steps into the park. Follow the steps around to the right and you will now meander in semi-circular fashion up Beechen Cliff. Keep going straight up the path.

When you reach the benches at the top, sit down. This is the best view of Bath there is. Follow round the hill behind you to your right for a bench that commands a view over Widcombe Valley; you'll see Prior Park at the far end of your view. Between the two views is a path that leads down to some increasingly steep steps, a path ominously known as Jacob's Ladder. You will have to go down it, eventually, though there is time yet for admiring the view.

When you do descend, turn right at the first road you meet: Alexandra Road. Seconds later, turn right and head up Lyncombe Hill. Shortly, turn left and walk down the treacherously steep Forefield Rise, (not Forefield Place) where you meet up with Prior Park Road behind Widcombe Crescent. Cross Prior Park Road and head straight up the adjacent path to the rear of the Crescent. Turn right and follow the small road until you reach the front of the Crescent. Parade as well as your legs permit and then turn left onto Widcombe Hill and walk to the bottom of the road. On your left is a backpackers' hostel called the White Hart, which has got a smashing back garden, though heed that you will need at least another hour's good sunlight if you intend to complete your perambulation from here today.

Main strollers, up these stairs with you. It's a good, stiff climb but the rewards are commensurate

National Trust countryside too? What myriad joys the Perambulator affords!

FROM THE CANAL UP TO SHAM CASTLE AND BACK DOWN TO PULTENEY BRIDGE

There's only one more significantly excruciating hill climb left to do on the Bath Perambulator, and it is preceded by a deceptively pleasant wander along the canal towpath. Turn right past the White Hart and head right onto the canal path yards later. Follow the path to the left, cross the first road you meet (Pulteney Gardens) and continue along the towpath until you reach a small white bridge on the right (Widcombe Lock). Cross the bridge and walk up the steps until you arrive at Sydney Buildings. Cross Sydney Buildings and walk up to Darlington Place; continue up the steps and follow the path up the back of Bathwick Hill, alongside National Trust-owned fields. At the end of the path, you'll meet Bathwick Hill proper.

You're tired now. Turn right and walk up Bathwick Hill for five to ten minutes until you reach North Lane on the left. Shuffle up North Lane and turn left onto North Road. That's the last climb over. You can coast it from here, providing it's not dark, in which case you're in serious trouble because we're about to go into the woods.

About 200 yards down North Road you will see a signed Public Footpath (not the bridleway) on the other side of the road. Follow the path through the woods to a stone stile leading into a field. The path continues left; there is a gate on the right that also leads into the field. Enter the field and follow round its lower side to Sham Castle. Admire it. Admire the view, then continue down the signed path, through the woods and fields, cross the golf course drive and slip down the muddy bank to North Road again. Turn right and 200 yards later take the path on your left. This leads between small fields down to Cleveland Walk. Cross the road and walk down Sham Castle Lane. At the bottom, turn right and then left onto Sydney Road. Cross over to Great Pulteney Street, head for the Bridge and reward yourself.

This is the path you want. Not the bridleway. That's for horses

Journey's end. Phew

Sham Castle: A Mockery Of A Sham

Built by Richard Jones in 1762, Sham Castle is a mock castle – all façade and no dungeons. Viewable from the garden of his Town House in the city, it was put up to show off Ralph Allen's Bath Stone. The castle is illuminated at night, but let us hope you reach civilisation before then.

OLD BATHONIAN

WILLIAM BECKFORD

(1760-1844) 19, 20 & 21 LANSDOWN CRESCENT

William Beckford was a wealthy recluse and eccentric with a notorious temper. His father – a Lord Mayor of London, England's first sugar plantation millionaire and a notorious slaver – died when William was just ten. Inheriting a vast fortune (£110 million in today's money) and his father's Fonthill estate in Wiltshire, Beckford swiftly embarked on a lifetime's pursuit of 'the pleasures', in the process amassing a huge collection of great works of art and a highly controversial reputation.

Though he was married and had a daughter, Beckford's relationship with the ten-year-old William Courtenay, the future 9th Earl of Devon, scandalised society. In 1784 he was charged with sexual misconduct, robbing him of a peerage and a career in politics and turning him against the outside world. He fled with his wife (who refused to testify against him) and daughter to Europe. His wife died in Switzerland giving birth to their second daughter. After collecting an astonishing array of artwork, Beckford eventually returned to England, walled himself in at Fonthill with an army of retainers and became a recluse.

At Fonthill during 1796 Beckford one day decided: "I am growing rich, and mean to build towers." And he did indeed build a tower – Fonthill Abbey. But impatient Beckford built it too high – and of wood and substandard cement – and one night in 1825 it blew down. But Beckford had already sold the Abbey for a good price and moved to Bath, where he bought, in succession, 19, 20 and 21 Landsdown Crescent, ensuring, he hoped, that he wouldn't be disturbed by the "beastly jinglings of some piano".

He connected the three houses with a bridge at drawing room level. Beckford also bought land behind the Crescent and, with the young architect Henry Goodridge, he built a new tower – from where he could see both Fonthill and what he called the "finest prospect in Europe". According to Goodridge, as the tower grew Beckford would cry "Higher!"

When his tower was completed it was stocked with a collection of treasures that art collectors today would weep at. Included in it were paintings by Rembrandt and Raphael, exquisite poetry and an astonishing array of rare books. But few saw Beckford's hoard while he was alive, as he seldom admitted visitors. Beckford's own reputation as an author was enhanced with his acclaimed 1834 Gothic romance *Vathek*, a bizarre tale about the adventures of the shockingly greedy, cruel Caliph Vathek and his final descent into Hell.

Beckford's secluded lifestyle encouraged much gossip in chattering Bath and the papers were full of lurid stories of "exotic and unholy rites". Few of the tales were true, but certainly Beckford rode with a cavalcade of dogs and outriders and he also retained from his days at Fonthill a dwarf named Pero, who according to one rare visitor to Lansdown Crescent, was "stationed in the vestibule of the house with no apparent duty whatsoever".

In his last years Beckford wrote two well-received travel books and, for himself, a collection of acid anecdotes in which he vented his spleen at the aristocracy. He died in 1844, aged 83, after inadvisedly going out in a rainstorm. Typically, all Bath, after whispering behind its hands about him for so long, turned out to see his funeral cortège and the bells of the Abbey were duly muffled. It was his wish to be buried with his dogs in a tomb by his tower. But the ground was unconsecrated and only later was his body moved there. His collection of art was sold off after his death but some of it can be seen today in his tower.

You can visit Beckford's Tower, and ascend its winding staircase, from Easter to October. [See the Attractions section for more details.]

HISTORY OF BATH TIMELINE

It's not all just pigs, Romans, Georgians and Jane Austen, you know. Oh. Apparently it is…

10,000-6,000 BC Rain sinks to a depth of about 2km below the surface, where it is cooked before gushing forth from the city's three hot springs.

c8,000 BC Hunter-gatherers camping on the hills surrounding what is now Bath visit the hot springs.

c100 BC The Belgae, an Iron Age tribe of farmers and craftsmen, build shrines around the springs to Sul.

43 AD The Romans invade Britain. Unlike some other tribes, the Belgae offer little resistance and are swiftly Romanised.

c65 The Romans, who value the benefits hot springs bring, set to work transforming the muddy bog into Aquae Sulis, a famous temple and health resort.

c391 The Christian Roman emperor Theodosius rules. Pagan temples like the one at Aquae Sulis are shut down.

c400 The Roman Western Empire is under attack from all sides and Aquae Sulis is abandoned. It is the beginning of the Dark Ages. Ideas such as grand buildings and public sanitation will disappear. Just a few Roman Britons remain in the city.

c500 The roof of the Great Bath falls in, the drains silt up and Aquae Sulis begins to decay.

c510 The Battle of Badon. The Britons (according to legend led by King Arthur) defeat the invading Saxons – possibly at Solsbury Hill, east of Bath.

577 The Battle of Deorham, a few miles north of Bath. Aquae Sulis is sacked by the Saxons.

c675 Building a convent which soon becomes a monastery, the Saxons rename Aquae Sulis "Hat Bathu" (hot baths). They use only a small part of the crumbled Roman bathing complex.

c750 A monk describes the city's decaying Roman remains in the haunting poem *The Ruin*: "Wondrous is this masonry, shattered by the Fates. The fortifications have given way, the buildings raised by giants are crumbling…"

781 A large and splendid abbey church is built which becomes an important religious centre.

c878 Alfred the Great defeats the Danes at nearby Westbury in Wiltshire. When not busy fighting he lays out Bath's street plan, preparing the way for it to flourish as a market town.

973 Edgar, the first King of all England, is crowned at the abbey church.

1086 Population of Bath: 890.

1088 After an unsuccessful Norman rebellion against William the Conqueror levels Bath, Bishop John of Tours buys the city for 500 pounds of silver and becomes the first ever Bishop of Bath and Wells by transferring his seat of power from Wells to the wealthy Bath Abbey. Work soon begins on a huge cathedral.

1106 Interested in the medical benefits of the hot springs, John of Tours builds the King's Bath. Around this time the first Hot and Cross baths are also built. Public bathing is back in Bath.

c1136 The writer Geoffrey of Monmouth sows the seeds of the legend of King Bladud and the founding of Bath [see panel below].

1180 Bishop Reginald Fitz Jocelyn's founds St John's Hospital by the Cross Bath so that the sick poor of the city can benefit from the waters.

1256, Henry III visits the city and as a joke has one of his knights thrown into the King's Bath fully clothed. Such events add to the city's growing fame.

1348 The Black Death reaches Bath. At the plague's height two priests a week die in the city.

1379 Population of Bath: 1,025.

1449 Shocked by the number of "privy parts" on display, Bishop Bekynton bans naked bathing.

1499 The Norman cathedral having fallen into rubble, Bishop Oliver King

1136 THE LEGEND OF KING BLADUD

Bladud, "king of the Britons and the founder of Bath", is first mentioned by Geoffrey of Monmouth in his *Historia Regum Britanniae*, the colourful pseudo history of Britain that includes such merry tales as the story of Arthur, Merlin and the Round Table. The myth of Bladud was later added to and we now have the following story, which every Bathonian knows…

Bladud as a young prince was banished form his father's court after contracting leprosy. While wandering as a swineherd in the Avon valley, Bladud's pigs, which had also caught the disease, wallowed in the hot mud looking for acorns and were miraculously cured. Seeing this Bladud tried the mud himself and returned to court a hero completely healed. King Bladud then built a settlement and temple by the hot springs and thus Bath was born. The legend is remembered by the acorns that ring the top the Circus.

orders work on the present building, which is not actually an "abbey" at all but an ostentatious parish church.

1536-9 The Reformation. Henry VIII dissolves the monastery and strips the lead from the unfinished Abbey roof.

1562 Bath is a small town prospering from the wool trade. Suggesting a modernisation of bathing facilities and a separate Lepers' Bath, William Turner, the Dean of Wells, accuses the City Corporation of neglecting the baths and spending its money instead on "cockfighting, tennis, parks, banqueting, pageants and plays".

1572 John Jones' treatise advocates actually drinking the waters for your health. The fashion for "taking the waters" is about to begin.

1574 Queen Elizabeth visits Bath, orders the restoration of the Abbey and generally puts Bath on the map as a fashionable spa. Visits from future royals will also help to keep up Bath's profile.

c1576 The Queen's Bath, originally for diseased poor people, is built.

1590 Bath is granted city status by Elizabeth I. Authority over the city and the baths is handed to a city corporation comprised of a mayor, aldermen and councillors.

1609 Bellott's Hospital founded in Beau Street for the treatment of poor pilgrims to the city. Bath has become a famous destination for the sick.

1643 The Civil War reaches Bath. [see panel below].

1664 Animals banned from the baths.

1688 Thanks, apparently, to the miraculous waters, Mary of Modena, Queen of James II, bears a Catholic heir – sparking a Protestant uprising.

1699 Population o0f Bath: 3,000.

1643 THE BATTLE OF LANSDOWN

Bath itself wasn't of particular strategic importance in the Civil War, but the Battle of Lansdown which took place north of the city on 5 July 1643, was a seriously bloody affair nonetheless. After three assaults, the Royalists, under the command of Lord Hopton, forced the Parliamentarians, who were led by Sir William Waller, to retreat from the heavily fortified Freezing Hill, but the Royalists were left too fatigued and depleted to take Bath itself. The Parliamentarians then sneaked off during the night, leaving match-cord burning and pikes standing along a wall to fool the Royalists into thinking they were still defending the city. The Royalists would retreat to Devizes to fight another day – but not before a prisoner blew up eight barrels of gunpowder trying to light his tobacco, temporarily blinding the already injured Lord Hopton. According to the Royalist eyewitness Richard Atkyns:

The ammunition was blown up, and the prisoners in the cart with it; together with the Lord Hopton, Major Sheldon, and Cornet Washnage, who was near the cart on horseback, and several others: it made a very great noise, and darkened the air for a time, and the hurt men made lamentable screeches…

1705 Soon to become its new Master of Ceremonies, Richard "Beau" Nash arrives in the city. Bath's Georgian heyday is about to begin.

1706 The first Pump Room is built. Before this you could only drink water at pumps in the baths.

1708 Harrison's Assembly Rooms open. Now visitors have a place where they can meet, gossip, eat, dance and play cards.

1725 The then young architect John Wood the Elder draws the first plans of his vision for a second Rome full of pseudo palaces for the wealthy.

1726 Post service entrepreneur-turned-quarrier Ralph Allen starts digging Bath stone. A beautiful honey-coloured limestone that can be sawn or "squared up" in any direction, all of Georgian Bath will be built with it.

1727 The beautiful Minerva Head – the Roman ancient sculpture combining the Celtic deity Sul and Roman god Minerva – is unearthed in Stall Street.

1728 Eminent physician Dr William Oliver, who will invent the Oliver biscuit, comes to Bath. He calls for a larger pump room to be built.

1736 John Wood the Elder completes Queen Square.

1738 John Wood, Ralph Allen, Beau Nash and William Oliver collaborate to build the Mineral Water Hospital for poor, sick pilgrims to the city.

1748 John Wood the Elder completes North and South Parades.

1754 John Wood the Elder begins the Circus. It is completed by his son, John Wood the Younger, in 1768.

1771 Today's "New" or "Upper" Assembly Rooms are built by John Wood the Younger.

1773 Robert Adam builds Pulteney Bridge – though for 16 years the bridge will lead nowhere.

1775 John Wood the Younger finishes Royal Crescent.

1766 Christopher Anstey publishes *The New Bath Guide*. Not so much a 'guide' as a satirical review, the book's broad humour immediately elevates it to bestseller status. It's still on sale today.

1750 16-STRING JACK THE HIGHWAYMAN

The 'notorious' highwayman John Rann was born in 1750 at the Crown Inn, which then stood on an important coaching route. Known as a bit of a dandy despite his occupation, and as 'Sixteen String Jack' because of the eight string laces he wore to the knee on each leg of his breeches, Rann was hanged at Tyburn in London, aged just 24, for holding up a vicar at gun point on the road. The Rev Bell's pockets had been made lighter to the tune of six shillings and sixpence and a rather nice pocket watch.

1777 The Hot Bath is rebuilt by John Wood the Younger. The Leper's Bath is demolished to make way for it.

1784 The Cross Bath is rebuilt by Thomas Baldwin.

1789 Great Pulteney Street is finally completed but a financial crisis leaves the planned streets leading from it unbuilt. Bath's Georgian heyday is over. The seaside is now fashionable, people start coming to the city to settle and to retire rather than holiday and play cards.

1789 The Bath Improvement Act gives powers to the city to open up the hemmed-in baths and spruce up the city centre. Bath Street will be built and many other streets widened.

1799 The present-day Pump Room is completed.

1799 Population of Bath: 34,160 – Bath is now the eighth largest city in all of England.

1801 Jane Austen and her family begin their stay in the city. She completes *Northanger Abbey*. The Austens – minus Jane's father, who dies here – leave Bath in 1806.

1810 The Kennet and Avon Canal, which still runs through Bath, is opened.

1820s The spa is in decline. The *Bath Chronicle* calls Bath a "once-favoured" city.

1830 Royal Victoria Park opens.

1831 Reform Bill riots reach Bath [see panel, right].

1841 Isambard Kingdom Brunel's Bath Spa railway station opens.

1851 Population of Bath: 43,023.

1871 Many other Roman finds over the decades have been ignored and then, during work to repair a leak in the King's Bath, the Roman Great Bath is discovered. A major excavation is soon launched and the temple and bathing complex unearthed. It's a massive boost for the city's flagging fortunes.

1889 The Queen's Bath is demolished

1755 **ANIMAL TRAGIC** Georgian Bathonians were entertained by a variety of travelling shows, the most weird and wonderful of which were the menageries – dubious outfits that visited inns to display their array of exotic creatures. If you visited the Wheatsheaf at the right time in 1755 you would have seen eleven mammals, two sepulchre vultures and a no-doubt sorry-looking golden eagle. In 1757 the first crocodile hit Bath – followed by a dromedary, two leopards and a 'sea monster' (an unfortunate sea lion captured off the Siberian coast). At the Cross Keys in 1780 punters were entertained by the sight of an ape sitting in a chair holding a club and drinking from a bottle. Even more bizarre, and indeed unsavoury, were the freak shows – like Piddock's of the 1790s, which featured a three-legged colt and a two-headed heifer.

to make way for fashionable new douche and massage treatments. The new facilities are a big hit.

1904 Bath gets its first electric tram.

1911 Population of Bath: 69,173. Manufacturing industry has brought 20,000 people to the city in a decade.

1939 Regular bathing stops at the King's Bath.

1942 Bath is bombed in retaliation for Allied bombing of historic German cities. Hundreds of people are killed, many historic buildings are hit.

1948-1976 Bath spa treatments available through the NHS.

1973 In response to the flattening of great swathes of historic artisan housing and the rise of brutal "packing case" architecture in the city, a "Save Bath Campaign" gets underway.

1978 Bad news: a meningitis scare closes all the spa facilities. The Hot Bath, Beau Street and New Royal Baths are all closed. The Mineral Water Hospital is 'switched off'.

1981 Population of Bath: 80,771.

1987 The city of Bath is made a UNESCO World Heritage Site.

1990 Three million people are visiting Bath every year.

2006 The Thermae Bath Spa facilities open. The city's hot springs can be enjoyed once more.

2012 Four-and-a-half million people are visiting Bath every year.

1832 THE BILL, THE WHOLE BILL AND NOTHING BUT THE BILL

Before the 1832 Reform Act began the process of making Parliament more democratic, Bath had two MPs – both of whom were simply "nominated" by the City Corporation. It was such a cosy affair that in 1794 RP Arden, in appreciation of the support of his small bunch of electors, threw a private banquet at the Bear Inn on Union Street, where an impressive 128 bottles of – variously – port, claret, Madeira, sherry, hock and cider were drunk.

But Britain was changing and by 1831 a great crowd was marching down Pulteney Street to the Sydney Gardens Hotel (now the Holburne Museum) demanding – as rallies like it up and down the country were – "the Bill, the whole Bill and nothing but the Bill". That same year, after the House of Lords rejected the Reform Bill for a second time, the White Hart Inn on Stall Street was wrecked in a riot. A Captain Wilkins was meeting at the inn with some men he was to take to Bristol to help quell the unrest there. An angry mob followed him and burning faggots were thrown against walls, windows were broken and an attempted entry was beaten off with red-hot kitchen pokers before 300 constables were sworn in to disperse the crowd.

A year later the Great Reform Bill was passed. It modestly extended the vote in Bath from just 30 males to about 3,000.

Listings **Attractions**

Bath has always been a city associated with pleasure. And it's still true today that there are many entertainments and diversions worthy of your attention. There can't be many cities with more festivals than Bath, and there's a happily growing number of theatres and entertainment hotspots to visit. There's also lots to do with children, as we hope you'll see…

ABBEY AND ABBEY TOWER

Tel: 01225 422462

www.bathabbey.org

The 15th century Gothic Abbey is worth at least a quick look inside. It's mere steps away form the Roman Baths and admission is a suggested donation of around £2.50. All to gawp at: the fan-vaulted ceiling (matched only by Westminster Abbey's), the 52 windows (the reason the Abbey is known as the Lantern of the West); and 617 wall and 847 floor memorials (including one to Beau Nash under Pew 33 of the Nave). Outside, by the Great Doors, are the Bishop's mitres, olive trees and ladder to Heaven – reminders of Bishop Oliver King's legendary dream that is supposed to have inspired him to build the Abbey.

Volunteer stewards will be able to answer many questions thrown at them, while school and group guided tours (£3 per person) can also be booked.

Opening times: 1 April to 31 October – Monday 9.30am-6pm, Tuesday to Saturday 9am-6pm, Sunday 1pm-2.30pm & 4.30pm-5.30pm. 1 November to 31 March – Monday 9.30am-4.30pm, Tuesday to Saturday 9am-4.30pm, Sunday 1pm-2.30pm & 4.30-5.30pm.

You can also embark on a guided tour up the 212 steps of the Abbey Tower. If you do you'll visit the bell chamber, stand on the vaulted ceiling, sit behind the clock face and enjoy a spectacular view of the city from the roof.

Tower Tours take place: January to March – 11am, 12 noon, 2pm. April & May – 10am-4pm on the hour. June, July and August – 10am-5pm on the hour. September & October – 10am-4pm on the hour. November – 11am, 12 noon and 2pm. During Bath Christmas Market (24 November to 10 Dec) – every 45 minutes Monday to Thursday 1.30pm-6.00pm, Friday and Saturday 12pm-8.15pm). Phone for details of tours during the rest of December. Tickets are purchased from the Abbey shop on the day only. Advanced booking only for groups of over six.

ALICE PARK

Gloucester Road

Tel: 477101

You'll come across this park on the left-hand side of the London Road on your way out of town. The entrance is just a little way up Gloucester Road. It's perfect for learner cyclists, with a practice road laid out that puts the town planners to shame. The playground has all the stuff that toddlers love and a fence around it that parents love.

Then there's the Alice Park café, where Tony and Russ will be keen to welcome you in for truly great coffee, home-made snacks and cakes and even a beer if you're feeling up to it (see if you can guess which of the duo also plays bass with Somerset scrump-folk legends, The Wurzels).

In addition to good eats, Tony and Russ lay on a brilliant collection of events all year round, details of which can be found on alicepark.co.uk. From 'bark in the park' designed for dog lovers, to lots of free kids entertainments. And even when there's nothing special happening parents will appreciate the chance to slow down and listen to feel-good, soul-based live DJs most weekends at the café. And all the time the little darlings will exhaust themselves in the play area next door or cycle up and down the slope and round the track, or play football in the acres of space.

All this plus four well cared for tennis

courts and a pond with real dragonflies equals family heaven.

AMERICAN MUSEUM IN BRITAIN

Claverton Manor
Tel: 01225 460503
www.americanmuseum.org

Housed in a splendid neo-classical manor in a glorious spot above the Avon Valley, this is the only museum of Americana outside the US. Through a series of authentic period rooms it tells the story of colonial life until the end of the 19th century. The collection is noted for its historical quilts, furniture, folk art, Native American art and Renaissance maps of the New World. Highlights in the beautiful grounds include a café, North American trees, replica historical gardens and a Cheyenne tepee. The children can have fun dressing up as they learn about the Founding Fathers, Native Americans, the Civil War and more. The museum offers events and activities throughout the year, including seminars on literature and film, music events, workshops and children's activities.

Situated off the A36 just up the road from Bath, the museum is well signposted if you are driving. You can also take the 18 or 418 bus from the Bus Station. Get off just outside the University at The Avenue, from where it is a 10-minute walk. The museum is open from 10 March to 30 October, Tuesday to Sunday, 12noon–5pm. It is closed Mondays except during August. Admission (inc a voluntary £1 donation): adults £9, concessions £8, children £5, family (4) £24; various offers for school and group visits.

ASSEMBLY ROOMS/ MUSEUM OF COSTUME

Bennett Street
Tel: 01225 477789
www.museumofcostume.co.uk

The Assembly Rooms – John Wood the Younger's grand halls for dancing, music, card playing and tea drinking – were the social hub of Georgian Bath. The fine building's highlights include its million-pound-apiece chandeliers and Gainsborough's portrait of Beau Nash. There is also a café.

The basement of the Assembly Rooms is the perfect venue for the world famous Museum of Costume, where you can see some of the fashions worn when the Rooms were in full swing. The collection spans the late 16th century to the present day, and there is always a good temporary special exhibition on too. Audio guides, guided tours (11am and 3pm during the summer), group bookings, children's activities and study facilities are all part of the finely embroidered bag.

The Assembly Rooms and Fashion Museum are open every day from 10.30am except 25 & 26 December. The Assembly Rooms are occasionally booked for functions (on such occasions you will still be able to visit the Museum of Costume). If you wish to check whether the Rooms are open, call 01225 477173. Admission: adult for Fashion Museum & Assembly Rooms £7.25. Saver ticket including Roman Baths £15.50. Assembly Rooms only £2.00. Various offers for children, seniors, families and groups.

BATH AQUA GLASS WORKSHOP

105-107 Walcot Street
Tel: 01225 311183/319606
or 07825 561379
www.bathaquaglass.com/bath-visitor-attraction.html

Just a stone's throw from the city centre, everything glass is here: stained glass artists, glassblowing and a glass museum featuring stained glass windows dating from 1557. Family-friendly, the workshop's interactive glassblowing demonstrations (by appointment) get you blowing glass. Meanwhile the new shop next to the Abbey in the centre of town sells all manner of handmade glassware and jewellery including trademark aquamarine "Bath aqua glass", which gets it colour by being blown with copper oxide, one of the main minerals in the hot spring waters.

Interactive glassblowing demonstrations: Monday to Friday 11.15am and 2.15pm. Saturdays 2.15pm only. Admission: Adults £4; children, concessions £2.50; family (4) £10. For an extra £2.50 you get to blow your own glass bubble.

Glass production viewing times: Monday to Friday 10.15am, 12.15pm and 3.15pm. Admission: adults £2, concessions £1, children under 11 free.

MUSEUM OF BATH AT WORK

Camden Works, Julian Road
Tel: 01225 318348
www.bath-at-work.org.uk

Did you know cars were made in Bath in the 1920s? An antidote to all the Roman and Georgian stuff, this excellent and friendly

GO CYCLING

IN SPITE OF THE HILLS, BATH HAS PLEASANT CYCLEWAYS. ONCE YOU'RE OUT OF THE CENTRE

GET ON YOUR BIKE

There are plenty of places to cycle around Bath and the surrounding countryside and, with a bit of careful planning to avoid the hills, many of the routes aren't too much hard work for kids.

The Bath to Bristol Cycle Path was the first traffic-free route built as part of the National Cycle Network. The Path was built between 1979 and 1985 by the Bristol-based sustainable transport group Sustrans. It's ideal for children and runs for 15 miles along an old railway line. You can pick up the Path from several places in the City – for further details of where to find it, go to the route planner on the Sustrans website at www.sustrans.co.uk.

And as if the beautiful scenery wasn't enough to look at, the route also features a sculpture trail by artist Katy Hallet. There are a number of pleasant stop-off points along the route including Bitton Station (home to Avon Valley Railway) and the Wilsbridge Mill Nature Reserve with refreshments available at the Bird in Hand or Jolly Sailor at Saltford.

Equally as good, and just a little further away is the amazing Collier's Way. Linking Radstock with Frome and Dundas, there's 23 miles of easy cycling to be had across the old North Somerset Coalfields, with precious little of it on the road. The best section starts on the far side of Radstock and follows an old disused railway line through mile after mile of gently rolling countryside towards Frome. Pack some sandwiches and lashings of ginger beer for a perfect day out. As you gaze over the rolling green hills that stretch to the horizon you can remark, "I can remember when this was all coalfields".

Cycling along the Kennet & Avon Canal – either towards the town of Bradford on Avon or the other way towards Bristol – is very pleasant indeed.

There is a great variety of other beautiful routes to cycle in the area, from sedate rides to off-road challenges. The Bath & North East Somerset website has more details: www.bathnes.gov.uk/leisureandculture/sporthealthfitness/sport/Cycling/Pages/RidesandRoutes.aspx

The year 2012 sees the opening of the Two Tunnels Greenway, a beautiful new route using an old railway line that will create a 13-mile, largely traffic free, "Bath Half Marathon" circular route from the city out to Dundas Aqueduct and back via the canal towpath (www.twotunnels.org.uk).

Bath Bike Hire (www.bathbikehire.com, 01225 447276) is based at Bath Narrowboats at Sydney Wharf (under Bathwick Bridge at the bottom of Bathwick Hill, south of Sydney Gardens). There is no parking, but you can take a pleasant walk there along the canal path that runs through Sydney Gardens. £15 a full day for an adult. Bikes, seats and trailers for children also offered.

You can hire bikes from the Bath & Dundas Canal Company, based in beautiful countryside about five miles south of Bath (www.bathcanal.com, 01225 722292). 24-hour adult hire £16. Bikes, seats and trailers for children available.

Bath itself has also launched a "Boris bike"-style bike hire system offering four racks throughout the city, situated at Bath Spa Station, Orange Grove, Green Park Station (close to the canal), and the Holburne Museum (also perfect for the canal). Eight hours will cost you £15, four hours £8 (www.bikeinbath.com).

Maps and routes are available from Sustrans, 35 King Street, Bristol. Tel 0117 9268893, www.sustrans.org.uk

museum concentrates instead on Bath's recent industrial and social history. The museum tells the story of J B Bowler, a Victorian engineering and soft drinks firm. Covering an entire floor, the entire Bowler works and all its antiquated machinery has been restored and moved, lock, stock and barrel, to the museum. Keeping your hands refreshingly dirty, the exhibition also takes a look at Bath quarrying and cabinet-making and much else. Some of the machinery is in working order and there are regular demonstrations. Free audio guides are on offer, while guided tours can also be arranged. Schools activities take in drama, handling objects and interactive tours.

Open 10.30am-5pm from April to October seven days a week; November to April weekends only. Closed for all of December (though research visits to the museum's library and archives can still be arranged). Admission: adults £5; seniors, children, concessions £3.50; family £12. Groups £3 per person.

BATH RUGBY CLUB

Shop: 11 Argyle Street
Tickets: Recreation Ground, Spring Gardens 01225 325200
www.bathrugbyclub.com

On match days, the atmosphere in central Bath changes completely as the town centre becomes overrun with burly families on their way to the game. Land Rovers and other 4x4s are parked all the way up Bathwick Hill, and when the match itself kicks off there'll be people leaning over the railings on Johnstone Street and Pulteney Bridge trying to cadge a free view as TV helicopters circle overhead and the roar of the crowd can be heard all the way through town. Down at the ground there's a noisy and enjoyable ruck around the bars. If you go to see a match the greatest danger you'll face is being crushed by some 16-stone giant struggling past you with a tray of beers to take back to his mates. If he trips, you'll probably drown as well. After the match, particularly after a victory against a local rival such as Bristol or Gloucester, the city centre becomes a no-go area for anyone of a sensitive disposition as blue-and-white striped fans jostle ten deep in all the local pubs.

Rugby is in the blood round here, and it's not just the posh types who enjoy it. In fact the enjoyment of it is a pretty good way to tell the true Bathonian from the more recently arrived. Ask someone if they've heard what the football scores are on a Saturday afternoon and a genuine local will start talking about Leicester 23, Sale 15, and not tell you that Man Utd and Arsenal drew 0-0.

Local players are treated like royalty around here too, and many greats of the past live in or around Bath. There's unmistakeable local gargoyle Gareth Chilcott (who makes a great pantomime dame); Mike Catt (our cover star and for many the backbone of the great side of the '90s); and – look out ladies! – the handsome Jeremy Guscott still prowls the town.

Recently the club has become embroiled in a bit of local controversy over its home at the Rec, which has been leased by the club for more than100 years. Millionaire owner of the club Andrew Brownsword (he made his money out of greetings cards) put his

Bath Rugby Club: A brief history

1865 Bath Football Club is founded
1882 Herbert Fuller becomes Bath's first capped player in a game against Scotland
1885 Bath play 20 games, winning 17, drawing two and losing just one
1907 Racing Club de Bordelais become the first foreign team to come to Bath
1923 Six Bath players feature in the County Championship-winning Somerset side
1954 Bath goes on its first overseas tour, beating three teams in France
1975 Floodlights are installed at the Rec. The first evening game is against the Royal Navy
1986 The English League for Rugby is formed
1987-1996 Bath enjoy a period of incredible dominance, winning the league on seven occasions in just ten years, and turning Bath into a rugby mecca
1995 In an England international against Western Samoa, an incredible seven Bath players are capped: Dawe, Obugu, Ojomoh, Catt, de Glanville, Callard and Mallet
1998 Bath become the first British club to lift the European Cup
2004 Bath win their first league title after eight years of hurt
2010 A change of ownership and plans are announced for a brand-new 20-25,000 seater stadium in the city

considerable weight behind plans to build a brand new stadium at the Rec. Some local residents were not too pleased by the idea though and, led by an idealistic fellow called Neil Jackson, successfully challenged the club, arguing that the land was originally leased to them for the promotion of amateur rugby and other healthy pursuits, not for the erection of a profitable development. The arguments still rumble on, and it remains to be seen whether Bath rugby will one day move from its traditional home.

BECKFORD'S TOWER & MUSEUM

Lansdown Road
Tel: 01225 460705
www.bath-preservation-trust.org.uk/museums/bath

The 1827 retreat, gallery and library of Bath history's most wealthy eccentric. Well worth a visit – it's an atmospheric place – Beckford's Tower now houses a museum displaying some of the art, furniture, paintings, books and other precious things Beckford collected during his life, and at the top of its 154-step spiral staircase there is a spectacular view of the surrounding area. You can see as far as Wales! On a good day.

Located about one and a half miles from the city centre, the swiftest and most painless way to the Tower is the No 2 or No 4 bus from any point on Lansdown Road (the big hill just east of the Circus) or the Park & Ride bus from Queen Square. Get off at Ensleigh, by the MoD centre, and it's just a brief walk up the road from there.

The tower, which can cater for groups, is open Saturdays, Sundays and Bank Holiday Mondays from Easter until the end of October. It's open weekdays by arrangement. Admission: adults £3; seniors, students £2; children 5-16 £1.50; various family, school and group offers.

BOATS

Take the steps down to the river at the Great Pulteney Street end of Pulteney Bridge and between April and October you can catch a boat tour on the River Avon – either an hour upriver to the village of Bathampton, where you can get off and have lunch, or downriver towards the city. A number of boats operate – just board and pay. Prices are broadly similar – adults £8, children half that.

If you feel like messing about on the water you can hire a punt or rowing boat from the Victorian Bath Boating Station, which you can find at the end of Forester Road, off the A36 to Warminster, not far from the Holburne Museum. It's not a bad trek on foot, but you can take a boat there from Pulteney Bridge. *An hour will cost £7 per person and it's £3 per person per hour after that up to a maximum of £16. You can halve that for children. Free punting lessons and group offers are available (www.bathboating.co.uk, 01225 312900).*

Short trips on the Kennet & Avon Canal are available from Sydney Wharf under Bathwick Bridge at the bottom of Bathwick Hill (south of Sydney Gardens), where you can also hire a canal boat for anything from a few hours to a few weeks. The wharf has no parking. A pleasant walk there is along the canal path that runs through Sydney gardens.

BUILDING OF BATH COLLECTION

The Countess of Huntingdon's Chapel, The Vineyards, The Paragon
Tel: 01225 333895
www.bath-preservation-trust.org.uk/museums/bath

If you want to know all about Georgian Bath's buildings and how they were built – from the mining of their Bath stone to their furnishing and plasterwork – this the place to come. As well as films, paintings, displays and period tools aplenty, the small but beautiful B of B boasts a part of an original balustrade from Queen Square, an acorn from the Circus, and as its highlight a brilliant model of the city in miniature. Once you've been around the place you'll look at the city with new, knowledgeable eyes. For the kids there is Mr Macheath, a rat-about-town who knows Bath from its sewers to its attics. They can also go on a touchscreen journey about Georgian Bath and even design their own Georgian house. For older students, an excellent library and study area can be booked for research.

The museum is open Saturday to Monday 10.30am to 5pm mid-February until the end of November. Admission: adults £4; seniors, students £3.50; children £2. Various offers for schools, groups, study days and family events.

BUS TOURS

Bath is not big but a bus ride is a good way of seeing some of the sights if you find getting around and about hard work. City Sightseeing provides Bath's two official bus tours – a "City Tour" and a "Skyline Tour". The City Tour – which leaves from High Street outside the

Abbey once every 6-15 minutes in summer and every 20-30 minutes in winter – has 20 hop on and hop off stops throughout the city. The Skyline Tour, which leaves the Abbey every 20 minutes in summer and every 30-60 minutes in winter, takes you to the American Museum in the lovely Avon Valley and then on to some great views of the city from Prior Park Landscape Garden.

Prices (24 hours hop on and off): adult £12; children (5-15) £6.50; students, seniors £10, family (2 adult, 3 Children) £27.

DYRHAM PARK

Dyrham, South Gloucestershire
Tel: 0117 9372501
www.nationaltrust.org.uk/dyrhampark

A beautiful 17th century baroque mansion in an ancient deer park and gardens near the village of Dyrham 6.5 miles north of Bath. Used as a filming location for the 1993 Merchant Ivory film *The Remains of the Day*, the house was once the home of William Blathwayt, a politician and civil servant who used his wealth gained through bribes, gifts and the slave trade to give the house its stunning 17th-century Dutch pottery, paintings and furniture.

Guided tours of the house, tea, park trails and a play area are all on the menu. The house and gardens are open for periods throughout the year; check the website for details. Gift Aid admission: house, park & garden – £11.55, children £6, family £28.90. Garden & park – adult £4.65, children £2.35, family £10.30. Park only – adult £2.90, children £1.70, family £6.60.

FOOTBALL

Twerton Park, Twerton, Bath
Tel: 01225 423087
www.bathcityfc.com

Semi-professional football club Bath City currently play in the Conference National, the fifth tier of English football.

GOLF

Bath provides opportunities for players of all levels to spoil a good walk. Fore!

Victoria Falls Adventure Golf

Royal Victoria Park
Tel: 01225 425066
www.victoriafallsadventuregolf.co.uk

Situated at the Queen Square end of Victoria Park, we are talking 18 holes of family-friendly crazy golf here.

Adults £4, seniors and students £3.50, families (2 children) £12. Open 10am to sunset.

Approach Golf Club

Weston Road
Tel: 1225 331162, www.aquaterra.org/bath-approach-golf-course

Two fun and relatively undemanding pitch & putt courses on a hill just behind the Crescent.

Twelve hole round: adults £6.20, juniors £2.80. Eighteen hole round: adults £7.50, juniors £3.50. Club hire free; balls, tees, pencils available. Open weekdays 8.30am to sunset, weekends & bank holidays 7.30am to sunset.

Entry Hill Golf Course

Entry Hill, Bath
Tel: 01225 834248
www.aquaterra.org/entry-hill-golf-course

Non-threatening course just south of Bath.

Nine hole round: adult £10, juniors £4 (club hire – adult £2.50, junior £2; trolley hire – £2.50). Eighteen hole round: adult £15, juniors £5 (club hire – adult £4, junior £2.50; trolley hire – £3.50). Open weekdays 8.30am to sunset, weekends & bank holidays 7.30am to sunset.

Bath Golf Club

Tel: 01225 463834
www.bathgolfclub.org.uk

Known as Sham Castle (which borders the course), this course, established in 1880, offers great views of Bath from Hampton Down, east of the city.

Lansdown Golf Club

Tel: 01225 420242
www.lansdowngolfclub.co.uk

A course three miles north of Bath which also boasts superb views.

JANE AUSTEN CENTRE

40 Gay Street
Tel: 01225 443000
www.janeausten.co.uk/centre

With the help of period and reproduction costumes and objects and introductory talks once every 20 minutes, this small exhibition tells the story of Jane's Bath experience and the effect it had on her writing.

Open April to October 9.45am to 5.30pm (July and August until 7pm). Open November to April 11am to 4.30pm (Saturdays 9.45am to 5.30pm). Admission: adult £7.45, senior £5.95, children 6-15 £4.25, families £19.50. Various

VIBRANT VENUES

LOOKING FOR SOME LIVE ENTERTAINMENT? YOU'RE IN LUCK. HERE IS SOME OF THE BEST

KOMEDIA

22-23 Westgate Street, BA1 1EP
Tel: 0845 293 8480
www.komedia.co.uk/bath/

Comedy, live music, local talent, cabaret, club nights, film screenings, special events, kids' stuff – this lovely, lively pleasure dome has got it all going on, all the time (including great grub).

MOLES

14 George Street, BA1 2EN
Tel: 01225 404446
www.moles.co.uk

New York had Ceebee Geebees, Liverpool had Eric's, London had the Camden Falcon and Bath has still got Moles, the venue that continues to thrive at the heart of the South West live music scene more than three decades into its legendary history. See below for details of some of the bands that Moles championed at the start of their illustrious careers; visit the ticket office to make sure you're in the audience when tomorrow's musical history is made. Also home to regular comedy gigs, an ace café and a fabulous pub, too. Dig in.

Moles Legends. They played in Bath once....

Over the years plenty of rock legends have played in the sweaty shoebox that is Moles club...

Blur, Beverly Knight, Catatonia, Courtney Pine, The Cure, The Damned, Elastica, Eurythmics, Everything But The Girl, Gabrielle, Housemartins, James, Manic Street Preachers, Massive Attack, Moloko, Oasis, Ocean Colour Scene, PJ Harvey, Primal Scream, Pulp, Radiohead, The Smiths, Snow Patrol, Spiritualized, Suede, Supergrass, Terry Hall, The Coral, The Killers, Tori Amos, Toyah Wilcox T'Pau and Travis... The list is ending.

MISSION THEATRE

32 Corn Street, BA1 1UF
Tel: 01225 428600
www.missiontheatre.co.uk

It's been a Catholic chapel, a protestant place of worship and an air raid shelter. But today this 200-year-old, Grade 2 listed building with a fascinating history is home to Next Stage Theatre Company, who have turned it into a theatre (and youth theatre), arts centre, music venue and lovely little vegetarian bistro, complete with bar.

THE RONDO

St Saviours Road, BA1 6RT
Tel: 01225 463362
www.rondotheatre.co.uk

Friendly, welcoming neighbourhood theatre with a strong community vibe, also home to a writer's group, a youth theatre and a lively schedule of theatre-related workshops. Around 80 different companies bring a wide variety of theatre, music and live performances to the Rondo every year but there are only 105 tickets up for grabs for each performance, so advance booking is highly recommended if something grabs your attention. Blessed with a bar in the auditorium itself.

THEATRE ROYAL

Sawclose, BA1 1ET
Tel: 01225 448844
www.theatreroyal.org

One of the oldest working theatres in the country (built on the current site in 1805) continues to thrive today. It's posh, it's plush and it's generally packed to the rafters all year round, thanks to a well-considered, gently diverse programme that takes in everything from Alan Ayckbourn's latest Aga saga to works by somebody modern and cutting-edge who's surname begins with Z. Illustrious luvvie Peter Hall has graced the TRB at the helm of a summertime residency for eight (almost) consecutive years, there's a fabulous pub attached (the Garrick's Head) and there's a resident ghost. Tickets can be pricey, but the theatre releases 40 seats for £6 from 12 noon on the day of performances, and a limited supply of standing-only/£4 tickets are occasionally available for those of a sturdy countenance.

THE USTINOV

Monmouth Street, BA1 1ET
Tel: 01225 448844
www.theatreroyal.org
Established in 1997 (almost a decade after Peter Ustinov started the fundraising ball rolling), the Ustinov is the Theatre Royal's feistier, hipper little sister tucked away in her own studio-style flatlet around the back of the mothership herself. This chic little theatre presents a diverse range of performance-art related events (including a programme of their own productions) throughout the year; a recent refurbishment, meanwhile, has brought this truculent teenager bang up to date.

THE EGG

St John's Place, BA1 1ET
Tel: 01225 448844
www.theatreroyal.org
If the Ustinov is the Theatre Royal's little sister, the Egg is the Grand Dame's precocious niece. This former cinema is home to a vibrant, nationally-acclaimed contempo-glossy complex featuring an auditorium specifically designed for staging family-friendly events, all manner of workshop and rehearsal spaces, and a lively café (complete with tables on the traffic-free lane outside), forming the epicentre of the TRB's Young People's Theatre activities.

LITTLE THEATRE CINEMA

St Michael's Place, BA1 1SF
Tel: 0871 902 5735
www.picturehouses.co.uk/cinema/The_Little/
Friendly, cosy, independent little haven of silver screen merriment offering an experience far removed from the multiplex mayhem – and all the better for it.

CHAPEL ARTS CENTRE

St James House, 9 Lower Borough Walls, BA1 1QR
Tel: 01225 461700
www.chapelarts.org
Much-loved multi-media Mecca for all things alternative arts-related, including live music, cabaret, theatre, dance, poetry and multiple combinations on the themes. Great vegetarian café; vibrant vibe.

THE KING'S ARMS

3 John Street, BA1 2AT
Tel: 01225 425418
www.thekingsarmsbath.com
This 17th century former inn continues to offer fans of the old school pub scene welcome respite from the glossy high street pubs that increasingly dominate the city centre and exists to remind us all that the grass roots live music circuit is alive and most definitely kicking every Saturday night. Your feet will stick to the floor if you try to dance and a visit during daylight hours couldn't be described as either a tasteful or fragrant experience, but the regulars are a friendly bunch, the real ales are drinkable and there's B&B accommodation available for out-of-towners who want to party on beyond the encore.

group offers. Admission to the tea room and gift shop is free.

BATH POSTAL MUSEUM

27 Northgate Street
Tel: 01225 460333
www.bathpostalmuseum.co.uk

How did the son of a Cornish publican, the manager of a Bath theatre and a woman in black shape what is now an everyday activity all around the world? You can discover the answer to this question and more at this small museum located close to spot where the world's first postage stamp was sent in 1840. On offer too are more post boxes than you can shake a letter at, a clay letter dating from around 2,000 BC, and an archive collection that is available to researchers by appointment.

Open Monday to Saturday 11am-5pm (4.30pm winter). Admission: adults £3.50, seniors £3, children (over 6) £1.50.

MUSEUM OF EAST ASIAN ART

12 Bennett Street
Tel: 01225 464640
www.meaa.org.uk

Spread over four floors of a Georgian townhouse, this is the only museum in Britain dedicated solely to the art and culture of China, Japan, Korea and Southeast Asia. Some of the objects in its 2,000-strong collection of ceramics, jades, bronzes and bamboo carvings and much more date back to 5,000 BC.

The museum stages regular special exhibitions and has an active events programme. Its education programme caters to pre-schools, primary and secondary schools, colleges and universities.

Open Tuesday to Saturday 10am-5pm; Sunday noon-5pm. Closed Monday (except some Bank Holidays). Admission: adults £5, senior £4, students £3.50, children (13-18) £3.50, children (6-12) £2.00.

HERSCHEL MUSEUM OF ASTRONOMY

19 New King Street
Tel: 01225 338727
www.bath-preservation-trust.org.uk/ museums/bath

This tiny gem of a museum is tucked away down New King Street because this is the address from where in 1781 William Herschel discovered the planet Uranus. As your learn during your trip through the authentically restored townhouse and garden, Herschel's observations helped double the known size of the solar system and he also advanced telescope design. You'll also find out about his redoubtable sister and assistant Caroline – a notable astronomer in her own right. All on the menu: an award-winning 10-minute film about the Herschels narrated by Patrick Moore, Herschel's workshop (brought to life by a touchscreen), a replica telescope much like that used by Herschel himself, plus the homemade equipment that enabled him to measure the distance between galaxies and stars with amazing accuracy.

Architecture students will simply find the 18th century house interesting. Sirius the dog is a faithful guide through the house for youngsters, while workshops and playgroups are also offered.

The museum is open weekdays (except Wednesdays) 1pm to 5pm; weekends and bank holidays 11am to 5pm. Admission: adults £5, students £3, concessions £4.50, children £2.50, family (2 adults, 2 children) £12.00, groups £4.50 per person. Registered disabled visitors – who can enjoy a virtual tour of the house from the ground floor – £3.

HOLBURNE MUSEUM OF ART

Great Pulteney Street
Tel: 01225 388588
www.holburne.org

This Aladdin's Cave of treasures gathered by the eminent art collector Sir William Holburne includes priceless silver, porcelain, majolica, glass and bronzes, plus paintings by Turner, Guardi and Stubbs and portraits of Bath society by Gainsborough.

Newly extended and refurbished (the superb extension at the back was opened in 2011), the Holburne always offers interesting special exhibitions, workshops for schools and colleges, and has a very nice licensed café with garden to the rear.

The main museum and café is open, completely free of charge, Monday to Saturday 10am to 5pm and Sunday and Bank Holidays 11am to 5pm. Special exhibitions admission: £6.95, seniors £5.50; students, children £3; families (1 child) £12, (2 children) £16.

OLD ORCHARD STREET THEATRE & MASONIC MUSEUM

12 Old Orchard Street

Tel: 01225 462233
www.oldtheatreroyal.com
The first Theatre Royal outside of London, then a Catholic Chapel and now a Masonic Hall, this is one of Bath's hidden oddities. There are guided tours of the building on Tuesdays, Wednesdays and Thursdays at 11am and 2.30pm and at 2.30pm only on Saturdays. The tour finishes in the vaults, where there is now a grand Masonic Museum filled with rare Masonic artefacts.

Admission for tour & museum: adults £6, concessions £5, children (6-16) £3.50, family (2 Adults, 2 Children) £12. Groups of 10 or more by appointment only.

PRIOR PARK LANDSCAPE GARDEN

Ralph Allen Drive
Tel: 01225 833422
www.nationaltrust.org.uk/priorpark
In hills one-and-a-quarter miles from Bath is Bath stone quarrier Ralph Allen's splendid Bath stone mansion, built "to see all Bath, and for all Bath to see" by John Wood in 1742. The mansion itself is, alas, off limits (it is a private school), but its beautiful valley-set garden, designed by Capability Brown and the poet Alexander Pope, is still well worth a visit. On offer are stunning views of Bath, three lakes, a cascade, a grotto, a gothic temple and a rare (there are only four left in the world) and splendid Palladian bridge. The gardens are looked after by the National Trust. Guided group tours can be arranged, and there is a tea kiosk by the lakes.

There is no onsite parking – Prior Park is a green tourism site. You can catch a First no. 1 bus every 30 minutes from Dorchester Street (by the bus station). The gardens are also the last stop for the CitySightseeing Skyline Tour open-top bus, which leaves from the Abbey every 20 minutes in summer and every hour in winter (11am to 5pm). The gardens are open 11am to 5.30pm – seven days a week from mid-February to the end of October; weekends only November to mid-February. Gift Aid Admission/standard admission: adult £5.80/£5.25, child £3.25/£2.95), family £14.80/£13.45). £1 off adult admission with City Sightseeing or First bus ticket.

NO. 1 ROYAL CRESCENT

1 Royal Crescent
Tel: 01225 428126
www.bath-preservation-trust.org.uk/museums/bath
When you're done gawping at the Crescent, No. 1 provides a great chance to take a peek behind the world-famous façade at what indoor life was like for posh Georgian Bathonians. Inside No. 1 are a series of fabulously reconstructed and staged period rooms including a dining room set for dessert, a gentleman's study complete with port and pipes, a drawing room ready for tea, a bedroom fit for a Georgian and a busy Georgian kitchen. Best of all, extremely knowledgeable, story-stocked guides are in every room to bring the whole house to life.

No. 1 is open Tuesday to Sunday mid-February to the end October 10.30-5pm, November to mid-December 10.30-4.00pm. Also open Bank Holiday Mondays and Good Friday. Admission: adults £6.50, seniors and students £5.00, children (5-16) £2.50. Various offers for schools and groups.

ROMAN BATHS

Abbey Church Yard
Tel: 01225 477743/ 444477
www.romanbaths.co.uk
As you trek down through the steaming intestines that form the Roman Baths Museum you grow steadily more excited, and the main event at the bottom – the bathing complex and Great Bath itself – doesn't disappoint. In fact the memory of it will never leave you. The Gorgon, the Minerva Head, curse tablets, water, water everywhere… it's not be missed, even if you're in Bath for only a few hours. And if you're here in July and August, go during the evening, when the Great Bath is torchlit.

You can book a guided tour of the baths either for yourself or for a group. New, unobtrusive computer reconstructions take you back in time and help bring the place alive, and there are also both audio and printed guides in a variety of languages. Activity programs catering for school groups of all levels are on offer, as is a specially designed education space with a view overlooking the Great Bath. A new audiotour especially for children is also available, and researchers can book study space.

The Roman Baths are open daily (except on 25 and 26 December) at the following times: January-February 9.30am-4.30pm; March-June 9am-5pm; July-August 9am-9pm; September-October 9am-5pm; November-December 9.30am-4.30pm. Admission: adult £12 (£12.50

BATH: FESTIVAL CITY

BATH IS BLESSED WITH MORE FESTIVALS THAN IS FRANKLY DECENT. WE PARTY ALL YEAR

BATH LITERATURE FESTIVAL

March, www.bathlitfest.org.uk

Celebrating its 18th birthday in 2012, the Bath Literature Festival easily rivals Hay and Cheltenham's similar annual lit-fest shebangs in terms of style, content and line-up, ranging from the superstars to the brand new and obscure, taking in a thorough programme of related debates, workshops and events along the way. But we believe that the festival's artistic director (and award-wining documentary film maker, novelist and TV producer) James Runcie has, in just over two years at the helm, brought a whole new dimension to the bookish buoyancy of Bath; today, the Bath Literature Festival presents a programme as culturally diverse as the contemporary Heritage City itself.

THE BATH COMEDY FESTIVAL

April, www.bathcomedy.com

Inaugurated to the festival calendar in 2008 by professional creative entrepreneur Alex Timms, the Bath Comedy Festival attracts the cream of cutting-edge, contemporary comedy and a host of legendary comic stalwarts alike in one big glorious celebration of humour. Widcombe-based promoter Nick Steel took over the director's mantle in 2011 and continues to uphold and develop Alex's original vision, offering colourful, vibrant celebration of comedy in all its many guises, including stand-up, street theatre, film, plays, writers, artists, workshops, mime, speakers, cartoons and competitions in venues across the city.

THE INTERNATIONAL MUSIC FESTIVAL

May/June, www.bathmusicfest.org.uk

One of Bath's longest-running festivals (the first took place in 1948) continues to go from strength to strength and is today renowned and acclaimed across the globe for presenting a culturally-diverse programme that also serves to celebrate and promote Bath's many venues, concert halls and iconic architectural landmarks. Festival Director Joanna MacGregor (2006-to the time of writing) was largely responsible for bringing new audiences to this long-standing institution by introducing the popular 'Electronica' element to the festival in her first year, while the city-wide, free opening night party is a stand-alone, legendary event in itself.

THE BATH COFFEE FESTIVAL

May, www.bathcoffeefestival.co.uk

It may be the new kid on the festival block (est. 2010), but the Bath Coffee Festival has already firmly established itself at the heart of the Bath festive scene. For one weekend every May, the Bath Recreation Ground is transformed into a caffeine-addict's dream: hone coffee-making skills with the experts in the Demo Theatre before perfecting them at the Coffee Academy, meet coffee growers and producers from across the globe in the World of Coffee area, chillax in the Music Tent, live it up with the kids (the festival is extremely family-friendly) or shop until sundown in the market – you just ain't a coffee cohort until you've bean here and done it all.

THE BATH FRINGE FESTIVAL

May/June, www.bathfringe.co.uk

This glorious celebration of art in every format – from loudmouth performance to gentler pursuits – takes place every May/June. The legendary Bedlam Fair (a weekend-long, street-based programme of performance art merriment, culminating in the all-day Bedlam Sunday festival on Sawclose) also incorporates the FAB Fringe Arts Fair. A myriad of local venues and watering holes host various events, but the Spiegeltent (on the Recreation Ground) has to be the Fringe Festival's iconic epicentre: a magical, travelling, history-laden, in-the-round performance area wrought from artisan-crafted wood, canvas and thousands of shards of stained and mirrored glass, complete with a cafe/bar area, SpiegelGarden and a Fringe Kids Festival line-up all of its own. Keep the Fringe at the forefront of your mind when you're planning a festive season in the Heritage City; for many locals and tourists alike, this one is the biggest and best.

THE JANE AUSTEN FESTIVAL

September, www.janeausten.co.uk

The festival dedicated to the woman responsible for multiple costume dramas elegantly dominates Bath in early autumn every year. The most spectacular event of the festival has to be the Promenade, when Jane junkies from across the globe dress in 18th century Regency attire and parade through the streets of Bath led by the Town Crier. Elsewhere, an assortment of soirées, theatre performances, concerts, walking tours, talks, dancing and food-related events (yes, really!) provide a non-stop Austen-related feast. What Ms Austen would make of it all we can only imagine, for it is a truth universally acknowledged that she only lived in Bath for about four years and, shortly after leaving the city for good, declared Winchester to be a "far more charming, graceful environment than a spa town only really suited to short visits". Ah well; her legend lives on, even if she didn't.

BATH FESTIVAL OF CHILDREN'S LITERATURE

September/October, www.bathkidslitfest.co.uk

Similar to the big Bath Lit Fest but worthy of a stand-alone mention in its own right for (a) being totally dedicated to literary little 'uns and (b) offering lots and lots of stuff to capture the attention and imagination of big kids too (particularly those wanting to be the next JKR/Jaqueline Wilson, etc). Currently sponsored by the *Daily Telegraph*, the festival celebrated its fifth birthday in 2011.

BATH FILM FESTIVAL

November, www.bathfilmfestival.org.uk

Okay, it's not quite Cannes (nor Toronto, Berlin, Sundance or, erm, Leeds). But in true Heritage City festival style, the Bath Film Festival (established in 1991, and today counting Ken Loach, Peter Gabriel and Stephen Woolley amongst its patrons) punches well above its provincial weight, attracting some of the film world's most distinguished cinema-related luminaries and flaunting a programme that presents both illustrious international premieres of mainstream films and arthouse, auteur-wrought events.

BATH MOZARTFEST

November, www.bathmozartfest.org.uk

This glorious festival has been celebrating the legacy of Wolfgang Amadeus Mozart for over 20 years by presenting a suitably grand selection of concerts, posh suppers and Wolfie-related events in the kind of fine style we're sure the Maestro himself would have approved of.

FOOD AND DRINK

Events all year round

Given that Bath nestles at the epicentre of a region globally renowned for producing some of the best, erm, produce in the UK, the potential for an established food festival has, rather surprisingly, yet to be fully explored (or exploited). But things they are a changin'. In 2011, the inaugural Bath Good Food Awards set tongues and tastebuds tingling and brought gourmet glamour to the Heritage City; event organisers Guide2Bath are set to do it all again in autumn 2012, and plans are already in the pipeline for the kind of tie-in events (including a producer's market and special BGFA menus at participating restaurants) that'll help guarantee that this much-needed celebration of local food becomes a regular annual event. Meanwhile, Bristol's Love Food Festival made its debut appearance at Green Park Station (also home to the thriving Farmers' Market) in June 2011. The LFF has since revisited Bath several times since receiving their initial warm welcome; visit www.lovefoodfestival.com for forthcoming dates. And while we're on the subject of unique foodie celebrations, credit must be given to the annual Flavours of the West festival, held at upmarket, swanky shopping centre Milsom Place: a friendly goodie gathering with the atmosphere of an artisan farmers' market set against a refurbished historical backdrop, held in July every year.

July and August); with admission to Museum of Costume £15.50; seniors, students £10.50; child (6-16) £7.80; family (2 adults, four children) £34.00; various group offers.

SALLY LUNN'S EATING HOUSE & KITCHEN MUSEUM

4 North Parade Passage Bath
Tell: 01225 461634
www.sallylunns.co.uk

This is probably not the original bakery where Sally Lunn supposedly invented the Sally Lunn bun (it did stand somewhere down this alley), but it is very old nonetheless (possibly as old as 1620) and today it is the spiritual home of the bun. Inside you can enjoy a cuppa and not only a Sally Lunn with some clotted cream but also a sweet Bath Bun. After all that you'll positively run downstairs to the free museum to check out the original faggot ovens.

The Eating House and Kitchen Museum is open Monday to Saturday 10am-6pm and Sundays 11am-6pm. The restaurant is open Monday to Thursday 5pm-9.30pm, Fridays & Saturdays 5pm-10pm and Sundays 5pm-9pm.

SHAM CASTLE

North Road, Bathwick Hill

This mock castle (it is just a façade, albeit a thick one, and nothing else – even the windows are blocked) was built on the eastern Hills of Bath in 1762 to show off Ralph Allen's Bath stone. You are rewarded with fine views if you take on the climb to the castle.

Directions: after a healthy walk five to ten minutes up Bathwick hill, turn left into North Lane, then turn left onto North Road. Roughly 200 yards down North Road there is a signed Public Footpath (ignore the bridleway). Follow the path to a stone stile leading into a field. The path continues left to a gate on the right that leads into a field and on to the castle.

SOLSBURY HILL

Batheaston

This hill dominates the eastern end of Bath with its distinctive flat top, the site of the remains of an Iron Age hill fort. Local pop megastar Peter Gabriel immortalised the place in song in his debut solo single after his departure from Genesis and it can be a challenge to climb up without finding yourself humming a few bars. It's a great place to visit, and kids will enjoy it hugely and be satisfyingly tired afterwards. It's not just the getting there that's fun (there's a lovely walk from the centre of Batheaston, up past the church to the left, or even drive up Solsbury Lane and park the car pretty near the summit), it's the flat top that's best. Cows graze up here, it takes half an hour or so to go around, there's a little maze, some spectacular views and some jutting out stones that you can (safely) stand on and pretend you're flying. Imaginative types will love pretending they're celtic warriors or princesses. Gentle pleasures, to be sure, but all very charming.

STANTON DREW STONE CIRCLES AND COVE

Stanton Drew, near Bath
www.english-heritage.org.uk/daysout/properties/stanton-drew-circles-and-cove

The sleepy village of Stanton Drew lies 11 miles west of Bath and is home to the second biggest stone circle complex in Europe (only Avebury is bigger). Very impressive and atmospheric, it's a great half-day out. Dating to the Neolithic and early Bronze Age (around 3,000–2,000 BC) and dotted with burial chambers, the complex is made up of the "Cove" (three huge standing stones), a main stone circle, two smaller circles and three avenues (two of which link the main circle and north-east circle).

According to folklore the stones are a wedding party turned to stone by the devil as punishment for carrying on the celebrations into Sunday. The circles are apparently the dancers, the avenues the fiddlers and the Cove the bride, groom and drunken vicar. Another legend has it that the stones are uncountable. The superstitious John Wood, who was influenced by Stanton Drew and also Stonehenge when he built the Circus, reported in 1750 that when he tried to count them a thunderstorm broke out…

The Cove is in a convenient spot – the garden of the Druids Arms public house.

Admission to the circles: donation box. Open all year round.

STONEY LITTLETON LONG BARROW

Wellow, near Bath
www.english-heritage.org.uk/daysout/properties/stoney-littleton-long-barrow

In a field a mile south of the lovely village of Wellow (six miles south of Bath on the A367) is a chambered long barrow built during the

Neolithic period, around 4,000-2500 BC. You can crawl inside it if you're small and agile enough and don't mind being scarily cramped in a tight, dark space. The entrance leads via a vestibule into a passage with pairs of side chambers radiating from it. A great little trip, the barrow – which does involve a small trek across fields – is well signposted from the village. The village pub, the excellent Fox & Badger, can provide refreshment.

VICTORIA ART GALLERY

Bridge Street, Bath
Tel: 01225 477233
www.victoriagal.org.uk

Next to Pulteney Bridge, this excellent free public gallery boasts Gainsboroughs, Turners and Sickerts upstairs and a programme of special exhibitions on the ground floor. The gallery caters for school groups by appointment, while talks, tours and study facilities can be also arranged.

The gallery is open from Tuesday to Sunday 10am to 5pm (Sundays 1.30pm to 5pm) all year except Christmas Day, Boxing Day, Good Friday and New Year's Day. It is closed Mondays with the exception of some bank holidays.

VICTORIA PARK

Families travel from miles around to visit Victoria Park, Bath's finest piece of Victoriana. Not only is it host to a variety of events such as the Children's Festival, circuses, the Fair and the Annual Flower Show, there are many other reasons to visit the park…

The Park and Play Area

It's not just out-of-towners that see Victoria Park as a splendid day out. Bathonians bring a picnic to the play area (the best of its kind for miles around) and spend the day chatting to their friends while their kids run wild. The play area is manned by wardens, and it's an enclosed space so you can take your eyes off the nippers for the split second it takes to unwrap the sandwiches. The park and its wide spaces are an open invitation for kids to use their imagination. Fly a kite, play frisbee, or just run off some of that energy.

Victoria Park is also home to the world's most overfed ducks, who won't eat bread for love nor money. Many a child can be spotted disappointedly clutching a bagful of breadcrumbs, watching as the ducks flop fatly into the water and promptly sink.

Skate Park

Not for the faint hearted, but ideal for older kids who don't want to hang around with parents because it's fairly near the play area. Huge ramps covered in graffiti play host to hoards of wheel-wearing kids. CCTV monitors the area constantly, as do the park wardens.

City of Bath Botanical Gardens

Yes, the Botanical Gardens are nine-and-a-half acres of the finest collection of plants in the West Country. But what appeals to parents is the fact that it's an enclosed, dog-free zone, so you know you can't lose your kids (unless you try really hard), and they won't come running back to you covered in 'God-knows-what'.

Watching the hot air balloons

On a summer evening, take the kids to watch the hot air balloons slowly inflate and take off in the north-east corner of Victoria Park. It's magical. Saturdays between 6pm and 7pm are usually best, though they do gather in fewer numbers throughout the week.

KID'S DAYS OUT

GET THE CHARABANC OUT OF THE GARAGE, JAMES – WE'RE OFF ON A DAY TRIP!

AT-BRISTOL

Harbourside, Bristol BS1 5DB
Tel: 0845 345 1235
www.at-bristol.org.uk

The £97 million At-Bristol development is essentially the entire area to the north of the Floating Harbour and includes The Aquarium (formerly Wildwalk), At-Bristol (formerly Explore), and Millennium Square. It was *The Good Britain Guide*'s Family Attraction of the Year in 2001 and has won several other tourism and design awards, even one for its car park, which was named as one of the best in the UK by the AA in 2005. It was Visitor Attraction of the Year at the Bristol Tourism and Hospitality Industry Awards 2011 (which seems a bit 'jobs for the boys'), and both the *Guardian* and *Independent* newspapers featured it in their best family attractions.

At-Bristol hit financial problems and in August 2003 had to ask Bristol City Council for a £500,000 loan to cover running costs. Although it is undoubtedly a major family attraction, there are two things that got it off to a bad start: it's expensive and it was sponsored by Nestlé. Eventually Wildwalk closed down and was replaced by the Blue Reef Aquarium (which is nowhere near as good as Wildwalk was).

Explore: Science and natural forces are the themes of the two storeys of displays and exhibitions, many of them interactive. Highlights on the ground floor include putting the kids on a treadmill to lift water from one tank to another, several displays involving magnets and magnetic fields and a particularly visual film about the journey of a sperm. It's all a bit like *Tomorrow's World*, but without the lure of Maggie Philbin or the avuncular presence of Raymond Baxter. Upstairs, visitors get to enjoy a harp that uses lasers instead of strings and a gyroscopic briefcase with a 'mind of it's own'. The virtual beach volleyball court is a hoot once you get the hang of it and visitors can create their own music or play slap pipes. The TV studio is popular, as the kids play weather forecasters and newsreaders in front of computer-generated backgrounds. The large silver ball you can see from outside is the planetarium, where you can watch the universe go by.

Bristol Blue Reef Aquarium: A visit to the aquarium (which utilises 250,000 litres of water) is a pricey affair: a family ticket costs about £40, though you can come and go as you please for the day. Built on the site of what was At-Bristol's Wildwalk, it's not the biggest aquarium in the world by any stretch of the imagination, but there are some pleasant features, including an exotic coral reef tank and the allegedly "world famous" giant octopus Velcro (who didn't do much on our visit). The café is remarkably poor.

Time from Bath: 45 minutes

AVON VALLEY RAILWAY

Bitton Station, Bath Road, Bitton
0117 932 7296 (24 hour timetable)
0117 932 5538 (general enquiries)
www.avonvalleyrailway.co.uk

Take a trip along the former Mangotsfield to Bath, Green Park branch of the old Midland Railway in a genuine stream train. The kids will be captivated by all the smoke and noise. There are special Thomas The Tank Engine days for fanatics.

Open: Phone for details. Cost: Adults £4.50, over 60s £3.50, children (3-16 yrs) £3, family (2 Adults + 2 Children) £12.50

Time from Bath: 20 minutes

AVON VALLEY COUNTRY PARK

Pixash Lane, Bath Road, Keynsham
Tel: 0117 986 4929
www.avonvalleycountrypark.co.uk

A delightful day out for the whole family, the Avon Valley Country Park has always been a popular attraction and recent improvements make it an essential venue. Situated on the banks of the Avon, the Park comprises three areas: outdoors, the outdoor play area and the new indoor play area. Outdoors there's a pets' corner, mini train rides, quad bikes, a land train, river boat trips, rowing boat hire, a farm trail, falconry displays and more. The two play areas feature death slides and a soft play area, among other attractions.

Open: 10am-6pm every day except Mondays. Open Bank Holiday Mondays and Mondays during school holidays. Cost: Adults £5, children £4,50 (under-2s free), senior citizens £4.50, season tickets available

Time from Bath: 20 minutes

BOWOOD HOUSE

A4, between Chippenham and Marlborough
Tel 01249 812102
www.bowood-house.co.uk

Country house and gardens that boasts the best adventure playground in the West for children under 12. Bring a picnic and chill out in the sun while the young 'uns wear themselves out on the ropewalks and slides. Most of the items, including a superb pirate ship, have been designed by former boat builder Alistair Guy, using timber from the Bowood estate. Among the more recent additions are the thrilling space dive and curving tubular metal slides. There's a separate area for smaller children.

Open: Daily from April 1-October 31, 11am-5.30pm. Cost: House and gardens: adults £6.40, children (aged 5-15) £4.10, children (aged 2-4) £3.25, senior citizens £5.30

Time from Bath: 35 minutes

BRANDON HILL AND THE CABOT TOWER

Off Park Street, Bristol

One of the best things to do as a visitor to Bristol is climb the Cabot Tower: the views from the top are fantastic. You can see virtually the whole city and it's the only place where you'll get such a dramatic impression of Bristol past and present. Kids love huffing and puffing up the narrow spiral stairway and are usually fascinated by the distance finder at the top, which tells you how many miles it is to many of the major cities of the world and various places of local interest.

Brandon Hill Park is Bristol's oldest public space: it was given to the city corporation in 1174. It's an ideal place for a picnic if you've been shopping on Park Street or wandering round the docks. The play area on the Hotwells side of Brandon Hill has equipment for toddlers as well as more adventurous climbing frames for older children. Brandon Hill is full of greedy, tame squirrels, so take a bag of nuts along with you.

Open: Brandon Hill Park is open 365 days of the year. Cabot Tower is open from 8am until just before dusk.

Time from Bath: 45 minutes

BROKERSWOOD

Westbury, Wiltshire
01373 822238
www.brokerswood.co.uk

A country park situated in the 'last remaining corner of the ancient Forest of Selwood', it's had only five owners since William the Conqueror. It's an ideal venue for a family day out: the kids will scramble to get on the outdoor play areas, and for the younger ones there's an undercover area. A miniature railway is a firm favorite. For the budding green-fingered there's a chance to learn about conservation in the Woodland Heritage Centre and, if you're not too squeamish, there's the opportunity to teach your children how to fish. Also popular for birthday parties.

Open: Daily 10am-6pm, except Christmas Eve, Christmas Day, Boxing Day and New Year's Day. Cost: Adults £3, senior citizens £2.50, children (3-16yrs) £2, train £1

Time from Bath: 30 minutes

CITY MUSEUM AND ART GALLERY

Queen's Road, Bristol
Tel: 922 3571
www.bristol-city.gov.uk/museums

The City Museum combines all the old-fashioned qualities of a civic collection (stuffed animals and bits of flint from Severn Beach) with some excellent contemporary exhibitions and regular events for children. The stuffed animals seem to fascinate kids – especially the dodo and Alfred, the gorilla from Bristol Zoo. As for the wolverine and the tiger, they are just plain scary.

The museum has presence: it's as imposing and impressive inside as its magnificent Venetian Gothic façade would suggest. Hanging in the foyer is a reproduction Bristol Boxkite aeroplane, which featured in the 1963 film *Those Magnificent Men In Their Flying Machines*. It lends the entrance a surreal quality. The Egyptology gallery contains real mummies. The Family Fundays on the first Sunday of every month are popular with kids. The café at the back of the Museum does a special Munchkin Box and children's menu.

Open: Daily, 10am-5pm. Free

Time from Bath: 45 minutes

GLASTONBURY TOR

The Arthurian and other legends surrounding Glastonbury Tor make it a magical place to visit – and kids are not as immune to the myth as you might think. They also love huffing and puffing their way to the top (it's less of a climb than it looks but feels really high) and the views are breathtaking. If it's a blustery day you may want to keep a tight hold of your littler little 'uns – it can get mighty bracing up there.

Open: Always. Free

Time from Bath: 35 minutes

LONGLEAT

Near Warminster, off the A36
Tel: 01985 844400
www.longleat.co.uk

Watching the monkeys remove loose bits of car trim and wonky aerials in the Safari Park is great fun. Until it happens to you. Longleat is a big day out – in fact, you need more than a day to see everything. Apart from the Safari Park, with the giraffes, zebras, elephants, lions and tigers, there's also a safari boat trip where you can see hippos and sealions. Other attractions include the Postman Pat Village, Doctor Who exhibition, butterfly garden, maze, adventure playground, pets' corner and steam railway.

Open: House and gardens 10am-5.30pm, Safari Park 10am-4pm. Open daily except Christmas Day. Cost: Longleat Passport (includes everything), adults £14, child £11, under-4s free. Check prices for individual attractions

Time from Bath: 35 minutes

LYME REGIS OR THE GOWER

South Coast and South West Coast

Bath is within striking distance of 'proper' seaside and these are the two of the best bits of coast within two hours of the City. Lyme Regis is a charming Dorset seaside town with a small fishing harbour, good beach and the Cobb Wall, made famous by that Meryl Streep scene in *The French Lieutenant's Woman*. The Gower Peninsula is an Area of Outstanding Natural Beauty and boasts many fine bays and coastal walks. The high-sided Three Cliffs Bay is worth the walk down through the dunes; while Rhosilli and Worm's Head are part of one of the most invigorating lengths of coastline in Britain.

Time from Bath: Two hours

M SHED

Wapping Road, Princes Wharf, Bristol BS1 4RN, Tel: 0117 352 6600
www.mshed.org

Opened in June 2011 to replace the old Industrial Museum, the £27 million M Shed may have been a couple of years behind schedule and the odd £10 million over budget, but it's still a pretty impressive project. Somehow, the curators have managed to re-create the sense of clutter that was one of the most comforting aspects of the old Industrial Museum. There are some hi-tech, interactive gizmos, but not too many. M Shed is a 'people's museum'. It attempts (and succeeds) to define Bristol through the stories and achievements of its ordinary and extraordinary citizens. So here we will find the famous, such as Cary Grant and Massive Attack, alongside everyday Bristolians such as Princess Campbell (the first black ward sister) and George Pine who fought in the First World War and worked on Bristol trams and buses and told his story in 44,000 words of hand-written notes. There are three galleries (People, Places, Life), fantastic views across Bristol and, most impressive of all, it's all free.

Open: Closed Mondays except Bank Holidays. Cost: Free

Time from Bath: 45 minutes

SLIMBRIDGE

Off the M5 at Junction 13 or 14.
Tel: 01453 890333
www.wwt.org.uk/visit/slimbridge

Formed in 1946 by artist and naturalist Sir Peter Scott (son of Polar explorer Capt

Robert Falcon Scott), Slimbridge is a haven for rare waterbirds. You can view them from hides or from the Sloane Observation Tower with fantastic views over the River Severn. There's also a cinema, a wildlife art gallery and a tropical house where the hummingbirds hum.

Open: Daily except Christmas Day, 9.30am-5pm (4pm winter). Cost: Adults £6, children £3.60, under-4s free

Time from Bath: 35 minutes

SS GREAT BRITAIN

Great Western Dock, Gas Ferry Road, Bristol BS1 6TY, Tel: 0117 929 1843
www.ssgreatbritain.org

Built in Bristol by Brunel, the ss Great Britain was the world's first iron-hulled, screw propeller-driven, steam-powered passenger liner, and the only surviving 19th-century example of its type. It has now been restored and converted into a museum and visitor centre and is also available for hire as a banquet, wedding reception and conference centre. The ticket price includes entrance to the Maritime Heritage Centre (an exhibition on the history of shipbuilding in Bristol) and to The Matthew, a replica of the ship in which John Cabot sailed from Bristol to discover Newfoundland in 1497. The ss Great Britain won the Gulbenkian Prize for Museum of the Year 2006.

Open: Daily except December 24 and 25. Cost: Check website for latest prices, concessions, family tickets and group discounts, under-4s free.

Time from Bath: 45 minutes

WELLOW HORSE RIDING AND TREKKING CENTRE

Little Horse Croft Farm, Wellow
Tel: 01225 834376
www.wellowtrekking.com

A corporate activity centre with a sideline in family activities. If you fancy horse trekking they've got a horse to suit every size and ability of rider. They also cater for kids' pony parties or quad bike parties and even provide the food – all you need to bring is the cake (and the kids).

For booking and price details you'll need to give them a call

Time from Bath: 25 minutes

WESTON-SUPER-MARE

Bristol Channel

In the height of summer, or on Bank Holidays, Weston can be too busy to enjoy. But out of season it's a great place to spend a few hours. It has loads of beach, the Grand Pier, donkey rides, pleasant sea front walks and plenty of cafés. Weston is proper seaside; the only traditional seaside element it lacks is, er, sea – the water beyond the mud is actually the Bristol Channel. The Weston experience comes wrapped in an atmosphere of faded elegance and seaside tackiness. If you'd rather not acquire the full-on kiss-me-quickness of the resort, try the long, sandy – and far quieter – beach at Brean to the south.

Other attractions at Weston include the Aquarium on the Marine Parade seafront (01934 641603, www.sealife.co.uk), the Helicopter Museum on Locking Moor Road (01934 635 227, www.helicoptermuseum.co.uk) and the Kidscove indoor adventure centre (01934 417411, www.kidscove.co.uk). The Tourist Information Centre is at Beach Lawns near the seafront (01934 888800).

Time from Bath: 40 minutes

WOOKEY HOLE CAVES

Wells Somerset
01749 672243
www.wookey.co.uk

The legend of the Witch of Wookey will leave children wide-eyed in fascination, especially when they discover her frozen stone figure in the cavern. The guides are knowledgeable and up for a laugh, tempering the legend with just enough humour so as not to scare the poor mites too badly. A trek through the dark, dripping passageways and immense caves leads through to the Paper Mill and Museum. The Museum lets the side down a little bit: it manages to take a load of potentially interesting artefacts and turn them into a school parents' evening display. Shame. But the Victorian Arcade and Magical Mirror Maze are kiddie heaven; you can even buy pre-decimal old pennies to play the old arcade games.

Open: Every day except 17-25 December. Summer 10am-5pm, winter 10.30am-4.30pm. Cost: Adults £8.80, children (4-16 inclusive) £5.50, children under 4 years old go in free

Time from Bath: 20 minutes

Listings **Drinking**

Rather than provide you with a massive list of all the city's many identikit bars and local boozers, we've carefully selected a few of our own favourite watering holes in and around Bath for you to try. We hope you enjoy them as much as we do…

APPLE TREE INN

Shoscombe
01761432263
www.appletree-inn.co.uk

If you fancy a pint and a meal in the country you could do worse than head for this stone-flagged 18th century farmhouse on the picturesque Colliers Way walking and cycling route (www.colliersway.co.uk/wellow_to_Shoscombe.php). The Apple Tree's considerable charms include Thatchers and Westons ciders (eight of them!), a no-thrills pub grub menu to soak it all up and a beer terrace with fine views over rolling Somerset hills. You could get used to the country life…

Opening times: Monday to Tuesday 7pm-11pm; Wednesday to Friday 12 noon-2.30pm & 7pm-11pm; Saturday to Sunday 12 noon-11pm.

BELL INN

Walcot Street, Bath
01225 460426
www.walcotstreet.com

A bohemian oasis off the beaten tourist track, the Bell is a laid back watering hole that positively encourages you to let it all hang out and forget about Romans, Georgians, spas and shopping. All on offer: an impressive array of nine very good ales (you'll do well to get through that lot), a roomy and pleasantly battered interior, and a courtyard garden that's beautifully peaceful on an afternoon and busy by night. The Bell is famous as a Bath music venue. Monday and Wednesday evenings and Sunday lunchtimes, when jazz, folk and blues can be found playing, are always very well attended. Other delights include pizza, falafels and enchiladas, bar billiards and table football. Child friendly.

THE BOATER

Argyle Street, Bath
Tel: 01225 464211

This rugby pub (it's a kick from the Recreation Ground) boasts a spacious weirside courtyard. If you want to take the weight off your feet for a bit with a cold drink, it's a peaceful option away from the bustle of the city. Very busy on match days and popular with students term-time evenings.

THE BOATHOUSE

Newbridge Road, Bath
Tel: 01225 482584
www.boathousebath.com

Very cheesy big riverside pub – but it's in a lovely setting just out of town, you can get fed, and there's plenty of space for the kids.

COEUR DE LION

Northumberland Place, Bath
Tel: 01225 463568
www.coeur-de-lion.co.uk

It's not only small, it's Bath's smallest pub! Though the Volunteer Rifleman's, just around the corner, is not far behind. Think small living room, halve it and then add a few swinging pint glasses to edge past and some shopping bags to trip over and you have it. Dating from around 1749, the Coeur's beautiful front features a fine Victorian stained glass window. Now owned by local brewery Abbey Ales, the beers are good, while a hearty pub grub menu is on offer to provide ballast. If you're lucky you can grab a table outside in the pretty lane. Ale and pub aficionados should definitely look in.

CROSS GUNS

Avoncliff
Tel: 01225 862335 or 867613
www.crossguns.net

Fantastically set canal and riverside pub in Avoncliff, near Bradford-on-Avon dating back to the 15th century. The gardens are simply lovely. The food (served 12-2pm, 6.30-9pm; light bites 12-9pm) you will find welcome if you've cycled here through the lovely Limpley Stoke Valley, and it may bolster you too if you're taking on the pleasant (think country lanes and paths), 3.5-mile Two Valleys Walk to The Inn at Freshford.

FOX & BADGER INN

Railway Lane, Wellow
www.foxandbadger.co.uk

A lovely, lovely country local in a beautiful village setting. The delights include: traditional country decor (various stuffed animas keep a beady eye on the place); Cheddar Valley cider (you may be informed that it'll "make your toes curl" – which it does); and an extremely varied menu (everything from an all-day breakfast to slow roast belly pork to four types of ploughman's – you won't be able to choose). After all that you'll be pulling on corduroys and offering to shift hay bales! On the Colliers Way walking and cycling route [See 'Cycling' in the Attractions chapter for more on this great cycle route]. Seating out the front of the pub.

Opening times: Monday to Thursday 11.30am-3.30pm & 6pm-11pm; Friday to Saturday 11.30am-11:00pm; Sunday 11.30am-10.30pm.

GARRICK'S HEAD

7 & 8 St Johns Place, Bath
Tel: 01225 318368
www.garricksheadpub.com

This chic-ishly uncluttered establishment is the sister pub of the King William. Next door to the Theatre Royal (you can accidentally nudge the drink of famous luvvies here), this used to be Beau Nash's House. And the Beau would have approved that the Garrick's always offers a good selection of well-kept ales plus five excellent local ciders too. Meanwhile, its dining room offers a quality West Country-sourced menu and bar snacks. Try the triple-cooked chips with homemade mayonnaise – they help soak up a pint very pleasantly indeed [see Eating]. And, always nice on a warm day, this is one pub where you can sit outside on the pavement and watch the world go by – a rarity in Bath.

GEORGE INN

Mill Lane, Bathampton
Tel: 01225 425079

This hulking, many-roomed and beamed old pub is not going to win many prizes – we're talking tourist fare here – but it's a traditional (and much needed) break and turn around point after a walk up the canal.

HALL & WOODHOUSE

1 Old King Street, Bath
01225 469259
hall-woodhousebath.co.uk

This recent addition to the city centre's pub landscape used to be Bonham's auction room. Extensively refurbished inside (it cost a fortune!) it now looks and feels like a classy big city pub. The main reason to come here is the beer though, which is straight from the Hall & Woodhouse Brewery just down the road in Dorset. Try the Tanglefoot, but be warned that it lives up to its name. The food's okay too, and it's somewhere you can take your mother.

HARE AND HOUNDS

Lansdown Road
01225 482682

Just an average pub situated at the top of the Lansdown road on the outskirts of Bath, with average beer and average food, and somewhere we only recommend you visit for one reason: THE VIEW. It's breathtaking, and sitting in the extensive garden up here you can drink it in for hours. Somewhere to take people to impress them with your insider knowledge…

HOP POLE

7 Albion Buildings, Upper Bristol Road
Tel: 01225 446327, www.bathales.com

If you're walking up the river path towards Bristol, or enjoying Victoria Park's many delights, this is a lovely port of call. The Hop Pole offers famously scrumptious seasonal pub nosh, a lovely pretty beer garden and very well kept ales (this is a Bath Ales pub). Just across the road from the pub is Victoria Park's children's play area.

INN AT FRESHFORD

Freshford
Tel: 01225 722250
www.theinnatfreshford.co.uk

This 16th-century village inn on the banks of the River Frome in Freshford is on the beautiful Two Valleys Walk, a 3.5-mile walking route that takes you, conveniently, to the waterside pub the Cross Guns at Avoncliff. Food served 12-2.30pm, 6.30-9pm Monday to Saturday; 12-5pm Sunday. Lovely cycling round here too.

KING WILLIAM PUB & DINING ROOMS

36 Thomas Street, London Road,
Tel: 01225 428096
www.kingwilliampub.com

The sister pub of the Garrick's Head, this urban gem off the tourist way has built its reputation on its locally sourced menu, ales and ciders. If you're exploring Walcot Street or are in the vicinity of the Bell or the Star it's certainly worth dropping in, and if you book a table here you'll get a lovely meal and fine booze.

MANDALYNS BAR

13 Fountain Buildings, Lansdown Road
Tel: 01225 425403
www.mandalyns.co.uk

Pink Paper South West pub of the year 2006 and recently refurbished, this is Bath's fun, friendly, party-going gay venue. All part of the party: happy hour 6-9pm, quiz night Tuesdays, games night Wednesdays, karaoke Thursday and Sundays, cocktail night Fridays. Saturday night is guest DJ night. Closed Mondays; open from 6pm rest of the week (and until 2am on Thursday, Friday and Saturday).

OLD GREEN TREE

12 Green Street, Bath
Tel: 01225 448259

Anyone interested in old pub culture needs to visit this place (and also the Star). Relaxing in the Green Tree's three oak–panelled rooms is the public house equivalent of smoking a pipe. A great place to meet both locals and visitors, it's also so cosy that you'll be guaranteed to strike up conversation with the neighbouring table or the regulars "holding forth" at the bar. Alongside the pub's three regular beers are three guest ales that are always sourced from within about 80 miles, while a traditional pub grub menu includes a famously rare beef platter with horseradish. Just beware the tempting array of gins and whiskys! Or, alternatively, throw yourself into them with gusto, remembering that in the Green Tree notions such as "time" and "pressing engagements" are abstract absurdities to be ignored. Mobile phone reception is, happily, very poor in here too.

OPIUM

Grove Street
Tel: 01225 332 321
www.opiumbars.com

Prettily decorated little late-night hideaway under Pulteney Bridge. The bar area is small but always bustling with cocktail shakers. To the left, a curtained doorway leads to a sumptuous cavern of low tables and private crannies. Popular at the weekends with the more discerning hen night crowds looking for a 'late one'.

PIG AND FIDDLE

2 Saracen Street
01225 460 868
www.thepigandfiddle.co.uk

Decent, independent, city centre pub that has a lot to recommend it: big-screen sport, decent ales, darts, outside area, okay food and lots of space. It does get packed with students though, so if that puts you off, it's best avoided in the evening. Great location makes it a good meeting place, and sitting outside on a summer evening watching Bath's citizens bustle past is rarely a chore. You'll even manage to top up your tan in the middle of winter here thanks to the Pig's ever-so-slightly controversial patio heaters.

RAVEN

6-7 Queen Street
Tel: 01225 425045
www.theravenofbath.co.uk

The Raven has become something of a legendary watering hole thanks to excellent ale that has seen it included in the CAMRA Good Beer Guide every year since 2006. Whether it's a dark porter so dense that light itself cannot escape from it or a bright pale ale so crisp and fragrant you'll think you've died and gone to beery heaven, the Raven's perfect pints will soon have you abandoning your plans to visit the Crescent. Add to the heady mix a guest cider, meat and veggie pies from legendary Bristol Pie tycoons pieminister, and the Raven's famously friendly service and you have an exemplary modern boozer. If the downstairs looks busy don't worry – there is more drinking and dining room upstairs.

ST JAMES WINE VAULTS

10 St. James's Square
www.stjameswinevaults.co.uk

A small but vibrant and respected local situated just behind the Crescent, the St James sports a cosy upstairs bar that gets pleasantly busy of an evening, plus a downstairs Cellar Bar hosting live music, including regular jazz nights, local bands and open mic nights. A great alternative night out, 'Jimmy's' even has a (small!) pool table.

SALAMANDER

John Street, Bath
01225 428889
www.bathales.com

The main talking points of this cosy city-centre Bath Ales pub are its excellent beers and its quality pub grub. After a couple of pints of Wild Hare, the small plates and starters always seem very tempting indeed. Rarebit or hot sausages & mustard anyone?

STAR INN

23 The Vineyards, The Paragon,
Tel: 01225 425072
www.star-inn-bath.co.uk

Best taken with a pinch of snuff (which is free on request), the Star, with its acres of oak panelling and 19th-century bar fittings, is a living museum and a much respected and vibrant boozer into the bargain. Like the Old Green Tree, you won't find any music or fruit machines here. What you will find is a series of rooms that have a hushed, almost church-like atmosphere by day and a pleasantly bawdy one by night. In short, it's a must visit for anyone interested in English pub tradition. Dating to about 1760 (the workers who built the Paragon were paid from here), the building is Grade II listed – and so are some of the older regulars who sit at the small bar on a bench affectionately known as "Death Row". The ale selection always has something for all tastes and livers, and the Bass is served from a jug. Nice. No menus as such here but there are rolls and bar snacks aplenty, and on Sundays you're looking at free sausage rolls and cheese. Add a shove-halfpenny table and this is a pub pilgrimage not to be missed.

WHEATSHEAF

Combe Hay
01225 833504
www.wheatsheafcombehay.co.uk

An ancient (the building is a farmhouse dating from 1576) hulking foodie pub three miles from Bath set in ridiculously idyllic countryside. Well worth a trip out here for the good restaurant and pleasant garden. The menu is at the pricy end of the market but there is an early bird menu served 6.30-7.30pm Tuesday till Friday. Lunch 12p-2.30pm; dinner 6-9.30pm. Friday and Saturday 6-10pm. Closed Mondays.

VOLUNTEER RIFLEMAN'S ARMS

3 New Bond Street Place, Bath
01225 425210

Old school, in the best sense, city centre boozer just around the corner from (and little bigger than) the Coeur de Lion. If you think it's cosy downstairs, there's an even smaller room upstairs. Worth a visit for the good ale and for the fact that pubs like this are fast disappearing. Traditional, homecooked pub grub is on offer here, and there are a couple of tables outside in the quaint alley. Can become cheerfully full of an evening – prepare for some shoulder rubbing!

WHITE HART

Widcombe Hill, Bath
Tel: 01225 338053
www.whitehartbath.co.uk

If you're doing any canal towpath walking this is a nice place to start or finish at. The secluded, walled beer garden is the central attraction here – not big but very relaxing. You can also eat from a fairly modern pub menu, and you can book both rooms and dormitory beds here too.

Listings Eating

There's so much great food in Bath that you could navigate your way around the Heritage City using your tastebuds alone as a guide. Instead we recommend you use our listings as an indispensable route map – you're about to embark on a rather more methodical voyage of discovery, taking in everything from the tastiest portable treats to glorious gastro feasts by way of boisterous breakfasts, terrific takeaways and top shopping opportunities.

Go forth, binge out… and be sure to tell 'em that Naked sent you.

The symbolic breakdown
How many tenners get one person a substantial repast plus a drink (alcoholic where applicable) in one of the restaurants listed here?

£ *one (or even less)*
£+ *one or two (if you go for upper echelon menu prices)*
££ *between two and three (for the full-on experience)*
£££ *big bucks, best splurged on big occasion celebrations*
*T *takeaway option available*

Restaurants

Americana

FIREHOUSE ROTISSERIE
2 John Street, BA1 2JL
Tel: 01225 482070
www.firehouserotisserie.co.uk
Vibrant California-inspired grub (think steaks, salads, modern Tex-Mex) largely courtesy of the rotisserie that lends its name to this bright'n'breezy contemporary bistro tucked away on a cobbled side street. *Guide £+*

HUDSON BAR & GRILL
14 London Street, BA1 5BU
Tel: 01225 332323
www.hudsonbars.co.uk
Stylishly sassy but never frivolously flashy, this 'Sex and the City' experience brings a little bit of Upper East NY to the top of Walcot Street, courtesy of the same charismatic impresario (Richard Fenton, since you ask) responsible for the Firehouse reviewed above. Classic combinations of sublime steaks, salads and pan-global medleys – all impeccably sourced and perfectly presented – can be enjoyed in either the laid-back, cushion-strewn bar or upstairs in a chic dining room that casually radiates discreet glamour. It's a bit pricey, but hey – you're worth it. *Guide ££*

Modern British

BROWNS
Orange Grove, BA1 1LP
Tel: 01225 461199,
www.browns-restaurants.com
Fairly formulaic, fashionable food courtesy of one of the UK's first franchises, but worthy of a visit for the elegant surroundings and gorgeous al fresco terrace offering top views of the Abbey. *Guide £+*

CIRCUS
34 Brock Street, BA1 2LN
Tel: 01225 466020
www.thecircuscafeandrestaurant.co.uk
Dine in true modern Bath style either at a pavement table on the picturesque thoroughfare that links the iconic Circus with the uber-iconic Royal Crescent, or indoors in contempo-genteel, modern bistro surroundings. Menus thrum with impeccably

sourced integrity, and we heartily endorse the return of the lesser-spotted 'elevenses' selection. *Guide £+*

COSY CLUB

Unit R4, SouthGate, BA11TP
www.cosyclub.co.uk
A local, independent venture (albeit another link in a small chain: see also Velo Lounge) in SouthGate? Yes indeed! The general locale may be a bit bland, but the Cosy's ambience and grub most certainly isn't. Wallet-friendly all-day menus run the whole gamut from breakfast until well beyond sunset, and includes top tapas and hearty, homecooked, comforting yumminess such as pies, burgers and scrumptious sweet treats. We're lovin' the al fresco balcony, too. *Guide £*

GASCOYNE PLACE

1 Sawclose, BA1 1EY
Tel: 01225 445854
www.gascoyneplace.co.uk
Is it a gastropub? Is it a bar? Is it an uppercrust dining experience in an elegant supper room? Is it all about jazz in the lounge, or fizz on the mezzanine? Go forth and discover the answers to all these questions for yourself, as this lively Sawclose cornerstone is whatever you want it to be, whenever the mood strikes – and comes highly recommended. *Guide £+*

GREEN PARK BRASSERIE

Green Park Station, BA1 1JB
Tel: 01225 338565
www.greenparkbrasserie.com
Decent, largely locally sourced grub served up in a former Victorian railway station HQ that today combines covered terraces to both front and rear of the building with a bar and several areas indoors, all put to very good use during regular live jazz shebangs. *Guide £*

HALL & WOODHOUSE

1-3 Old King Street, BA1 2JT
Tel: 01225 469259
www.hall-woodhousebath.co.uk
Formerly a branch of Bonhams Auctioneers, today a tarted-up social epicentre for Bath's suited and booted/spray tan crowd – which is a shame, really, as the rooftop garden (open to diners only), some surprisingly eclectic décor flourishes and the reasonably decent all-day menus are rather appealing. Plus great ales from this renowned Dorset brewer. *Guide £+*

UPPER CRUST: GO ON, PUSH THE BOAT OUT!

BATH PRIORY HOTEL

Weston Road, BA1 2XT, Tel: 01225 331922, www.thebathpriory.co.uk
Nestling in the leafy environs of Bath's version of the Hollywood Hills, the BPH is the epitome of the Brit version of full-on glamour: a gracious, gorgeous, gourmet experience. Head Chef Sam Moody – overseen by affable executive hob god Michael Caines – sure knows how to turn out a memorably impressive plate of grub, and service is second to none. *Guide £££*

DOWER HOUSE AT THE ROYAL CRESCENT HOTEL

16 Royal Crescent, BA1 2LS, Tel: 01225 823333, www.royalcrescent.co.uk
Want a red carpet experience at the heart of Bath's most iconic crescent? This is it: a paean to refined élan from aperitif to nightcap, but still somehow refreshingly unsnooty. *Guide £££*

LUCKNAM PARK

Colerne, Nr Bath SN14 8AZ, Tel: 01225 742777, www.lucknampark.co.uk
Acres of picturesque private parkland, an equestrian centre, a spa and an assortment of wood-panelled drawing room bars combine to offer a distinctly distinguished destination experience, with dining options of a chic, airy brasserie adjacent to the sparkling spa and a more formal, trad-luxe affair in the hotel's main house. Both are overseen by Executive Chef Hywel Jones, who flaunts a Michelin star to confirm his superstar status. Posh? You got it. *Guide £££*

OLIVE TREE

Queensberry Hotel, 4-7 Russel Street, BA1 2QF, Tel: 01225 447928
www.thequeensberry.co.uk
Smart, stylish, triple-AA Rosette winning food in surroundings to match. If the hushed atmosphere in the dining room becomes too stifling, make your way to the Old Q Bar for a more laid-back, quirky experience or decamp to the charming al fresco urban oasis outback. *Guide £££*

HOLE IN THE WALL

16 George Street, BA1 2EN
Tel: 01225 42524
www.theholeinthewall.co.uk
Originally opened in 1952 by charismatic, legendary chef George Perry-Smith – who aimed to serve real home-cooked food in a convivial environment at a time when eating out in the provinces was a rigid, formal experience, the Hole has earned itself longstanding Bath institution status. It may not be quite as characterful or atmospheric today as it was in the good old days of yore, but it offers a contempo-cosy, reasonably satisfying experience and set menu/early dining deals that make for veritable bargains. *Guide £+*

KOMEDIA CANTEEN

22-23 Westgate Street, BA1 1EP
Tel: 0845 293 8480
www.komedia.co.uk/bath
Cheerful diner attached to the entertainment pleasuredome that is Komedia. Established by tousle-haired toff and champion of chickens Hugh Fearnley-Whittingstall, the KC is now an independent venture, but grub still adheres to fundamental RCC principles regarding seasonality, sourcing and urban-meets-rustic stylings, and can be enjoyed as a stand-alone experience or as a set menu in conjunction with Komedia shows bearing the 'Meal Deal' logo. Weekend breakfasts are perfect but pricey, kids are very well catered for. *Guide £+,*

BRILLIANT BREAKFASTS

BOSTON TEA PARTY
Kingsmead Square
- Granola, muesli and porridge; bagels and waffles; full-on Full English (including veggie versions), all made from locally sourced ingredients

RIVERSIDE CAFÉ
below Argyle Street
- Truly scrumptious, sumptuous breakfast menu to be enjoyed against a backdrop of the best weir view in town

GUILDHALL MARKET CAFÉ
Guildhall Market
- For their good old-fashioned, traditional fry-ups, we salute the GMC

JAZZ CAFÉ
Kingsmead Square
- Bacon buttie perfection

WILD CAFÉ
Queen Street
- From fruit pancake stacks to locally sourced Full English by way of eggs Florentine and Benedict

LIME LOUNGE

11 Margarets Buildings, BA1 2LP
Tel: 01225 421251
www.limeloungebath.co.uk
Dinky, vibrant bistro on a gorgeous traffic-free lane within Bath's most des-res neighbourhood just a croissant-toss away from the Royal Crescent and the Circus. All-day menus and al fresco seating complete the staycation experience. *Guide £*

MARKET

Sawclose, BA1 1EY
Tel: 01225 330009, www.marketbath.com
Merry, multifaceted affair featuring a spacious, partially covered/heated terrace at the heart of the Sawclose scene serving fresh, fuss-free food (burgers, pizzas, salads, steaks, tapas) at down to earth prices all day long. *Guide £, *T*

MENU GORDON JONES

2 Wellsway, Bath BA2 3AQ, Tel: 01225 480871, www.menugordonjones.co.uk
According to the Heritage City foodie grapevine, the new Bath food revolution starts here… at a tiny, unassuming former café next door to McColls newsagent and over the road from a Co-op. Don't expect a formal, traditional menu or much space to move around in (the restaurant has room for a maximum of 14 diners); do expect a fantastical version of the best intimate supper party you've ever attended, courtesy of a chef who skilfully cartwheels his way across the tricky tightrope between down-to-earth and utterly stellar. Highly recommended. *Guide ££*

RAPHAEL

Upper Borough Walls, BA1 1RN
Tel: 01225 480042
www.raphaelrestaurant.co.uk
Smart food in a softly lit, well-heeled

environment, particularly popular with the more mature pre-theatre crowd. *Guide £+*

SALLY LUNN'S
4 North Parade Passage, BA1 1NX
Tel: 01225 461634, www.sallylunns.co.uk
Tourist hotspot within a 15th century building, now a shrine to the (actually rather dull) buns apparently invented by a young Huguenot refugee who came to Bath over 300 years ago. Today, Sally would no doubt be amazed by the enduring popularity of her baps; personally speaking, we're incredulous. *Guide £+*

TILLEYS BISTRO
3 North Parade Passage, BA1 1NX
Tel: 01225 484200
www.tilleysbistro.co.uk
Both décor and menus at this distinctly characterful, unashamedly (but not, we don't think, consciously) 1970s-style bistro are charmingly eccentric. Mix'n'match from a selection of small, medium and large dishes, the best of which focus strongly on regional classics… but not necessarily the south west region. Enjoy hearty, creamy sauces and a good selection for vegetarians to boot… See what we mean about eccentric? Still, legions of longstanding fans love it, and so do we. *Guide £+*

THE TRAMSHED
Beehive Yard, BA1 5BD
Tel: 01225 421200
www.thetramshedbath.co.uk
It may be the most commercial venture to be found along the Walcot Street 'strip' but those in search of flexible refreshment opportunities may well find it worth making a pitstop at the end of the line. The faux NY loft stylings grate a little, but the partially covered, heated terrace gives great alfresco sofa. *Guide £+*

VELO LOUNGE
30 Moorland Road, Oldfield Park, BA2 3PW, Tel: 01225 344663
www.thelounges.co.uk
This welcoming bar-diner oozes bonhomie and brings the genuine 'neighbourhood bistro' experience to Bath, from breakfast to serious suppers by way of lunchtime light bites, tapas, scrumptious sweet stuff and – wa-hey! – some seriously cocky cocktails.

WOODS
9-13 Alfred Street, BA1 2QX
Tel: 01225 314812
www.woodsrestaurant.com
Yet another Heritage City institution, established in the 1970s and still very well patronised today. The airy bar-brasserie area at the front is home to perhaps the liveliest tables in the house, but the softly-carpeted, more formal dining room is worth a visit, if only to peruse the racehorse-related artefacts that line the walls. The classic British/European menus, meanwhile, don't frighten those horses with any unexpected high jinks, but food is generally consistently good. *Guide £+*

Fish

LOCH FYNE
24 Milsom Street, BA1 1DG
Tel: 01225 750120, www.lochfyne.com
Unusually for a franchise, Loch Fyne – with its classy, glam dining room, lovely back garden and menus flaunting wholly sustainable, fabulous fresh fish – doesn't send us into a fractious frenzy; in fact, we highly recommend it. *Guide £+*

Fusion

GIRAFFE
6 Dorchester Street, BA1 1SS
Tel: 01225 463333
www.giraffe.net
A simple link in a massive chain specialising in crowd-pleasing, family-friendly, unchallenging 'global' grub. Quirky décor flourishes flaunt an admirable attempt to distinguish this split-level funkateria from the more soulless food outlets that largely dominate the shrine to Mammon that is SouthGate. *Guide £*

JIMMY SPICES
8 Dorchester Street, BA1 1SS
Tel: 01225 426802
www.jimmyspices.co.uk
Another ever-expanding national chain that – rather surreally – brings together the flavours (although we use that word loosely) of Thailand, China, India, and Italy on an array of hotplates and woks from which folk of a not-so-sophisticated palate can help themselves, all-you-can-eat buffet style. *Guide £*

Turkish

MARMARIS

4-5 Grand Parade, BA2 4AN
Tel: 01225 461946

Step back in time into an old-school Turkish taverna affair complete with a busy takeaway counter, waistcoated waiters, fading murals and a rickety sweet trolley laden with fruit salad, trifle and sticky Turkish pastries. Food is based around a traditional mezze/moussaka/kebab theme, and the resulting bill is usually a pleasant timewarp experience too. *Guide £, *T*

Italian

AIÓ

7 Edgar Buildings, George Street, BA1 2EE
Tel: 01225 443900
www.aiorestaurant.co.uk

The name translates from the Sardinian as 'come and join us' – and who are we to argue? Step away from the prosaic pastas and pizzas offered at similarly themed havens of la dolce vita and discover the joys of the fregola (a plumped-up version of cous cous) that accompanies huge platters mainly featuring chargrilled fresh fish, chicken and steak dishes. Veggies are well catered for too, and there are al fresco opportunities both on the wide pavement out front and in the tiny courtyard to the rear. *Guide £+*

AQUA

86 Walcot Street, BA1 5BD
Tel: 01225 471371
www.aqua-restaurant.com

Popular, familiar Italian-themed menus served in a rather theatrical chandelier/candlelit dining room that – due to echoing acoustics and a see-and-be-seen layout – generally appeals to party animals rather than quiet tables-for-two. *Guide £+*

BOTTELINO'S

5 Bladud Buildings, BA1 5LS
Tel: 01225 464861, www.bottelinos.net

Cheerful trattoria/pizzeria offering a taste of Italian grub the like of which somebody's mamma probably used to make a long time ago. Lovely terrace with a great view and plenty of space downstairs for those nights when only a table for 20 will do. *Guide £,*T*

ENZO'S

39 Gay Street, BA1 2NT
Tel: 01225 427919
www.enzo-ristorante.co.uk

Chef/proprietor Enzo Piscopo calls his menu 'authentically Neapolitan'; we call it traditional, reliably sturdy Italian fare, from antipasti to zabaglione by way of pizzas, pastas, risotto and grills. *Guide £+*

JAMIE'S ITALIAN

10 Milsom Place, BA1 1BZ
Tel: 01225 510051
www.jamieoliver.com/italian/bath

Pukka fare from the man who started his life in the public eye as the Naked Chef before setting his sights on heading up a national food revolution (fully clothed, of course). If you want to sample Jamie-style, Italianesque grub against a lively backdrop that looks like the set for his latest TV series, this is the place to do it – if, that is, you're paziente enough to tolerati the long queues. *Guide £+*

JOYA

6 Newmarket Row, BA2 4AN
Tel: 01225 460240

A thoroughly easy-going Italian-themed bar/diner experience offering weir views from the first-floor dining room and menus that fail to get all confusionale about the "modern Italian" idiom, relying on a blend of really good Italian imports and the best of British sourcing to present clean, fresh dishes packed with flavour – which is, after all, what decent Italian food is all about. *Guide £+*

MARTINI

8-9 George Street, BA1 2EH
Tel: 01225 460818
www.martinirestaurantbath.com

Long-established, convivial pizza/pasta bistro popular with parties. The pasta is perfectly cooked, and the waiters charming or smarmy, depending on your outlook. *Guide £+*

REAL ITALIAN PIZZA CO.

16 York Street, BA1 1NG
Tel: 01225 330121

Pizzas fresh from a woodfired oven in the open kitchen are served alongside massive salads and ice cream courtesy of the proper gelateria next door. Venture out onto the walled courtyard to the rear for unique rear views of the Abbey. *Guide £, *T*

GLORIOUS GASTROPUBS

BATH HAS A HANDFUL OF VERY FINE RESTAURANTS THINLY DISGUISED AS PUBS

The British gastropub is just what its name suggests: a pub that offers a lot more than the standard pint-accompanying, chips-with-everything fish, steak or lasagne fare, generally specialising in a unique combination of a top-class restaurant in an informal pub or inn environment. The atmosphere and social mix of the well-patronised local doesn't necessarily have to be sacrificed in the name of Gastro, but menus will offer an array of imaginative, seasonal delights made from ingredients sourced from local suppliers. Prices, therefore, tend to reflect such quality (expect to pay £10+ for a main course), but in theory you can drop into a G-spot for a quiet drink and a packet of crisps (although it has to be said, your pint will be chosen from a selection of lesser-spotted microbrewery specialities, the wine list will be thoughtful and eclectic, and the crisps more likely to be of the Kettle variety than the football player-endorsed type). But if you're after the best pub grub in Bath at peak times, booking is essential.

MARLBOROUGH TAVERN

35 Marlborough Buildings, Bath BA1 2LY
Tel: 01225 423731
www.marlborough-tavern.com
Double AA Rosette-endorsed top notch scoff with a perfect pedigree served up in cosy but chic surroundings. A walled, partially covered garden to the rear turns into the ultimate Bath social hotspot when the sun comes out to play, but the sturdy highlights on the MT menus really come into their own during the gloomier months when classy comfort food is called for.

Regular events ('real' fish and chips, steak and Malbec celebrations, set price lunch deals, etc) bring bargains to the table, but the frequently changing à la carte selection turns the spotlight on the true taste of the Tav. Those who like their grub satisfactorily straightforward will revel in soups known locally as the best home-made examples in Bath followed by Butcombe beer-battered fish served with proper chips and mushy peas, while razor clams and goose barnacles, slow-roasted Charolais Jacob's Ladder and the suggestion of a cherry foam with the dark chocolate pot keep foodie fashionista attention levels up.

GARRICK'S HEAD

7 & 8 St Johns Place, Bath BA1 1ET
Tel: 01225 318368
www.garricksheadpub.com
See King William.

KING WILLIAM

36 Thomas Street Bath BA1 5NN
Tel: 01225 428096
www.kingwilliampub.com
In 2004, Charlie and Amanda Digney left London and made their way to Bath with their young family. Calling on Charlie's experience gained at working at well-known London gastropub The Anchor and Hope in Waterloo, the couple have since opened two of the best gastropubs Bath has ever seen (as well as another, The Oakhill, in deepest, darkest Somerset.)

Their first foray was taking over the King William, which despite it's chi-chi address is in fact on the London Road – the main road into Bath from the East. Formerly an iniquitous and legendary cider den and unofficial pharmacist, the Digneys transformed the 'King Billy' into the sort of pub they liked. The locals liked it too, and so did restaurant critic Giles Coren, who raved so hard about it in the *Times* that people travelled for miles to visit.

Their next step was to take over the Garrick's Head and deliver a classy but classless thesp hangout adjacent to the Theatre Royal.

Both pubs are particularly proud of maintaining their proper pub roots, meaning you'll always be as welcome in their bar(s) as you are in their distinctly stylish dining rooms. While some folk may not be so keen on the GH's rather dark interior (which explains why the exterior tables on the traffic-free lane/patio to the front of the pub are generally very well-patronised, even during drizzly weather), the menus rarely divide opinion.

A typical grub-fest at the Garrick's might include a starter of potted Cornish crab with toasted Bertinet sourdough, a main of Warleigh Lodge pork loin accompanied by slow-cooked pig cheek and puy lentils followed by a rhubarb jelly trifle, but take note: the bar food menu (in particular the burgers/fish and chips) offers a selection of exceedingly wallet-friendly, sturdy suppers, while the classic Sunday roasts are legendary.

Menus at the King Billy, meanwhile, tend toward a more flamboyant array of foodie fabulosity (hence the Coren commendation): an ostensibly downhome selection such as devilled lambs kidneys on toast, fish soup with gurnard, mackerel and cod, new potatoes and garlic mayonnaise and blackberry and apple crumble may arrive at your table flaunting a flurry of cheffy twists and treats, but little to detract from the earthy sensibilities at the heart of the matter.

THE CHEQUERS

50 Rivers St Bath BA1 2QA
Tel: 01225 360017
www.thechequersbar.com

Loved by lively locals and snooty national food critics alike, this enduringly popular neighbourhood boozer (and little sister for the Marlborough Tavern, on the previous page) strikes the perfect posh pub/glorious grub balance, especially since it ditched the 'fine dining' supper room upstairs and made its classic menu (soups, casseroles, pies, roasts, burgers etc, all made on the premises) available to all. A recent winning dinner at Chequers included pressed ham hock set in parsley jelly, red wine braised beef with butternut squash and horseradish emulsion and lemon and raspberry meringue posset crumble, but we have it on very good authority that even the burgers are the best in Bath.

HOP POLE

7 Albion Buildings Bath BA1 3AR
Tel: 01225 446 327
www.bathales.com/our-pubs/pid/the-hop-pole

Don't be put off by the seemingly prosaic location on a busy, traffic-heavy artery; once inside (or even outside, in the gorgeous private garden out back) this characterful urban oasis, you'll find a traditionally styled home-from-home overseen by luscious local brewery Bath Ales.

While real ale fans flock to the Hop for their regular Gem/Barnstormer/Rare Hare (etc) fix, many more are attracted by the kind of imaginative fare-with-flair that's kept this welcoming hostelry at the top of the Bath Gastropub league since before the careworn idiom was invented. Sociable sharing platters (the one that includes the homemade scotch egg is highly recommended), pork sausage rolls with piccalilli or corned beef pasties with HP Sauce could be taken as a pint-accompanying nibble or enjoyed as a prelude to a menu that might (if you're lucky) include Neston Park game pie, crayfish and mackerel fishcakes, and SPA-ale battered fish and chips. If you like what's on offer here (and our bet is that you very much will), sign up for a Loyal Hare Force loyalty card and reap heap big rewards at all Bath Ales hostelries in the region.

ONE BEAUFORT

1 Beaufort West, Bath BA1 6QL
Tel: 01225 334050
www.onebeaufort.com

Discover upper-crust Modern English classics infused with chef-led Gallic inspirations far (but not too far) from the madding crowds of the city centre.

Superchef Christophe Lacroix is as adept at reinventing traditional British classics (beef hash cakes; beer battered fish and chips; sticky toffee pudding) as he is as ensuring that his beloved French inspirations maintain their illustrious reputation at the top of the gastro charts. His pates, tourte d'agneau, onglet aux echalottes et al may have their roots in Christophe's homeland but all ingredients are locally sourced before being turned into a pub grub tour de force on the premises. Voila! Tres chic.

RIVER CANTEEN

Spring Gardens Road, Bath BA2 6PW
Tel: 01225 424800

This glorious new addition to the Bath Italian restaurant scene has absolutely nothing to do with Hugh Fearnley-Whittingstall's River Cottage Canteen but everything to do with freshly prepared, quietly glamorous contemporary and traditional Italian food served up in a characterfully stylish former boathouse with an upper-level al fresco balcony that offers the a great view of the weir. Beware though, the lunchtime menu is distinctly café-style and bears little relation to the à la carte. *Guide ££*

RUSTICO BISTRO ITALIANO

2 Margarets Buildings, BA1 2LP
Tel: 01225 310064
www.rusticobistroitaliano.co.uk

Tiny, super-pretty, fully authentic family-run Italian bistro based around an open kitchen. Pavement tables on the traffic-free lane out front. Highly recommended. *Guide £+*

SOLO PIZZA

2 Milsom Place, BA1 1BZ
Tel: 01225 444439

Excellent coffee, Italian pastries, antipasti, salads and freshly baked pizzas best enjoyed at a covered outside table at the heart of this upmarket shopping complex. *Guide £, *T*

SOTTO SOTTO

10 North Parade, Bath BA2 4AL
Tel: 01225 330236, www.sottosotto.co.uk

This stylish, subterranean, contemporary trattoria is a fairly recent addition to the Bath eating out scene. Already, though, the green shoots of a great reputation are beginning to flourish. Expect upmarket, top-notch representations of Italian classics with a contemporary twist in cosy but cool surroundings. *Guide ££*

STRADA

Beau Nash House, Sawclose, BA1 1EU
Tel: 01225 337753, www.strada.co.uk

Slick, Italian-themed menus in the kind of grand surroundings (formerly the home of uber-dandy Beau Nash) that belie the fact that this chic eaterie is actually part of a national franchise – until it dawns on you that there's not much passion behind the superficially welcoming vibe. *Guide £+*

LOVED UP

CASANIS

Saville Row

- The intimate little table-for-two in the window has to be the most romantic table in town

HUDSON BAR & GRILL

London Street

- Follow on from a cocktail in the candlelit, cushion-strewn bar by smooching over plenty of dishes to share in the contempo-elegant dining room upstairs

BISTRO LA BARRIQUE

Barton Street

- A menu that lends itself to sharing

RAJPOOT

Argyle Street

- Cosy booths and plenty of tucked-away tables for two

BEAUJOLAIS BISTRO

Chapel Row

- Great for impressing a date… as long as you can convince proprietor JP that now is not the time to share his latest naughty joke with you

Japanese/Sushi

YEN SUSHI

11-12 Bartlett St, BA1 2QZ
Tel: 01225 333313, www.yensushi.co.uk

This charmingly cheerful, independent, Japanese-themed canteen offers the hottest seat in town for the inquisitive gourmet: non-stop sushi, makizushi, tepanyaki, ramen and more, resulting in the foodie version of the perfect model train set up, a lap-dancing club for scoffers, or tapas for the jaded, depending on your perspective. *Guide £, *T*

YO! SUSHI

Milsom Place, BA1 1BZ
www.milsomplace.co.uk

A smallish link in the huge international chain credited with introducing British diners to the

Japanese kaiten-zushi (conveyor belt), hidden in a semi-subterranean corner of the Milsom Place complex. The food's pretty good, though we consider the addition of mayonnaise to some otherwise authentic dishes a gastronomic atrocity. *Guide £, *T*

Mexican

LAS IGUANAS

12 Seven Dials, Sawclose, BA1 1EN
Tel: 01225 336666, www.iguanas.co.uk
It's a shame that Bath only has one Latin-American themed diner. Fortunately though, Las Iguanas keeps the colourful flag flying in fine style, courtesy of a lively fiesta of Mexican/Brazilian food, including interesting tapas. The pretty little courtyard at the front, meanwhile, adds to the party-on vibe when the sun is shining. *Guide £+*

MEAT-FREE MAGNIFICENCE

DEMUTHS
North Parade Passage
- Face-free fabulosity

THE PORTER
George Street
- Huge portions of thoroughly decent, proper pub grub, all of a totally vegetarian persuasion

METROPOLITAN CAFÉ
New Bond Street
- Vibrant veggie food in contempo-cosy surroundings

GREEN ROOM AT THE MISSION THEATRE
Corn Street
- Eclectic elevenses and lively lunches attached to Bath's own version of Islington's Almeida theatre (well, sorta…)

YUM YUM THAI
Kingsmead Square
- Okay, the YYT isn't strictly vegetarian-only. But for offering almost everything on their menu in a meat-free format, they deserve a mention here

Middle Eastern

ARABESQUE

Podium Shopping Centre, Northgate Street, BA1 5AL, Tel: 01225 481333
www.arabesquebath.co.uk
Candlelit, cushion-strewn, tented-ceiling, evocative, authentic Lebanese exotica… at the top of a shopping centre escalator, above a supermarket. The fixed-price, unlimited serve-yourself lunchtime buffet – a wholly authentic Arabian Nights affair, from Armenian sausages to Zahra Maglia – is, quite rightly, the stuff of local legend (an equally legendary £6.95 per head at the time of going to press). *Guide £*

CAFÉ DU GLOBE

1a North Parade, BA1 1LF
Tel: 01225 466437, www.caféduglobe.co.uk
We like this place more for the cheerful, brazen eccentricity of the experience than the actual quality of the food – although, having said that, when it's good, it can be very good. But anyway, this pretty-but-prosaic shoppers paradise caff (with pavement seating out front) morphs into a candlelit Moroccan bistro post-sunset, when Moroccan classics (mezze, tagines, couscous, etc), reflect the owner's Casablanca roots. Oh, and there's also a bazaar in the basement, selling Berber jewellery, teapots and Moroccan babouche; bizarre indeed, but rather sweet. *Guide £+*

Spanish/Tapas

LA PERLA

12a North Parade, BA2 4AL
Tel: 01225 463626, www.la-perla.co.uk
If you loved Minibar, you'll adore La Perla: think of it as Minibar+ (the + denoting an extended menu of their legendarily gorgeous gourmet tapas, now supplemented by proper paella and more). But even if you have no idea what Minibar was (for sadly, it is no more), fandango along to this glamorous vaulted cavern and prepare to flamenco with their award-winning Spanish chefs (who also run occasional cookery classes). *Guide £+*

LA TASCA

36 Broad Street, BA1 5LP
Tel: 01225 466477, www.latasca.co.uk
Assembly-line tapas and paellas. *Guide £*

Pan-Asian

HONG KONG BISTRO
33 SouthGate, BA1 1TP
Tel: 01225 318500/316088
www.hongkongbistro.co.uk
Functional, efficient, utilitarian canteen adopting a 'pile it high, sell it cheap' ethos revolving around huge portions of noodle/rice-based dishes. Expect speedy service, value-for-money prices and not-very-friendly staff. *Guide £*

PANASIA ORIENTAL RESTAURANT & BAR
2 George St. BA1 2EH
Tel: 01225 481001, www.panasia-uk.com
A bling-laden experience (sequined walls! sparkly curtains! staff wearing gowns fashioned from jewel-coloured silks!) flaunting an equally dazzling menu that travels from contemporary sushi to traditional Szechuan by way of soups, noodles and rice dishes… and fabulous cocktails. *Guide £+*

WAGAMAMA
1 York Buildings, George Street, BA1 2EB
Tel: 01225 337314, www.wagamama.com
Canteen-style pan-Asian dining chain, famous for its rapid-noodle formula and lively range of fairly healthy, freshly cooked Far Eastern fancies. It's more rapid refuel than relaxing repast, but it's definitely fun. *Guide £, *T*

Thai

MAI THAI
6 Pierrepont Street, BA2 4AA
Tel: 01225 445557
Sparkly, kitsch décor, sweet staff and really, really good classic, Brit-friendly Thai food served in intimate surroundings – little wonder, then, that booking is a must on Friday/Saturday evenings. *Guide £, *T*

SALATHAI
8 Pierrepont Place, BA1 1JX
Tel: 01225 484663
www.salathai-bath.co.uk
Competent, contemporary Thai diner at street level with slightly more formal, traditional but cosy dining areas downstairs. Food is reliably, consistently good. *Guide £, *T*

THAI BALCONY
1 Seven Dials, Sawclose, BA1 1EN
Tel: 01225 444450
Bath's most elegant Thai restaurant offers a theatrical dining experience (glamorous décor, beautifully décorated tables, staff adorned in authentic Thai costume), fortunately, the menus complement first impressions and food offers maximum impact too. *Guide ££, *T*

THAI BASIL
90a Walcot Street, BA1 5BG
Tel: 01225 462463
www.thaibasilbath.com
Food is as fresh and pretty as the décor at this well-heeled, recently refurbished temple to all things Thai. *Guide £+, *T*

THAI BY THE WEIR
16 Argyle Street, BA2 4BQ
Tel: 01225 444834
www.thaibytheweir.co.uk
Contemporary and traditional Thai delights alongside a smattering of pan-Asian crowd-pleasers at wallet-friendly prices. If you spot an empty table on the tiny balcony overlooking the weir, grab it fast. *Guide £*

YUM YUM THAI
17 Kingsmead Square, BA1 2AE
Tel: 01225 445253, www.yumyumthai.com
Fans of frills and frippery may not feel entirely at home in this straightforward little Thai canteen, but whatever the Yum Yum may lack in terms of fanfare it fully makes up for with its organic/free-range/MSG-free pledge, its vegetarian versions of almost all dishes on the menu, its crunch-busting prices and its friendly, efficient service. *Guide £+*

Vegetarian

DEMUTHS
2 North Parade Passage, BA1 1NX
Tel: 01225 446059, www.demuths.co.uk
Longstanding, nationally acclaimed, multi award-winning gourmet veggie/vegan bistro on the lane aka Bath's Prettiest Olde Streete. Sparklingly fresh, innovative menus constantly evolve according to seasonal fluctuation and market availability, resulting in one of the most thoughtful, imaginative selections to be found in the Heritage City – and it's all totally face-free. Also runs a Cookery School. *Guide ££*

Chinese

HOI FAAN

41-42 St James Parade, BA1 1UQ
Tel: 01225 318212, www.hoifaan.com

The very basic ambience here shouldn't put you off – the grub cooked up in the Hoi Faan kitchen is most definitely a welcome addition to the limited availability of decent Chinese food in Bath. It's always full of chinese students from the nearby college looking for home-style cooking, so they're doing something right. Portions are massive, the dim sum is delightful, the chicken's feet are – erm – crunchy. *Guide £+, *T*

HON FUSION

25 Claverton Buildings, BA2 4LD
Tel: 01225 446020, www.honfusion.com

Seriously good, fully authentic Chinese food (including really, really good dim sum and some lesser-spotted regional rarities) served up in down-to-earth but cheerful surroundings. Highly recommended. *Guide £+, *T*

OCEAN PEARL

Podium Shopping Centre, Northgate St, BA1 5AL, Tel: 01225 331238
www.oceanpearl-bath.co.uk

A vast range of familiar Far Eastern delights (usually around 35+ dishes to choose from/ mix'n'match) piled high on serve-yourself buffet hotplates every lunchtime and evening Fill-your-own takeaway boxes (£3.50 lunch, £4.50 dinner at the time of going to press) are particularly good value for money. MSG headaches are a myth, but if you're ever going to suffer one, it'll be here. *Guide £+, *T*

PEKING CHINESE

1-2 New Street, Kingsmead Square, BA1 2EF, Tel: 01225 461750/466377
www.pekingrestaurantbath.co.uk

Depending on your fondness (or lack thereof) for the 1980s, the Peking Chinese will either float your boat or make you seasick. A proliferation of pink dominates on the décor front, while signed photos/endorsements from some distinctly days-of-yore 'celebrities' line the walls – or rather, the spaces on the walls that aren't already taken up by embroidered flock representations of some of China's most iconic landmarks. Food, too, offers a similarly retro approach: Cantonese-, Szechuan- and Peking-inspired 'classics', most definitely engineered to appeal to 80's-era British palates, not quite resulting in a 'so bad, it's good' experience, but definitely within such parameters. *Guide £+, *T*

REAL CHINA ORIENTAL BUFFET

Unit 3, Kingsmead Leisure Complex, 5-10 James Street West, BA1 2BZ
Tel. 01225 332677
www.therealchina.co.uk

Eat-all-you-like, serve-yourself Chinese buffet livened up a bit by a teppanyaki kitchen theatre (fresh dishes made from your choice of ingredients, prepared before your very eyes). Not particularly memorable, but makes for a convenient speedy pitstop en route to an Odeon multiplex screening. *Guide £+*

Indian

BOOJON TANDOORI

28 Charles Street, BA1 1HU
Tel: 01225 429429/429529
www.boojontandoori.com

Friendly neighbourhood BYO affair serving distinctly non-oily curries with all the requisite accompaniments. Popular with big parties, students and loved-up couples alike. Highly recommended. *Guide £, *T*

CURRY MAHAL

31 Belvedere, Lansdown Road, BA1 5HR
Tel: 01225 789666/789501
www.currymahal.net

This charming, old-school curry house has been providing the folk who live on the hill with their chilli fix for many a long year. *Guide £, *T*

DESH

10 Chelsea Road, BA1 3DU
Tel: 01225 314413/463388

Popular, inexpensive, straightforward neighbourhood Indian eatery. BYO policy means that the drink prices are up to you. *Guide £, *T*

EASTERN EYE

8a Quiet Street, BA1 2JS
Tel: 01225 422323/466401
www.easterneye.co.uk

'Posh' curry, Bath style (ie, in former Georgian

townhouse surroundings). Once you've worked your way through the massive (and, in some cases, slightly bizarre) list of 'celebrity endorsements' at the start of the menu, every dish is flagged up with highlighters denoting heat, sugar, nut, wheat and dairy content. Is this Bath's best curry house? You decide. *Guide £+, *T*

JAMUNA
9-10 High Street (entrance in Cheap Street), BA1 5AQ
Tel: 01225 464631
www.jamuna-cuisine.com
Traditional Indian restaurant with no pretensions towards anything else offering splendid views of Bath Abbey. *Guide £, *T*

THE MINT ROOM
Lower Bristol Road, BA2 3EB
Tel: 01225 446656
www.themintroom.co.uk
Tradition meets modernity in bright'n'breezy, contempo-glam surroundings. *Guide £+, *T*

MOUCHUCK
136 Wells Road, BA2 3AH
Tel: 01225 333449
www.cityofbath.co.uk/mouchuck
Straightforward, unfussy neighbourhood BYO curry canteen. *Guide £, *T*

PANAHAR
8 Moorland Road, Oldfield Park, BA2 3PL
Tel: 01225 471999/471899
The Moorland Road locals love Panahar – and it's easy to see why: good fun, good food and affable staff, plus a BYO policy that no doubt keeps business thriving at the off licence conveniently situated just across the road. *Guide £, *T*

PREMIER
4a Argyle Street, BA2 4BA
Tel: 01225 462323/442955
It may not be either the first or the best curry house in Bath (despite the fact it's upstairs from – and closely related to – a hot contender for both titles; see below) but late last-ordering times (11pm week nights; later at weekends) make Premier a popular post-pub haunt. *Guide £, *T*

RAJPOOT
4 Argyle Street, BA2 4BA
Tel: 01225 466833/464758
www.rajpoot.com
If it wasn't for the exotically dressed doorman wearing full Raj regalia (a local landmark in his own right) you could easily bypass the 'poot and end up in the far less dazzling Premier (see above) at street level instead. So allow that doorman to usher you down, down and down again, until you reach an evocative, barrel-vaulted subterranean curry cave.

Downstairs is a bit like the Tardis, really, as you struggle to work out where all the space has come from. There are two bars and several discrete eating areas; the plush, booth-lined affair at the heart of the matter being home to the restaurant's most wanted tables. Food (which has won many awards, including Best Indian Restaurant in the South West at the 2010/11 British Curry Awards) revolves around authentic, upper-crust versions of classic Indian faves alongside a small selection of fascinating, lesser-spotted regional specialities. Highly recommended. *Guide £+*

ATMOSPHERIC AL FRESCO

BISTRO LA BARRIQUE
Barton Street
- The walled garden to the rear is one of Bath's best kept sunspot secrets

CÔTE
Milsom Place
- The courtyard! The courtyard! The courtyard!

RUSTICO BISTRO ITALIANO
Margarets Buildings
- Pavement tables on one of Bath's prettiest, traffic-free lanes

MARKET
Sawclose
- The spacious, partially covered/heated patio is the ultimate summertime see-and-be-seen Sawclose hotspot

HALL & WOODHOUSE
Old King Street
- The only open-air, rooftop dining room to be found in town

YAK YETI YAK

12 Pierrepont Street, BA1 1LA
Tel: 01225 442299
www.yakyetiyak.co.uk

Guardian food critic John Lanchester recently made known nationally that he loves this place; even if you harbour a massive mistrust of such endorsements, it's our bet that you'll find something to yak about here too. Laid-back, cosy and unique (to Bath, at least), find thoroughly decent, well priced, authentic, homemade Nepalese grub (including excellent vegetarian options) which you can, should you so wish, enjoy authentic Nepalese style: lounging on floor cushions around a foot-high table. *Guide £+*

French

BEAUJOLAIS BISTRO BAR

5 Chapel Row (off Queen Square), BA1 1HN Tel: 01225 423417
www.beaujolaisbath.co.uk

It was established way back in 1972. It was gutted by fire in 2005 only to rise from the ashes, phoenix-like, around a year later. It's run by a charismatic eccentric who's one part "Allo 'Allo"s René François Artois and two parts all his own work. And it's très, très bon. Highly recommended. *Guide ££*

BISTRO LA BARRIQUE

31 Barton Street, BA1 1HG
Tel: 01225 463861
www.bistrolabarrique.co.uk

Proper French food (confits, tatins, rillettes, crepes, balotines, etc) served in tapas-sized, mix'n'match portions: voila, c'est chef/proprietor Michel Lemoine's 'petits plats' menu, best enjoyed avec un verre du rosé in the gorgeous walled garden or Parisian-style, on the pavement tables out front. *Guide £+*

BRASSERIE BLANC

Queen Square, Bath BA1 2HH
Tel: 01225 434105
www.francishotel.com

At the time of going to press, the Francis Hotel is, quite literally, under wraps as a complete refurbishment (and new ownership) gets set to unveil in May. And when the dust sheets drop, a brand new branch of Brasserie Blanc – complete with spacious outdoor seating area – will be revealed. Expect top notch, classic French brasserie fare at wholesome prices in contempo-glam surroundings courtesy of long-established celebrity chef Raymond Blanc (and, probably, plenty of blank looks from the head honchos of the independent restaurants in the near vicinity who are going to need your support more than ever before). *Guide £+*

CAFÉ ROUGE

15 Milsom St, BA1 1DE
Tel: 01225 462368, www.caférouge.co.uk

Franchise-style franglais food (albeit of a reasonably high quality). *Guide £+*

CASANIS

4 Saville Row, BA1 2QP
Tel: 01225 780055, www.casanis.co.uk

Swooningly pretty and uber-romantic, this softly lit haven of bonhomie totally sums up that quintessentially Gallic sense of effortless, multi-faceted good taste. Highly recommended. *Guide ££*

CÔTE

27 Milsom Place, BA 1 1BZ
www.cote-restaurants.co.uk

TEATIME TREATS

PUMP ROOM

Abbey Churchyard

- The ultimate high tea hotspot

REGENCY TEA ROOMS

Gay Street

- Cute…in a Jane Austen-related way

BATH BUN TEA SHOPPE

Abbey Green

- A paean to one of Bath's most legendary indigenous sweet treats

CAKE CAFÉ

SouthGate

- Take a break from the full-on commerciality of the shopping centre itself and treat yourself to a slice of independent Bath

LE PARISIEN

Shires Yard

- Perfect patisserie

Tel: 01225 335 509
It may be yet another franchise to threaten the Heritage City's glorious independent eateries (and this one gives the dagger another quarter-turn, as it's leapt into the space vacated by the much-loved Moon and Sixpence when it went bust in 2011). But credit where it's due: the brasserie-style food served here ain't half bad, while the fact that it can be enjoyed in the characterful courtyard or on the upper-level terrace within the stylish Milsom Place shopping complex earns Côte extra brownie points. Just don't make a habit of fraternising with the enemy, okay? *Guide £+*

Cafés

ADVENTURE CAFÉ

George Street, BA1 2ED
Tel: 01225 462038,
www.adventure.000space.com
A bit like a licensed version of Central Perk (oh come on, surely we're allowed one 'Friends' reference when talking about cafés?). Suntrap patio to the rear, pavement tables out front and affable, easy-going menus from breakfast to burger-fuelled beyond.

THE BATH BUN TEA SHOPPE

2 Abbey Green, BA1 1NW
Tel: 01225 463928,
www.thebathbun.com
It may be stuffed to the gills with tourist-trap frills and fripperies (staff dressed in period Regency costume, a plethora of olde worlde stylee stylings, etc), but the BBTS gives great cake (and a choice of 18 varieties of tea to slurp with it).

BATH BAKERY CAFÉ

37 Moorland Road. BA2 3PN
Tel 01225 481477, www.bathbakery.co.uk
Illy coffee, panini, homemade soup, sarnies, sweet and savoury pastries, cakes and what are possibly the best sausage rolls in Bath, all to be found in a lively, bustling environment at the heart of the Moorland Road shopping experience. **T*

BEN'S COOKIES

21 Union Passage, BA1 1RD
Tel: 01225 460983, www.benscookies.com
Dinky little cookie bakery specialising in funky, chunky freshly-baked cookies (priced by the kilo) to take away or enjoy at a table on the traffic-free lane out front with a mug of really good coffee. **T*

BERTINET BAKERY

6 New Bond Street Place, BA1 1BH
www.bertinet.com
Croques monsieur, tartines, soups, savouries and what we believe to be amongst the very best cakes, pastries and viennoiserie in Bath, all to be enjoyed with a vintage pot of boutique loose leaf tea, a bowl of coffee or the finest hot chocolate this side of the off-piste experience, all courtesy of award-winning doughboy Richard Bertinet.

BONGHY-BO'S

2-3 Barton Court, Upper Borough Walls, BA1 1RZ, Tel: 01225 462276
Tucked away in an unlikely location behind the smart shops on New Bond Street, this almost hidden gem is loved by those who claim to have 'discovered it'. If you're not familiar with exiting Laura Ashley's tradesman's entrance, take the stairs under the archway that lead up from Upper Borough Walls and you'll come across a gorgeous little split-level courtyard that gives way to a friendly, funky refectory within, featuring an open kitchen that churns out quiches, jacket spuds, sarnies, cakes etc all day long, alongside – and here's a glorious, unexpected twist that we bet you didn't expect – a selection of noodle/rice dishes on a Far Eastern theme.

BOSTON TEA PARTY

Kingsmead Square, BA1 2AE
Tel: 01225 313901
www.bostonteaparty.co.uk
This longstanding Bath café society hotspot gets packed to capacity when town is busy – fortunately, the big terrace out front offers a spacious alternative to sitting knee-to-knee with those at the table next door at peak times. It's not a particularly wallet-friendly affair, but a strong emphasis on ethical sourcing, environmental responsibility and hearty, wholesome grub (including particularly splendid breakfasts) adequately compensates for the surcharge. **T*

BRIDGE COFFEE SHOP
Pulteney Bridge, BA2 4AY
Tel: 01225 483339
Just over the road from the one below, find breakfast, baguettes, pasties, sausage rolls, sweet treats etc at this fuss-free café and takeaway overlooking the weir. *T

CAFÉ AU LAIT
7 Pulteney Bridge, BA2 4AX
Tel: 01225 338007
Just over the road from the one above, find cakes, gateaux and pastries, quiches, jacket potatoes, salads, sandwiches, baguettes etc at this recently refurbished café overlooking the one over the road that overlooks the weir. *T

CAKE CAFÉ
5 SouthGate, BA1 1AQ, Tel: 01225 789010
Owned by the same team behind the Bridge Coffee Shop (see above the one above), this lively little hubbub of refreshment merriment keeps the local independent flag flying in SouthGate. As the name suggests, this is a cake-focused cafeteria, but breakfasts, lunches, etc, go large here too. *T

CAFÉ DU GLOBE
1a North Parade, BA1 1LF
Tel: 01225 466437, www.caféduglobe.co.uk
By day, a prosaic shoppers/office workers' pitstop (albeit a pretty one). By night, however, it's something else entirely… [see listing in Restaurants, above].

CAFÉ LUCCA
The Loft, 1 Bartlett Street, BA1 2QZ
Upper-crust, well-heeled Tuscan-themed venture within a très stylish shopping hub.

CAFÉ RETRO
18 York Street, BA1 1NG
Tel: 01225 339347, www.caféretro.co.uk
Independent café-restaurant specialising in massive breakfasts and plenty of easygoing, homemade fare of the pasta/panini/burger/salad/veggie option variety all at down-to-earth prices. Eat-in customers can swoon over excellent Abbey views from the first floor, while Retro to Go (next door) has to be one of the nicest daytime food-on-the-hoof takeaways in Bath. *T

CAFÉ SHOON
14 Old Bond Street, BA1 1BP
Tel: 01225 445309, www.caféshoon.co.uk
Bagels, well-dressed salads, homemade cakes and splendid views across the Heritage City's rooftops from this slick cosmopolitan café situated above a chic urban outfitters.

CHAPEL ARTS CENTRE CAFÉ
Lower Borough Walls, BA1 1QR
Tel: 01225 461700, www.chapelarts.org
There ain't no meat anywhere on the fresh, eclectic menus at this unpretentious, arty culture vulture hangout attached to a thriving arts centre. *T

CORAL QUAY CAFÉ
8/9 New Bond Street Place, BA1 1BH
Tel: 01225 446362, www.coralquay.co.uk
The food on offer above this gift shop specialising in crafty global ethnica, is of the fairtrade, largely organic, locally sourced persuasion – but that doesn't always justify the high prices. Good coffee, though, and gluten-free options are a welcome sight. *T

COLONNA & SMALLS ESPRESSO ROOM
6 Chapel Row, BA1 1HN
Tel: 01225 446362
www.colonnaandsmalls.co.uk
Coffee aficionados' paradise, home to truly great brews served with a healthy side of coffee-fascism. Ask for milk in your filter coffee. Go on. We dare you. *T

EAT5STAR
14 Kingsmead Square, BA1 2AD
Tel: 01225 330555, www.eat5star.com
The best bacon butties in Bath? We think so. *T

EGG CAFÉ
St John's Place, BA1 1ET
Tel: 01225 823408, www.chandosdeli.com
The coffee's good (if a tad pricey), the sarnies are nicely stuffed, the cakes are scrumptious and the pavement tables are a great place to stalk celebrity thesps using the Theatre Royal's stage door. If only someone would tell the kids who frequent this prestigious young people's theatre complex to keep the noise down! *T

FINE CHEESE CO.
29-31 Walcot Street, BA1 5BN
Tel: 01225 483407, www.finecheese.co.uk
Posh prandial paradise within the ultimate cheese lovers' Mecca. *T

GOURMET SCOFFS
9 Terrace Walk, BA1 1LN
Tel: 01225 471137
Uncomplicated, straightforward, fresh, frill-free fare including thoroughly decent breakfasts. *T

GREEN ROOM AT THE MISSION THEATRE
32 Corn Street, BA1 1UF, Tel: 01225 428600, www.missiontheatre.co.uk
Delightful, totally vegetarian theatre-café serving freshly prepared, homemade elevenses, scrumptious cakes and lunches. *T

GUILDHALL MARKET CAFÉ
Guildhall, High Street, BA1 5AW
Tel: 01225 461593
Need a break from the flashy antipasti, artisan cheeses and posh tarts that are quietly starting to dominate this increasingly foodie market? Go forth and binge on the wallet-friendly, not-too-greasy greasy spoon fare in the utilitarian surroundings of a typical English market caff, the last of its kind in Bath. *T

HANSEL UND GRETEL STRUDEL BAR
9 Margarets Buildings, Brock St, BA1 2LP
Tel: 01225 464677
www.hanselundgretel.com
The kitschest café in Bath (that's a compliment) downstairs from a street-level shop packed with Tyrol/Alpine-related knick-knackery. The strudel sets a benchmark standard by which all strudel should henceforth be judged, and the hot chocolate is rich enough to constitute a stand-alone lunch.

JACOB'S COFFEE HOUSE
6 Abbey Churchyard, BA1 1LY
Tel: 01225 758132, www.juicemoose.com
Fresh, wholesome grub with an emphasis on local, organic and free-range ingredients, Abbey Churchyard/Pump Room views from the covered patio. *T

JAZZ CAFÉ
Kingsmead Square, BA1 2AA
Tel: 01225 329002
www.bathjazzcafé.co.uk
This long-established, independent café-bistro deserves special credit for starting the Kingsmead Square coffee house revolution that continues to thrive today. Breakfast bacon butties (a heap of rashers twixt two doorsteps of freshly baked bread) have earned well-deserved, local legendary status – if one of these doesn't sort your hangover out, nothing can. Also hosts regular live jazz events. *T

RAPID REFUELLING ON THE HOOF

WAGAMAMA
York Buildings
- Noodle-doodle a go-go

WHOLE BAGEL
Upper Borough Walls
- Make like a New Yorker and grab a salt beef bagel-to-go.

YEN SUSHI
Bartlett Street
- Snatch fresh sushi directly from the conveyor belt

SAUSAGE SHOP
Green Street
- If you're not too sure about whether sausage'n'mash is a viable walkabout option, this is your one opportunity to find out. Or you could wimp out of the challenge and take your bangers on a baguette instead…

HONG KONG BISTRO
SouthGate
- Wallet-friendly pan-Asian grub served so speedily it's almost thrown at you

JIKA JIKA COFFEE HOUSE & CANTEEN
4a Princes Buildings, George St, BA1 2ED
Tel: 01225 429903, www.jikajika.co.uk
Can be a bit too self-consciously 'cool' to be totally chillaxing, but worthy of acclaim for lively menus driven by local inspiration, including substantial breakfasts, hearty sandwiches/warps/flatbreads, real pizza, homemade cakes and interesting specials. *T

KINDLING
9a Claverton Buildings, BA2 4LD
Tel: 01225 442125
www.kindlingcoffee.co.uk
Breakfasts, sarnies, homemade sweet and

savoury pastries (including veggie options) and cakes feature strongly amidst a solid selection of local, organic, homemade and fairly traded fare served in welcoming, child-friendly surroundings with an authentically unforced 'neighbourhood' vibe. *T

LA CROISSANTERIE

14 Northumberland Place, BA1 5AR
Tel: 01225 469641

No surprises to be found on the shopper/tourist friendly menus based on sandwiches, baguettes, pastries, etc, but worthy of a mention for the location (and al fresco tables) on a pretty, traffic-free lane. *T

LE PARISIEN

Shires Yard, BA1 1BX
Tel: 01225 447147, www.leparisien.co.uk

Even if the upmarket, snooty-ish boutiques, galleries and – increasingly – food franchises in and around the Milsom Place shopping complex ain't your thang, the lovely Le Parisien is a classless, all-things-to-all people experience: a laidback but lively brasserie featuring French bistro-style décor at entry level and sofas for lounging around on upstairs. But really, it's all about the courtyard: a spacious, characterful, cobbled affair, with generous umbrella coverage and heaters making it an all-weather outdoors hotspot. Breakfasts go large here (whether continental or full English), and heartier lunchtime offerings include croques, steak frites, chunky Medi-themed soups and stews and extremely well-filled baguettes and wraps. The proper patisserie selection, meanwhile, is highly recommended. *T

PARTY ON!

LAS IGUANAS

Seven Dials

- Fiesta in fine, Latin American-themed style aided by a celebratory combination of cocktails and tapas

AQUA

Walcot Street

- Big parties are welcome at this Italian-themed, dolce vita experience

BOOJON TANDOORI

Charles Street

- Table for 30? No problem! Just make sure you give the lovely staff advance notice (and remember to stock up on your BYO bar supplies en route)

THE CORK

Westgate Buildings

- Staff here go the extra mile to accommodate party people of all persuasions

GREEN PARK BRASSERIE

Green Park Station

- Super-flexible attitude to big parties, from the grand (weddings, etc) to smaller, more informal affairs

LIME LOUNGE

11 Margarets Buildings, BA1 2LP
Tel: 01225 421251,
www.limeloungebath.co.uk

Chic in an unforced, non-snooty way, this fully licensed café/bistro offering al fresco tables on one of Bath's prettiest traffic-free lanes serves up all-day delights (including breakfasts) that gently give way to a lively, modern-Brit bistro menu as the sun sets.

MANGIA BENE

5-6 St James Street, BA1 2TW
Tel: 01225 336106

Teeny, tiny, almost doll's house-proportion deli with a small café attached, serving classy breakfasts, lunches and teatime treats best enjoyed at a pavement table overlooking a very pretty square. *T

METROPOLITAN CAFÉ

15 New Bond Street, BA1 1BA
Tel: 01225 482680
www.bloomsburystore.com

This small but unclaustrophobic little café above Bloomsbury gift shop doesn't make a big song and dance about being a wholly vegetarian, largely organic affair; instead, it just quietly gets on with the job in hand, rustling up all-day breakfasts, ciabatta, sarnies, tarts, salads, soups, cake, etc, all from locally sourced, totally meat-free ingredients.

MISSION BURRITO

4 New Street, Kingsmead Square BA1 2AF
Tel: 01225 442599,
www.missionburritos.co.uk

Boisterous, freshly prepared burritos alongside a range of classic Tex-Mex inspired fascinators. If you don't fancy taking your fajita for a fandango, there's limited seating available within a lively canteen environment. *T

MOLES MUSIC CAFÉ

14 George Street, BA1 2EN
Tel: 01225 404405, www.moles.co.uk

Part of the Moles mini-complex, specialising in thoughtfully eclectic, sociable sharing platters, boisterous 'Sunday Session' roasts and all manner of tantalising nibbly stuff alongside drinks, cakes, etc.

PATISSERIE VALERIE

20 High Street, BA1 5AJ
Tel: 01225 444826
www.patisserie-valerie.co.uk

A bustling café to the rear of a cake counter flaunting the most exquisite range of gorgeous gateaux, posh tarts, etc that it's possible to imagine being rustled up in a franchise-operation kitchen. Free wi-fi but barely enough space to open your laptop.

PRESTO

7 Abbey Churchyard, BA1 1LY
Tel: 01225 338803, www.pastypresto.com

Okay, it's another chain. But pavement tables offer a ringside seat when there's live street entertainment going on in front of the Pump Room, and the freshly baked pasties are seriously good. Beware, however, of the franchise curse – sorry, health and safety rules – that translates as not-very-hot coffee. *T

PUMP ROOM

Abbey Churchyard, BA1 1LZ, Tel: 01225 477782, www.romanbaths.co.uk

Set in the elegant environs of the Roman Baths complex, staff in starched uniforms, live classical music and a butler dispensing complimentary glasses of spa water (which, by the way, tastes like stagnant pond water – you have been warned) turn this neo-classical salon into one of Bath's most civilised, traditional afternoon tea experiences… except when those naughty naked jugglers are putting on a free, live show directly in front of the windows (see above).

REGENCY TEA ROOMS

40 Gay Street, Queen Square, BA1 2NT
Tel: 01225 443000, www.janeausten.co.uk

Yet more Regency-themed afternoon delights (see also the Bath Bun Tea Shoppe and the Pump Room), this one is set above a shrine – sorry, visitor centre – entirely dedicated to Bath's legendary one-time writer in residence, Jane Austen. Those who aren't of the po-faced persuasion are asked to leave their pride and prejudices with the top-hatted doorman.

ROMAN BATHS CAFÉ

11 Abbey Churchyard, BA1 1LY

At the time of writing, there's a major redevelopment refurbishing the recently vacated, split-level building at the heart of Abbey Churchyard – and it's about time too, as the café that used to live here was about as shabby and listless as a tourist trap caff-gaff can get. The new venture promises to be a suitably elegant addition to the Roman Baths complex, featuring a casual ground floor café and a more formal restaurant on the first floor, both of which will offer stunning views.

ROSCOFF DELI

18 Northumberland Place, BA1 5AR
Tel: 01225 469590, www.roscoff.co.uk

Sicily meets the West Country at this funky, flair-packed deli-caff. *T

ROYAL PAVILION CAFÉ

Royal Victoria Park, BA1 2NR
Tel: 01225 448860

In a quietly eccentric manner, Swiss mountain chalet meets traditional British tearoom at this charming park life hotspot offering swoonsome views across the city from the tiny balcony and tables under the trees out front. Hot tip: keep a close eye on those fearless squirrels – they stop at nothing to grab a nibble on your sausage roll. *T

SALLY LUNN'S

4 North Parade Passage, BA1 1NX
Tel: 01225 461634, www.sallylunns.co.uk

Only bother with this one if you can cope with long queues of tourists and find the ensuing disappointment when you're finally seated at a rickety table in claustrophobic surroundings easy to digest. Given the many fresh, lively alternatives we have highlighted elsewhere in this section, Sally's buns are well past their sell-by date.

SAME, SAME BUT DIFFERENT

7a Princes Buildings, Bartlett Street, BA1 2ED, Tel: 01225 466856

Fully licensed café-bar/bistro/tapas haven hybrid on a picturesque, traffic-free lane, open until midnight Thursday to Saturday.

SAM'S KITCHEN

61 Walcot Street, BA1 5BN
Tel: 01225 481159
www.samskitchendeli.co.uk

Casually stylish café and deli specialising in seasonal, locally sourced, imaginative grub, from light bites to sturdier treats served up in artfully eclectic surroundings. **T*

SECRET GARDEN CAFÉ AT PRIOR PARK GARDEN CENTRE

Prior Park Road, BA2 4NF
Tel: 01225 427175
www.priorparkgardencentre.co.uk

Bright and breezy café with an al fresco patio at the heart of a lively garden centre, where most of the ingredients that make up the daily-changing, homemade fare on the menu are sourced from the local producers who supply the garden centre's farm shop. Lovely.

BATH INSTITUTIONS

THE HOLE IN THE WALL

George Street

• Established in 1952

BEAUJOLAIS BISTRO AND BAR

Chapel Row

• Established in 1972

RAJPOOT

Argyle Street

• Established in 1980

WOODS

Alfred Street

• Established circa 1982

FIREHOUSE ROTISSERIE

John Street

• Turns sweet 16 in 2012

TAMBO PERUVIAN KITCHEN

1 Grove Street, BA2 6PJ
www.tamboperuviankitchen.co.uk

An authentic taste of Peru has come to Bath, courtesy of Peruvian-themed sandwiches (yes, really) and a small but perfectly formed range of street food (empanada, papa rellena, etc). The chilli hot chocolate, meanwhile, delivers more kick than a donkey with sunstroke, but be warned: the fun ends at 3pm every day.

TEAHOUSE EMPORIUM

22a New Bond Street, BA1 1BA
Tel: 01225 334402
www.teahouseemporium.co.uk

Tranquil teahouse in an atmospheric 18th-century cellar below a shop dedicated to all things tea.

TEA TIME

12 Dorchester Street, BA1 1SS
Tel: 01225 444990

Charming, independent café offering welcome respite to SouthGate centre shoppers and travellers using Bath Spa Railway Station (just across the road).

TIME OUT

Guildhall Market, BA2 4AW

American milk bar-themed café-diner at the heart of the Guildhall market.

WILD CAFÉ

10a Queen Street, BA1 1HE
Tel: 01225 448673, www.wildcafé.co.uk

There are so many good things to be said about this cheerful little café that it's difficult to know where to start. So take the basic information as a guideline (that'll be locally sourced, seasonal, sustainable produce used to rustle up brilliant breakfasts, hearty lunches and downhome tea-time treats, mostly cooked before your eyes in an open kitchen) and form your own opinion. **T*

YMCA

International House, Broad Street Place, BA1 5LH, Tel: 01225 325900
www.bathymca.co.uk

Is this one of Bath's best kept secrets? Not if you're one of the thousands of backpackers who make the YMCA their holiday home every year. But not a lot of people know that the efficient little canteen here is open to non-hostel dwellers too; make like a village person and find homecooked favourites at exceedingly wallet-friendly prices tucked away behind a courtyard reached via a quaint little alleyway or ancient stone steps.

Grab'n'go

Many of the restaurants and cafés listed here offer grub-to-go options (hence our handy, helpful **T* signage). But there are some lovely ventures that cater specifically to hoofers only; we hereby present you with a speedy run-down of the places we believe provide the best takeaway options in the Heritage City.

Daytime Delights

BUTTER PAT

18 Upper Borough Walls, BA1 1RJ
Tel: 01225 310184
Freshly made sandwiches, baguettes etc, with a side order of the possibility of meeting the building's resident ghost. Feeds hundreds of local workers every day.

CORNISH BAKEHOUSE

11a The Corridor, BA1 5AP
Tel: 01225 426635
1 Lower Borough Walls, BA1 1QR
Tel: 01225 780432
www.cornishbakehouse.com
Cornish pasty central – at two locations.

DEVON SAVOURIES

19 Lower Borough Walls, BA1 1QU
Tel: 01225 442099
Ditto the comment above, but from Devon instead (fight it out among yourself as to which you prefer).

HIPPIE SHAKE

20 Moorlands Road, BA2 3PW
Tel: 01225 466200
www.hippieshake.co.uk
For goodness sake, why wouldn't you want to shake it all about at this quirky, stylish sanctuary of all-things-shake-related? The

Bath Farmers' Market

In contemporary foodie circles, regional Farmers' Markets hold near-legendary status. But the original – and, many would argue, still one of the best – of the bunch celebrated its sixteenth birthday in 2012… and what an extraordinary teenager Bath Farmers' Market has turned out to be.

Regular stallholders (we refuse to single any of them out for particular attention; that'd be akin to asking a mother to choose her favourite child) at the market's Green Park Station HQ estimate that up to 2,000 people leap out of bed to be first on the forecourt every Saturday morning, where they'll browse, taste and, of course, shop from a splendid array of around 30-40 regular traders and occasional guests, all from within a 40-mile radius of Bath. Vegetables, meat, fish and bread; cheese, paté, wine, eggs; plants, flowers, herbs and more constitute an ever-evolving selection of largely organic, free-range seasonal produce traded in a buzzing, friendly atmosphere far removed from the bland, vacuum-packed experience offered by the big-name supermarket nearby. And while the ruthless, pile-it-high, sell-it-cheap loss-leading 'bargains' offered by such supermarkets continue to influence how many people tend to shop today, awareness of the value – in both moral and financial terms – of buying local produce from local traders continues to intensify.

Bath Farmers' Market benefits both the local community and the wider environment by promoting and supporting small, independent, local businesses, producers and artisans who use far less energy- and waste-intensive production, transportation and packaging methods than the bland, branded, big business alternatives – and therefore aren't obliged to pass the surcharge for such overheads on to their customers. Shopping here also offers a simply lovely experience, too; you're unlikely to glean such a friendly, informative, advice and inspiration-laden exchange in aisle 34 of your nearest faceless corporate food retail behemoth. Tasty? We think so. See you there!

Bath Farmers' Market: Green Park Station, Bath BA1 1JB. Every Saturday, 8.30-1.30pm; www.bathfarmersmarket.co.uk

attention-grabbing array includes lots of dairy-free, low-fat and diabetic-friendly options alongside all kinds of other sweet treats and drinkable delights. Try the 'Mega Bad Boy', an 80-ounce shake! Bucket provided, charmingly.

INTERMEZZO EXPRESS

32 Barton Street, BA1 1HH
Tel: 01225 466583
Gurt big fat baguettes, sarnies, etc, are generously over-stuffed to order from the deli counter.

LES MUNCHIES

Kingsmead Square, BA1 2AF
Tel: 01225 480779
Slightly annoying name; far-from-annoying array of ace goodies-to-go.

MONTGOMERY'S

10a Queen Street, BA1 1HE
Tel: 01225 338803
Over 40 sandwich fillings available at any one time, resulting in the possibility of thousands of combinations.

PICNIC IN THE PARK

16 Lark Place, BA1 3BA
Tel: 01225 461620
Why pack your own park picnic when somebody else has already done it for you?

SHAKEAWAY

3 Beau Street, Bath BA1 1QY
Tel: 01225 466200, www.shakeaway.co.uk
Almost a decade of assaulting teeth enamel and alarming overly-fussy, diet-nazi parents has not swayed Shakeaway from its noble goal. Put simply, they mash up your favourite sweets and add them to a milkshake. The result is proof that the simple ideas are usually the best, as anyone who's ever slurped their way happily through a Reese's Buttercup or Curly Wurly milkshake will confirm.

SUBWAY

11 Westgate Street, BA1 1EQ
Tel: 01225 789958, www.subway.co.uk
Young people who insist on having their takeaways fully endorsed by a massive, annoying advertising campaign love it.

TASTY 1

14a Manvers Street, BA1 1JH
Tel: 01225 444288
Catching the train? We suggest you forgo the dubious 'pleasures' of the on-board catering service and stock up at this conveniently located haven of fresh loveliness (just across the road from the Railway Station) before you start your journey.

THYME

27 Westgate Street, BA1 1EP
Tel: 01225 780078, www.thymefood.co.uk
If you don't agree that Thyme is the best takeaway sandwich/soup/salad etc pitstop in town, we want to know why.

Sunset... and beyond

AL FALAFEL

3 Monmouth Street, BA1 2AJ
Tel: 01225 311133
It may not serve up the best kebabs in town (that particular commendation goes to Marmaris [see Restaurant listing]), but when the post-revel munchies strike, there are far worse late-night options to stagger into.

BILLY BURGER

St Saviours Road, Larkhall, BA1 6RT
Tel: 01225 313393
www.eatmyburgers.co.uk
Burger paradise, alongside a range of hot dogs, jackets, fries, potato skins, hash browns, garlic bread, etc, to further confound your fast food urges. Free local delivery for £10+ orders.

CHILLIES

2 Lambridge Buildings, Larkhall, BA1 6RS
Tel: 01225 443030
www.chilliesbath.co.uk
Top-notch traditional and contemporary Indian grub. Free delivery service and online ordering service.

FISH & CHIPS

Upper Borough Walls, BA1 1RJ
Tel: 01225 330195
The name says it all, really. Well it would, if it also included sausages, pies, mushies, canned drinks, etc – but then again, that'd be a bit clunky, wouldn't it?

FORTUNE COOKIE

378 Wellsway, BA2 5RN
Tel: 01225 832223
www.fortune-cookie.uk.com
Worthy of a special mention for the Japanese udon noodle dishes and several lesser-spotted far-flung specialities (curry trigon samosa, anyone?) in amongst a classy, classless selection of classic Chinese food. Home delivery 6-10pm daily (£1.50 delivery charge within a three-mile radius)

GOLDEN PLAICE

13a Cleveland Place West, BA1 5DG
Tel: 01225 338288
Thoroughly decent, old-school chippie.

MOGHUL

140 Walcot Street, BA1 5BL
Tel: 01225 464956
Long-established, traditional Indian takeaway. The Chicken Jalfrezi is legendarily spicy.

MR D'S

8 St Georges Place, Upper Bristol Rd, BA1 3AA, Tel: 01225 425204
Van at night on Milsom St/Orange Grove
The late-night fast-food fanatics who patronise Mr D's mobile van in search of cheesy chips would call it a Bath institution. Ah well, needs must when many pints have been slurped.

PEKING CHEF

84 St Kilda's Road, Oldfield Park, BA2 3QJ
Tel: 01225 425685
Quality Chinese and Thai cuisine from an absolutely massive menu, available to take away or order for delivery between 5-11pm (min order for delivery £6, delivery charge £1 within two-mile radius, £2 thereafter).

PIZZA FRESCA

1 Wellsway, Bear Flat, BA2 4QL
Tel: 01225 429776
Fresca pizzas.

RUPOSHI

3 Sussex Place, BA2 4LA
Tel: 01225 337294
Small, friendly Indian takeaway with a long-established reputation for high quality fare.

SCHWARTZ BROTHERS

4 Sawclose, BA1 1EY
Tel: 01225 461726

102 Walcot Street, BA1 5BG
Tel: 01225 463613
If one was to issue a guide to food in Bath without mentioning Schwartz Bros' freshly flame-grilled burgers (best topped with their legendarily good garlic mayo and accompanied by a stack of fries), one would doubtless be lynched by hordes of Bathonians who grew up on them, and continue to revisit their youth today (if, that is, the queues of spring chickens creating their own happy memories don't prove too rowdy to endure).

SEAFOODS

38 Kingsmead Square, BA1 2AA
Tel: 01225 465190
www.fishandchipsbath.co.uk
This long-established, award-winning café and

LITTLE PEOPLE

THE BEAR

Wellsway

- A mini vintage kitchen, wooden toys, colouring books and their own menu keeps little ones well away from the tantrum zone.

THE EGG CAFÉ

St John's Place

- If there's a more child-friendly family hangout located in Bath, we've yet to come across it

KOMEDIA

Westgate Street

- High chairs, baby-changing facilities, a microwave for heating baby food, a spacious buggy park and stay-and-play/ childcare services courtesy of Mulberry Kidz – waaaaargh!

GIRAFFE

Dorchester Street

- Kids' menus clearly created with picky eaters/fussy teenagers in mind

YO! SUSHI

Milsom Place

- There's no stress about keeping attention levels up at this colourful, cartoon-ish healthy fast food franchise takeaway (with pavement seating, and gloomy room downstairs) has earned a similar status to Schwartz Bros (see above): you simply haven't tasted Bath until you've scoffed a Seafoods fish supper – a prime catch indeed.

Specialist food shops

If you've got the time and the inclination, the domestic angels responsible for keeping the family larder buoyant can conduct a thoroughly practical, down-to-earth food shopping trip around Bath without stepping into a single supermarket. But it's also possible to take a very upmarket voyage of prandial discovery just for fun; even browsers with no intention of splashing the cash are welcome to a free tasting session in many of the city's loveliest gourmet emporiums – just don't tell them we sent you in the direction of a free lunch.

BARTLETT & SONS

10-11 Green Street, BA1 2JZ
Tel: 01225 466731
www.bartlettandsons.co.uk
This traditional family butcher probably hasn't changed that much since it was established in 1931, except for the fact that these days the locally-sourced produce clearly states its chemical/additive-free status. Sausages and burgers are made in-house, and there's a good selection of cooked meats, cheeses, pastries, pickles and – occasionally – cakes, too. It's also home to Bath's best value sandwiches…

BATH BAKERY

3 Chelsea Road, BA1 3DU Tel: 01225 421702 / 37 Moorland Road, BA2 3PN Tel 01225 481477, www.bathbakery.co.uk
A real bakery, selling real bread, pasties, pies, sausage rolls, croissants and cakes. The Moorland Road branch has a café too. **T*

BATH DELI

31 Bathwick Street, BA2 6NZ
Tel: 01225 316265, www.bathdeli.co.uk
Do 'a Nigella' and get everything you need for a posh buffet (local cheeses, artisan bread, Wiltshire ham, charcuterie, olives, salads, patés etc) here, at non-scary prices. Want to do a full-on Delia and create dinner without lifting a finger (or opening a packet)? The freshly prepared dishes-to-go constitute the most upmarket ready meals in town (despite what Waitrose would have you believe). **T*

BATH HUMBUG

Guildhall Market, BA2 4AW
Sweet little traditional sweetshop.

BERTINET BAKERY

6 New Bond Street Place, BA1 1BH web: www.bertinet.com
Explore the full range of legendary baker Richard Bertinet's carb-laden loveliness, including his award-winning sourdough and a signature selection (rustic epis, fougasse, baguettes, focaccia, etc) alongside all manner of tarts, cakes and pastries and viennoiserie. Don't want to take it away? Stay put at the lovely café upstairs.

BEST OF BRITISH

12 Broad Street, BA1 5LJ
Tel: 01225 448055
www.bestofbritishdeli.co.uk
Nope, not the Bath headquarters of the latest dodgy political party, but a sweet little mini-cornucopia of organic British produce with a small café and takeaway/delivery opportunities too. **T*

CHANDOS DELI

St George Street, BA1 2EH
Tel: 01225 314418
Egg Cafe, St Johns Place, BA1 1ET
Tel: 01225 823408, www.chandosdeli.com
This award-winning deli (with small café at rear) has been bringing classy foodie inspirations (including superb antipasti and fab cheeses) from around the world to Bathonians for many a year. Also responsible for the café at the Egg Theatre. **T*

CULPEPERS

28 Milsom Street, BA1 1DG
Tel: 01225 425875, www.culpeper.co.uk
There may be lavender pillows, thyme bubble bath and non-edible aromatherapy products in the window, but venture toward the back of the shop and discover a wide range of herbs, spices, stock/soup bases etc, alongside interesting relishes, pickles, honey, homemade jams and ready-blended Thai/Indian/Italian herb/spice combinations.

DA VINCI ITALIAN DELI

33 Wellsway, Bear Flat, BA2 4RR
Tel: 01225 471850, www.davincideli.co.uk

Crack the gourmet version of the Da Vinci code in this authentic little corner of Naples overseen by charismatic godfather of Italian grub Vincenzo Bartolo and his lovely missus Joanne. What this pair doesn't know about the Italian cheese, coffee, ham, wine, antipasti, fresh pasta, bread, oils and olives that line the shelves or languish on the deli counter here isn't worth knowing – oh, and they also rustle up excellent coffee/splendiferous sarnies to take away or enjoy in the tiny little garden or on one of two pavement tables. *T

FIELDTOFEAST

Tel: 07971 719279, www.fieldtofeast.co.uk

Based an olive stone's throw away from the Heritage City's Farmers' Market, this utterly splendid service specialises in bringing together all manner of upper-crust, top-notch scrumptiousness sourced from producers and artisans in the South West region, with which they fill a selection of glorious hampers and picnic baskets and/or create sumptuous spreads for dinner parties and event catering; lovely stuff!

FINE CHEESE CO.

29-31 Walcot Street, BA1 5BN
Tel: 01225 448748, www.finecheese.co.uk

The epicentre of a venture dedicated to British and European cheeses from the classics to the adventurous/obscure in a style as far removed from the uniformity of the supermarket cheese counters as you can get. Proprietor Ann-Marie (the "Queen of Cheese") Dyas seeks out small artisan producers and suppliers to line her (refrigerated) shelves with the real McCoy of dairy-related hard (and soft) stuff alongside an Aladdin's Cave of all kinds of everything else, including gourmet grocery products from olive oil and homemade chutney to fine wine, chocolate, and sweet and savoury delights. Gives great gift; lovely café attached. *T

GOODIES

2a St Saviours Road, Larkhall, BA1 6RJ
Tel: 01225 336033, www.goodiesdeli.co.uk

English and continental deli with in-store French bakery. Freshly baked bread available throughout the day alongside specialist beers, organic wines and an inspired selection of cheeses, olives, baguettes, pastries, etc. *T

GUILDHALL DELICATESSEN

8a Guildhall Market, BA2 4AW
Tel: 01225 427195

Wide range of continental and local meats, homemade cakes, olives, jams and chutneys, cheeses and vegetarian, Indian and Italian specialities, with takeaway options. *T

LONDON ROAD STORES

3 Cleveland Place East, London Road, BA1 5DJ, Tel: 01225 336307

Beyond the crates of soap powder, tins of beans and cheap lager deals, this longstanding local convenience store flaunts an excellent source of lesser-spotted (in Bath, anyway) West Indian cooking supplies, from spices and sauces (including the infamous West Indian hot pepper range) to fresh produce such as yams, mangoes, plantains, ackee and coriander. In keeping with such an eclectic theme, freshly baked bhajis, pakoras and Greek pastries often appear on the counter.

MANGIA BENE

5-6 St James Street, BA1 2TW
Tel: 01225 336106

Dinky, chic little deli specialising in a small but perfectly formed, enticing range of largely Mediterannean-sourced cheeses, smoked and cured meats, wine and champagne, handmade chocolates, tempting sweet stuff, etc. Small café attached. *T

MINERVA CHOCOLATES/BATH CHOCOLATE MUSEUM

15 Abbey Church Yard, BA1 1NA
Tel: 01225 464999
www.bathchocolatemuseum.com

If this chocoholic Mecca didn't insist on displaying really gross chocolate boobs (complete with the kind of misshapen nipples that make you wonder if the maker has ever encountered real breasts in his life) in the window, we'd have nothing but praise for this venture. As it is, a massive range of indulgent, flamboyant confectionery (including handcrafted chocolates based on characters and fables from Bath's past, hence the 'museum' in the title) go some way to making up for the head honcho's Benny Hill-style bad taste, and the café serves up what's probably the best hot chocolate in Bath. Also conducts live chocolate-making demos/workshops (women beware: polo necks advisable).

MR SIMMS OLD SWEET SHOPPE

26 Westgate Street, Bath BA1 1EP

Candy cornucopia!

NIBBLES

Stall 53, Guildhall Market, BA1 4AW
Tel: 01225 460213

A smaller (and, dare we say it, more affordable?) version of Bath's other dedicated cheese shops, selling quality cheeses from around the UK and further afield alongside British and continental bacon and hams.

PAXTON & WHITFIELD

1 John Street, BA1 2JL
Tel: 01225 466403
www.cheesemongers.co.uk

Established in 1797 and holders of no less than three Royal Warrants, P&W are master purveyors of traditional English and continental cheeses, luxury olive oils, pickles and preserves, alongside all manner of cheese-related equipment; for such an eminently upmarket experience, one should expect to pay premium prices.

POLISH DELICATESSEN

James Street West, BA1 2BX

Solid range of traditional Polish foodstuffs, including some fascinating sweet treats and a fine line in smoked sausage.

PRIOR PARK GARDEN CENTRE FARM SHOP

Prior Park Road, BA2 4NF
Tel: 01225 427175
www.priorparkgardencentre.co.uk

Hooray, a farm shop that negates the need for trekking all the way to an actual farm! Loads and loads and loads (honestly, we can't stress just how much!) of locally sourced produce from various farmers, dairies, bakers, kitchens, breweries and imaginative artisans mostly from within around a 12-mile radius of Bath. Visit towards closing time to benefit from bargain prices for fresh produce.

RAISIN FINE WINES

132a Walcot Street, Bath BA1 5BG Tel: 01225 422577 www.raisinwine.co.uk

The rather elegant brainchild of former Harvey Nichols Sommelier Colin Bell (who, by the way, fought off competition from El Bulli, the Fat Duck and Fifteen Sommeliers to win the title of 'Sommelier of the Year') offers a scrumptious, thoughtful selection of fine wines alongside tasting sessions, corporate services, party planning (with free glass hire), case discounts and all manner of wine-related, slurpable events. Tastings notes come as standard with every tipple on offer, which come with price tags designed to appeal to all wallets. Hoorah!

REAL ITALIAN ICE CREAM COMPANY

17 York Street, BA1 1NG
Tel: 01225 330121

Serves up exactly what the name suggests. **T*

REAL MEAT CO.

7 Hayes Place, BA2 4QW
Tel: 01225 335139, www.realmeat.co.uk

Established over 21 years ago and still thriving today, thanks to contemporary market forces that dictate that any meat on our modern-day menus has been reared according to a strictly monitored welfare code and lacks hormones, growth promoters, pre-emptive medication and additives. Rather bizarrely, perhaps, an excellent vegetarian larder range dominates one side of the shop, while ready meals and pies (all made in-house), dairy produce (and alternatives), free-range eggs, chocolate, breakfast cereals, puddings, wholefoods and preserves complete the Real experience.

SAUSAGE SHOP

7 Green Street, BA1 2JY
Tel: 01225 318300
www.sausage-shop.co.uk

Banger central, from the award-winning Aldridge sausage to venison by way of scrumpy, duck, chorizo and global exotics all too numerous to list here, alongside vegetarian, vegan and gluten-free varieties, award-winning black pudding, olives, mustards, cured continental meats and locally famous pork pies. Takeaway hot sausages of the day (served on a massive baguette or with a mountain of proper mash) constitute a splendidly sturdy lunch-on-the-trot. **T*

SEASONS WHOLEFOOD

10 George Street, BA1 2EH
Tel: 01225 469730

Wholefood haven serviced by knowledgeable, helpful staff and offering a variety of veggie/vegan larder/fridge/frozen essentials alongside dietary supplements and homeopathic remedies. Takeaway counter serves frozen yogurts in summer, homemade soups in winter, plus sandwiches, salads, etc. *T

TEAHOUSE EMPORIUM

22a New Bond Street, BA1 1BA
Tel: 01225 334402
www.teahouseemporium.co.uk
All manner of teas, tisanes and infusions from the traditional to obscure varietals and loads of tea-themed paraphernalia to accompany it.

THAI BALCONY MINI MART

40 Monmouth Street, BA1 2AN
Tel: 01225 337213
If you can't get a table at the popular Thai Balcony restaurant, do it yourself at home instead (with, might we suggest, a little bit of help from Rick Stein's *Far Eastern Odyssey* recipes and advice from the charming, informative staff). This is the Bath epicentre of everything Thai, from store cupboard ingredients (noodles, dipping sauces, exotic fruit in cans, jars, soup bases) to frozen dim sum/fish, fresh herbs and spices, massive, crunch-busting sacks of rice and freshly cooked Thai ready meals to take home. Oh, and handbags. And jewellery.

THOUGHTFUL BREAD CO.

Green Park Station Market
Tel: 01761 239074
www.thethoughtfulbreadcompany.com
@thoughtfulbread
This fun, funky, ethically minded, environmentally friendly bakery supplies many of Bath's best restaurants, cafes and delis. If you've got the Twitter bug, the bakers are well worth following for product updates and behind-the-scenes high jinks and gossip.

Open Tuesday to Saturday.

VOM FASS

Shires Yard, BA1 1DN
Tel: 01225 447660, www.vomfass.net
Exquisite liquids (oils of the culinary/non-edible essential variety, vinegars, wines, liqueurs and spirits) available straight from the cask. They tend to be more gift-orientated than fit for practical purpose at home.

WHOLE BAGEL

4 Upper Borough Walls, BA1 1RG
Tel: 01225 333259,
www.thewholebagel.co.uk
More of a takeaway than an actual shop, but one of the few places in Bath where you can buy freshly baked, cholesterol-, preservative-, GM- and additive-free bagels from a range that includes multi-seed, jalapeno, olive and sun-dried tomato or good old plain. Can't be bothered filling your own at home? Make free with the deli display of fillings, including smoked salmon and cream cheese, pastrami, 'Nutty Swiss' and breakfast options. *T

A UNIQUE TASTE OF BATH

THERE ARE SOME FOODIE DELIGHTS THAT YOU CAN ONLY FIND IN BATH...

CUTE BUNS AND CHEESEBOARD BISCUITS

Okay, let's get something straight: the Bath Bun and the Sally Lunn bun are not – we repeat, not – one and the same thing. The Sally who gave the Lunn its name was a Huguenot refugee – but she wasn't actually called Sally. Instead of bothering to find out her real name, the bakery who originally ~~exploited~~ kindly gave sanctuary to this resourceful French teenager named her after the way she described the shape of the crescent-shaped bun that she originally created, referring to is as a 'sol et lune'. And so it came to pass that the (in)famous bun was born: a big, bland, spongy thing that you can dress up or dress down according to the time of day: when the sun goes down on jam 'n' cream afternoons, the Sally Lunn puts its savoury outfit on and returns to the table pretending to be a South West version of the Yorkshire pudding.

Unlike these neutral, flavourless doughballs, the Bath Bun is unashamedly sweet and rich, and topped with crunchy sugar crystals. Early references to the Bath Bun date back to the late 18th century, and some food historians believe they were invented by Dr William Oliver, the 17th century physician and philanthropist who invented the Bath Oliver (the tasty disc that quietly adorns many an excellent cheese board today). It's most likely, however, that the Bath Bun was invented by another wealthy philanthropist (what is it with Bath and rich philanthropists?) Ralph Allen, who instructed his cook to create a cheap but filling treat for the families of workers employed on the Pump Rooms building site.

BATH CHAPS

Referred to by those in the know simply as 'chaps', these visceral treats are actually fatty little morsels of pig's cheek, salt cured or pickled in brine before being smoked, boiled, and rolled in seasoned breadcrumbs; seek 'em out at either the weekend Farmers' Market at Green Park Station, the Guildhall Market in the city centre or on menus at local gastropubs throughout the region.

THE OTHER WYFE OF BATH

If you're hoping for Chaucer's lusty, post-feminist icon to come bouncing along to your table at the grand finale of a supper in many of Bath's best restaurants, you'll be sorely disappointed when your order arrives. Cheese lovers, however, won't feel short changed at all, as the Wyfe of Bath that many menus refer to is an organic, handmade, semi-hard cheese, not dissimilar to Gouda but with a stronger taste and chewier texture. This distinctive cheese (and its equally popular relatives Bath Soft, Kelston Park and Bath Blue) is made by artisan cheese maker Graham Padfield, a third-generation dairy farmer based in Kelston, just a mile or so up the road from Bath city centre. All Graham's award-winning cheeses are handmade from organic milk to the farm's own recipes, but we declare Graham's Wyfe – described by the man himself as "succulent and bouncy, redolent of buttercups and water meadows" – to be the nicest one in his collection.

Bath Soft Cheese: www.parkfarm.co.uk

BATH SPA WATER: PUMPING POMP AND CEREMONY

The neo-classical salon that dominates the street level entrance to the Roman Baths complex offers the ultimate English High Tea experience, served to you by unobtrusively efficient staff. But one team member in particular is bound to catch your eye. Bedecked in full Georgian footman regalia (including black knickerbockers, white stockings and silver buckled slippers), the Pump Room's Head Pumper is responsible for the auspicious task of drawing the warm, mineral-laden water on which the Heritage City was built directly from the

spa pump itself and offering all-comers a complimentary sample in a disposable plastic beaker (which is perhaps the point at which the pomp aspect of this particular ceremony falls apart a bit). Although undeniably rich in trace minerals, the water's restorative or healing properties have yet to be formally sanctioned by a reliable scientific source. But then again, nobody has declared it to have any detrimental properties, either – except in a sartorial sense. With its mildly sulphurous odour, cloudy hue and tepid dishwater taste, this ain't exactly Perrier. It does, however, offer you a true taste of history… served to you in a disposable plastic beaker by a man in tights.
The Pump Rooms
www.romanbaths.co.uk

GLORIOUS GRAPES

The four-acre Mumfords Vineyard (just a couple of miles to the east of the city) is home to a thriving family of over 5,500 vines that yield four types of grape, including Madeleine Angevine (the English strain of an old French white grape), Kerner (a variety of the classic German Riesling) and Triomphe, an Alsace grape that produces excellent red wine. Mumfords proprietors Tony and Margaret Cox use the grapes to produce three white, one rosé and one red variety, each of which have enjoyed a spotlight medal moment in various regional and national competitions.
Mumfords Vineyard
www.mumfordsvineyard.co.uk

SCRUMPTIOUS CIDER

This is prime cider-producing territory, and we're only sad that it's difficult to point you in the direction of an authentic old cider house to sample them in within the city walls. Time has done for them all, with the legendary Beehive the last to leave us. You'll find great local cider at many a pub in town though – The Garrick's Head usually stocks a couple, the Bell will find you some local varieties and The Raven can be relied upon to carry at least one on pump.

But if cider does catch your fancy in any way then we have two things to recommend. One is a trip to Dick Willows on the Box Road, a couple of miles out of town. Here craft cider is given the centre stage it deserves, from the staggering (often literally) array of local craft ciders to be sampled and purchased in the shop, to the excellent ciders they produce from scratch here. We can heartily recommend the tour of the factory in the company of the eponymous Dick.
Dick Willows, Box Road, Bathford BA1 7LR, Tel: 01225 859780, www.dickwillows.com:

Our second recommendation is that we relieve you of a few more coppers and induce you to buy our very own *Naked Guide to Cider*. It's every bit as good as this book, and offers a fascinating insight into the growing West Country phenomenon of craft cider. You'd – frankly – be mad not to buy a copy.
The Naked Guide to Cider is available from www.tangentbooks.co.uk or any good bookshop or even Amazon if you must but we hardly see any money from those grabbing beggars.

BACK TO SCHOOL

Forget all notions of the old 'domestic science' classes; these days, contemporary cookery classes are hip places to hang out. In the '60s, snooty, complicated Cordon Bleu courses were the dish of the day for any self-respecting debutante or wannabe domestic goddess; four decades on, and a whole host of Bath chefs are ready and waiting to share their skills in a totally snoot-free environment.

For those who prefer face-free food, Rachel Demuth (hob goddess at the helm of the long-established veggie/vegan haven Demuths) regularly shares her skills with eager groups of followers though instructive, interactive workshops that focus on unpretentious and uncomplicated veggie food at her dedicated Vegetarian Cookery School, which also acts as a host to a glamorous roll call of guest foodies who collaborate with Rachel to present all manner of masterclasses.
Demuth's Vegetarian Cookery School
www.vegetariancookeryschool.com

Compared to Rachel's two decade-plus relationship with the Heritage City, delectable doughboy Richard Bertinet may be a relative newcomer to the scene. But nevertheless his purpose-built cookery

school (established in 2005) offers courses that are the stuff of foodie legend, thanks in no small part to *Gourmet* magazine rating it as "one of the best cookery schools in the world". Cooks of all abilities can learn all they knead to know (sorry) from the master baker himself, or choose from courses that embrace such delights as the joys of classic bistro cookery, the art of Mediterranean-themed menus and how to create perfect pasta on a rich and varied prospectus
The Bertinet Kitchen
www.thebertinetkitchen.com

If you ignore the crude, distasteful aberrations that sometimes dominate the window display at the otherwise upmarket chocoholic haven Minerva Chocolates/the Bath Chocolate Museum (chocolate boobs? A certain 'master chocolatier' clearly needs to make himself a real girlfriend), you're in for a real treat. Minerva's Chocolate Initiation Workshops last for around two hours and are suitable for small groups of people aged 8+; truffles, ganache, proper drinking chocolate, chocolate logs – it's all going on!
Minerva Chocolates
www.bathchocolatemuseum.com

But if you prefer to boycott the boobies altogether, Nikki Cameron – Bath's award-winning cupcake queen (and driving force behind those yummy Country Cupcakes) – knows all there is to know about buttercream, icing sugar and all manner of sparkly things; spend a morning in her charming company before taking your personalised creations home in an equally pretty gift-wrapped box.
Country Cupcakes
www.countrycupcakes.com

Last but most certainly not least on our educational tour of Bath's food scene, the Flavours of Bath day out – described by the entrepreneurs behind the venture as "the ultimate food experience in Bath" – is the brainchild of Cookery Coach, a mobile cookery school that specialises in teaching British and European cuisine. Led by the company's founder, Nev Leaning, the day kicks off with a tantalising tour of the city's unique food shops and artisan producers before an afternoon cookery session taking place in Grade 2 listed townhouse No 3 Abbey Green, where participants get involved in an interactive session putting all those locally sourced, seasonal, freshly bought ingredients to good use. Great fun!
Flavours of Bath
www.cookerycoach.co.uk/flavours-of/bath

If all this has whet your appetite to take your domestic yearnings to the next level, take a peek at the City of Bath College prospectus. A selection of full, part-time and evening classes gather together under the general theme of Catering and Hospitality and cover everything from courses specifically aimed at beginners to NVQ courses in pro cheffing.
City of Bath College
www.citybathcoll.ac.uk

Listings Shopping

It would be an entirely feasible (albeit rather onerous) task to dedicate a PHD thesis to the subject of shopping in Bath: the whys, wherefores and history of such an activity would take up at least half the allocated space before practicalities such as the address of any given outlet is even considered. But even if a pedantic individual was inclined to embark on such a project, the chances are that, by the time the work was done, many of the listings, recommendations and comments would be redundant or outdated. As we don't claim to have either the inclination nor the need to provide a Bath shopping guide so inclusive that it ends up reading like a section of the Thompson Local, we hereby present a whistlestop tour of the distinctly different areas that we believe provide the nicest shopping therapy experiences in the Heritage City, naming names/specialist retailers as we come across them.

SouthGate/ Town Centre

↘ In 2010, the **SouthGate** development brought a distinctly noughties version of shopping as a 'leisure experience' to Bath in the form of a gleaming shrine to Mammon stuffed to the gills with High Street Big Names, including **Boots, Apple, Debenhams, Currys, Apple, Calvin Klein, Urban Outfitters, Tommy Hilfiger, Karen Millen** and **Kurt Geiger**. But the independents are slowly but surely finding a foothold here too, most notably stylish frock shop **Pretty Eccentric**, the kiddie-specific **My Small World**, the fascinating **Whitewall Gallery** and **Avon Valley Cyclery**. Main city centre thoroughfare Stall Street, meanwhile, is lined with yet more usual retail suspects (think **M&S, BHS, Anne Summers, HMV, Whittards, Clinton's Cards, Next, Thorntons, Superdrug, TopShop, Dorothy Perkins, Burtons, Wallis, Banana Republic, Clarks, Hush Puppies** – oh, you know: 'that' sort of thing). Apart from a handful of exceptions to the rule, many of the shops around these yer parts are bland, faceless, corporate and predictable, but hey, they all serve some sort of purpose (ie, emptying your wallet as fast as possible).

On a distinctly less commercialised note, however, an enthralling collection of indie art galleries, hairdressers, sweet/fudge emporiums and gift shops thrives around the general vicinity of the Abbey (check out the cutesy North Parade Passage in particular), with the longstanding, independent purveyor of all-things baby- and child-related **Eric Snook's Golden Cot** bookending the 'Abbey Quarter' on the Abbeygate Street side and smelly wax shop **Roman Candles**, New Age haven **Arcania**, school uniform specialists **Scholars**, quirky, globally-themed knick-knack emporium **Eureka** and melodious musical mayhem courtesy of **Sharps and Flats** keeping things lively on Terrace Walk/ Orange Grove. Just up the road from all this excitement, the **Guildhall Market** is home to a myriad of fiercely independent craft, DIY, pet, jewellery, leather goods, book and novelty stalls, with the food traders in particular providing a lovely alternative to shopping in **Waitrose**, just down the road. Talking of which... At the time of writing, **The Podium** shopping centre is subject to big changes, as the aforementioned supermarket recently announced their plans to expand their Bath home by taking over the entire ground floor of the complex, forcing existing businesses to flee the nest. Bath is holding its collective breath as it waits for the new **John Lewis** department store to open.

Milsom Street/ Milsom Place/ Broad Street/ New Bond Street

This whole area is very well served in terms of upmarket cash-splurging opportunities, with a healthy dose of independent traders dotted in and amongst a classy but familiar array of retail outlets. Alongside **Jolly's** on Milsom Street (the oldest department store in the country), find branches of **Square, Gap, Cargo, Reiss, Jaeger, Kaliko, East, Shoon, Ted Baker, Hobbs, Office, Waterstones, Paperchase**, the **Highgrove Shop, Comptoirs des Cotonniers** and **Vintage to Vogue** amongst the melange, with the glorious **Kitchens** cookware haven just off the main drag on Quiet Street and two distinctly individual jewellers (**Clive Ranger** for classic sparklies, **Justice** for contemporary designs) in the vicinity. Discerning gentlemen will find much to enjoy at luxurious European suit outlet **Gabbuci**, which stocks suits you won't find easily on the UK high street. Milsom Place, meanwhile, acts as a very stylish crossroads 'twixt Milsom and Broad Street, with New Bond Street providing the backbone. Seamlessly blending days gone by with tomorrow's innovations, Milsom Place offers a multi-level network of historical lanes and passages linked by wide stone staircases, futuristic lifts and elevated walkways that connect all-weather courtyards, al fresco piazzas and rooftop terraces, all lined with an exciting blend of high fashion outlets, gift shops, restaurants and cafés. Today the Place is a fashionistas paradise, home to the **British Designer's Boutique@FashionCapital, Traffic People** and **Hannah Dulcie's** lingerie lounge alongside chic homeware/gift shops such as **Quadri, Luma,** the **Salcombe Trading Company, Liquid Glass** and **Lilly Pola,**

WALCOT STREET/ LONDON ROAD

If contemporary commercial high street ventures fail to float your boat, the shops, watering holes and galleries that thrive along Walcot Street/London Road capture the imagination in a way that Big Brand marketing campaigns can only dream of aspiring to. Eclectic, funky and vibrant, the area has, since the 1960s, held the informal title of Bath's Artisan Quarter and still represents the essence of alternative life in Bath today, not least of all because the long-established pubs that line the route (the legendary **Bell** at 103 London Road, the **Star Inn** on The Paragon and the **Pig and Fiddle** on Saracen Street) are second to none in terms of the kind of character that an influx of franchises in Bath are apparently intent on sanitising for good. Grab your wallet; it's time to wander around Walcot.

Find classy home interiors inspirations from **Vita Interiors, Farrow and Ball, Coopers Kitchen Appliances, Broadleaf Flooring,** the **Framing Workshop**, lighting expert **Richard Hathaway**, all-things-Scandi haven **Shannon** and mini-department store (and furniture/flooring specialists) **TR Hayes. Walcot Reclamation** yard, meanwhile, is worth dedicating a whole afternoon of browsing to. On the fashion front, find vintage and retro bargains and delights in the **Yellow Shop** and **Jack and Denny's**, headwear for all occasions at the **British Hatter**, footwear for all occasions at **MasterShoe** and yet more fabulous footwear in those often tricky-to-source sizes at **After 8 Shoes**, but don't overlook the bargains to be found in the **Save the Children** and **Bath Women's Refuge** charity shops while you're pounding the pavements. Elsewhere on the eclectic shopper's shopping list, **John's Bikes,** the **Christian Science Reading Room, Sewing Machine Workshop, Minuteman Press, Reboot Computer Repair Shop** and the **Makery** craft workshop hub go some way to keeping all manner of imagination levels up. Have we left someone out? If we have, we apologise.

HIGHLY RECOMMENDED

HOW TO CHOOSE FROM SO MANY RETAIL OUTLETS? AH-HA, A HANDY GUIDE...

WONDERFUL WEDDING DRESSES

- **Traditional:** Clifton Brides, 11 St James' Parade, BA1 1UL Tel: 01225 447878 www.cliftonbrides.co.uk
- **Posh:** Caroline Castigliano (by prior appointment only), 5-6 Sawclose, BA1 1EN Tel: 01225 789900, www.carolinecastigliano.co.uk
- **Princessy:** Drop Dead Gorgeous, 4 Seven Dials, Sawclose, BA1 1EN Tel: 01225 444232 www.dropdeadgorgeousbath.co.uk

BUY/SELL VINTAGE

- **Bang on-trend:** Scarlet Vintage, 5 Queen Street, BA1 1HE Tel: 01225 338677 www.scarletvintage.co.uk
- **Long-established:** Frock Exchange, 10 Kingsmead Square, BA1 3AB Tel: 01225 461518
- **Classic:** Vintage to Vogue, 28 Milsom Street, BA1 1DQ Tel: 01225 337323 www.vintagetovoguebath.co.uk

NON-SNOOTY ART GALLERIES

- **Quirky:** Bo-lee, 1 Queen Street, BA1 1HE, www.bo-lee.co.uk
- **Chic:** Rostra & Rooksmoor, 5 George Street, BA1 2EJ Tel: 01225 448121 www.rostragallery.co.uk
- **Classic:** Beaux Arts, 12-13 York Place, BA1 1NG Tel: 01225 464850 www.beauxartsbath.co.uk

DAY SPAS

- **Yummy mummy:** Green Street House, 14 Green Street, BA1 2JZ Tel: 01225 426000, www.greenstreethouse.com
- **Glam:** Champneys, 20 New Bond Street, BA1 1BD Tel: 01225 420500 www.champneys.com
- **Long-established:** Frontlinestyle, 4-5 Monmouth Street, BA1 2AJ Tel: 01225 478478, www.frontlinestyle.co.uk

HOBBIES

- **Stitch up:** Sew'n'Sew, 11-18 Guildhall Market, BA2 4AW Tel: 01225 482648 www.bathguildhallmarket.co.uk
- **Model behaviour:** Bath Model Centre, 2 Lower Borough Walls, BA1 1QR Tel: 01225 460115, www.bathmodelcentre.com
- **Crafty:** The Makery, 146 Walcot Street, BA1 5BL Tel: 01225421175 www.themakeryonline.co.uk

GIFTS

- **Classy:** Bloomsbury, 15 New Bond Street, BA1 1BA Tel 01225 461049 www.bloomsburystore.com
- **Quirky:** Octopus, 5 Old Bond Street, BA1 1BW Tel: 01225 462372 www.octopusshop.com
- **Cute:** Pink Art, 9a York Street, Bath BA1 1LZ Tel: 01225 330121

ECCENTRIC EXPERIENCES

- **Taking 'that' Wizard song literally:** 25 December, 16 Cheap Street, BA1 1NA Tel: 01225 315555, www.december25.co.uk
- **Slightly sinister:** Build-A-Bear, 7 Southgate Street, BA1 1AQ Tel: 01225 463100 www.buildabear.co.uk
- **Just Do It:** Hansel und Gretel, 9 Margarets Buildings, BA1 2LP, Tel: 01225 464677 www.hanselundgretel.com

SOUVENIRS

- **Informative:** Tourist Information Centre Shop, Abbey Churchyard, BA1 1LY, www.visitbathshop.co.uk
- **Eclectic:** Pulteney Bridge Gift Shop, 15-16 Pulteney Bridge, BA2 4AY Tel: 01225 426161, www.pulteneybridge.com
- **The Ultimate:** Roman Baths Museum Shop, Stall Street, BA1 1LZ Tel: 01225 466766 www.romanbathsshop.co.uk

bespoke oil and vinegar merchants **Vom Fass** and floral abundance from **Anemone**. On the Broad Street side, find gorgeous independent department store **Rossiters of Bath**, a flagship **Cath Kidston** store, the utterly delightful knick-knackery haven that is **Kiss the Frog Again**, flooring/kitchen experts **Mandarin Stone** and a branch of sophisticated/special occasion clothes shop **Phase Eight**. New Bond Street, meanwhile, is home to the **Bloomsbury Gift Shop**, clothes by **Karen Millen, Fenn Wright Manson, LK Bennett, White Stuff, Coast, Jigsaw, Warehouse** and **Laura Ashley**, and shoe shop **Moda in Pele**. There are beautifying havens here too (**Space NK Apothecary, Molton Brown, the Champneys Day Spa**), alongside a branch of **Lakeland** (specialists in essential kitchenware) and brewmeisters the **Tea House Emporium** all waiting to be discovered. But whatever you do, don't overlook Green Street while you're in the area, home to superior clotheterias **Fat Face, French Connection** and **Maze**, the **Red Cross** charity shop, a **Scholl** shoe shop, pampering paradise the **Green Street Spa** and **Fashion Fabrics**, which sells exactly what the name suggests in an Alladdin's cave stuffed with fabric delights.

The Corridor/ Union Passage/ Northumberland Place

↘ Hip urban retailers such as **Free Spirit, Cult** and **Weird Fish** – all offering major appeal to the young skater/goth/stude crowd – today largely dominate The Corridor, one of the world's first dedicated retail arcades (built in 1825). But for subtler sophisticates, there's also a branch of outdoor/urban outfitters **Rohan** just around the corner in Union Passage, itself offering an eclectic mix of shops, including the charming **Silver Gift Shop** and the global/fairtrade bazaar that is **Coral Quay**, with classy bling from jeweller **Nicholas Wylde** just around the corner again on super-pretty Northumberland Place, also home to **Neil's Yard Remedies** and a collection of charming gift shops.

George Street/ Bartlett Street

↘ Ah, gorgeous George Street – and it's equally gorgeous, largely lady-centric clothes shops. **Instant Vintage, Prey** and **Via Appia** (actually on Bladud Buildings, across the lights at the non-bendy end of the GS 'strip') are the names on every chic, pretty girl's lips – if, that is, they haven't bagged Bath's Best Bargain frock in either the **Shaw Trust Charity Shop** or the **Oxfam Boutique**. Take a minor detour off George Street (the uninitiated should look for the Adventure Cafe and take the lane to the right of the frontage), and you're wandering up Bartlett Street, the picturesque, traffic-free lane on which you'll find the (also very girlie) **Mee Boutique** and the brand new, multi-faceted 'lifestyle shopping experience' that is **The Loft**: home to fabulous fashions from **Blue**, interior inspirations from **Obi and Moo** and the Tuscan-themed **Café Lucca**, all under one recently restored Regency-style building in one of the most characterful corners of the city, and just across the road from the fabulous **Bartlett Street Antique Centre**, which is home to around 160 stalls staffed by knowledgeable dealers and experts in the antique jewellery/clothing/homeware/ furniture/ceramics/art trade.

Pulteney Bridge

↘ It's a wonder that this tiny, ancient bridge (completed in 1773) hasn't collapsed under the weight of the many shops and eateries that keep the area on and around this elegant, weir-spanning erection so lively today. Find **Hampstead Bazaar** (Dame Judi Dench's favourite outfitters, don'cha know), stylish home stylists **Found** and **Grasse**, **Pulteney Bridge Gift Shop** (packed to the rafters with souvenirs and doll's house accessories), hi-fidelity specialists **Bang and Olufsen, the Mosaic Shop**, the official **Bath Rugby** store, a **Phase Eight** sales outlet, a **Smile** convenience store, a flower shop, sports shops, a traditional chemist/pharmacy, and not one but two charity shops (**Dorothy House** and **Oxfam**). Worthy of a stand-alone mention for being so very 'Bath', **Orvis**

BATH SHOPPING: LEFT OF THE CENTRE SCENE

MARGARET'S BUILDINGS

This charming, pedestrianised lane tucked away between the Royal Crescent and the Circus is home to an enchanting range of independent boutiques, galleries and antique shops. Don't miss **Alexandra May's** jewellery/gift/curiosity shop on the corner (the window display alone is good for a full half hour of browsing), the **White Room Gallery** (Brock Street), and **Bath Old Books** at the top of this lovely lane.

WIDCOMBE

Welcome to wonderful Widders, almost an independent state (of mind, at least). This community-driven haven centres around the main drag that is Widcombe Parade, home to the **Aga Shop**, **Corrie Schrijver's violin making/restoration services, Blazes Fireplace and Heating Centre, Bus Station Florists** (not really that convenient for the bus station, and all the better for it), **Roundabout** and **Second Hand Rose** (vintage/posh second-hand clothes for children/grown-ups respectively) a traditional chemist, a **McColls** convenience store, the **Two Dragons Gallery** and unique architectural model maker **Timothy Richards'** workshop, tucked away behind St Mark's Church, St Mark's Road.

MOORLAND ROAD/ OLDFIELD PARK

A whole host of independent butchers, bakers, hardware, pet and wholefood emporiums and a bookshop (and oh, okay, a **Sainsbury's Local**) interspersed with a delightful muddle of charity shops and some lovely, lively watering holes.

Outfitters (subtly dominating No 1 Pulteney Bridge) specialises in outfits specifically geared to hunting and fishing jaunts. Need a shooting shirt, gun case, Upland Lanyard, Barbour jacket or waterfowler's hat? This is the place to come.

BOOK SHOPS: READING MATTERS

UNLIKE MOST CITIES, BATH'S BOOK SHOPS SEEM TO BE PROLIFERATING PLEASANTLY

BATH OLD BOOKS

9c Margarets Buildings, BA1 2LP
Tel: 01225 422244
Browse a multi-faceted range of second-hand art, architecture, Bath specific, children's books and more (including collector's editions/original imprints) courtesy of a lively cooperative of friendly dealers, each of them experts in their various individual fields.

BATH VISITOR INFORMATION CENTRE

9c Abbey Chambers, Abbey Churchyard BA1 1LY www.visitbath.co.uk
Top-notch selection of guide books, photographic books, history books and more about Bath and the surrounding area. Everything you need to enjoy and get the most out of your visit to the city and plenty of titles that will help you plan day trips around the South West.

GEORGE BAYNTUN FINE BINDINGS & RARE BOOKS

Manvers Street, BA1 1JW Tel: 01225 466000, www.georgebayntun.com
Founded by Bath bookbinder and philanthropist George Bayntun (1873-1940), today globally renowned for being the last of the great Victorian trade binderies still in family ownership. Also stocks a fascinating collection of antiquarian/new bindings, well worth a browse (not least of all for an opportunity to digest the evocative atmosphere and historical surroundings).

GOOD BUY BOOKS

6 North Parade, BA1 1LF Tel: 01225 469625, www.goodbuybooks.co.uk
A comprehensive, frequently changing range of bargain books from publisher/booksellers overstocks (many at way less than half the RRP) to reasonably priced, high quality reprints with a good local history/guidebook section too.

MR B'S EMPORIUM OF READING DELIGHTS

14-15 John Street, BA1 2JL Tel: 01225 331155, www.mrbsemporium.com
This award-winning independent bookshop tucked away behind Jolly's offers an exceptionally warm welcome to browsers. A regular programme of events (including a book club and plenty of readings/signings) keep bookworms buoyant.

OLDFIELD PARK BOOKSHOP

43 Moorland Road, BA2 3PN
Tel: 01225 427722
Friendly, well-stocked independent book shop at the heart of a lively neighbourhood high street founded by affable, informative bookworm Harry Wainwright – a former regional manager of a national book-selling chain – in 2002, when he felt the urge to step away from the increasingly commercialised pressures of contemporary marketing and revisit his roots.

OXFAM BOOKSHOP

4-5 Lower Borough Walls, BA1 1QR Tel: 01225 469776, www.oxfam.org.uk
Impressively well-stocked, books-dedicated charity shop, packed to the rafters with previously owned all kinds of everything (in print form, at least) alongside valuable rarities and collector's items donated by altruistic lit-lovers.

SKOOBS BOOK STALL

40-42 Guildhall Market BA2 4AW
Tel: 01225 463133
www.bathguildhallmarket.co.uk
Long-established second-hand paradise, with the bound bounty helpfully sorted by genre (contemporary/classic/crime/romantic/science fiction, biography/children's/reference/travel etc). Staff are informative and helpful, and they'll offer you a good price to take your previously loved tomes off your hands too.

TOPPINGS & CO

The Paragon, BA1 5LS Tel: 01225 428111, www.toppingbooks.co.uk

Vibrant, friendly, independent bibliophile paradise offering a selection of around 45,000 titles to choose from at any one time. Free coffee served to browsers; visit the website for news of forthcoming events (Top Tip: Toppings regularly welcomes today's superstar authors to Bath)

WATERSTONES

4-5 Milsom Street, BA1 1DA
Tel: 01225 448515
www.waterstones.com

Bath's Biggest Bookshop (and familiar national high street stalwart).

WH SMITH

6-7 Union Street, BA1 1RT Tel: 01225 460522, www.whsmith.co.uk

Credited with being the first chain store company in the world (and responsible for creating the ISBN book cataloguing system), WH Smith started selling books in 1792. Today, the Bath branch is slightly more 1972 in overall vibe, but there are plenty of best-selling bargains to be found.

THE WORKS

13 Westgate Street, BA1 1EQ
Tel: 01225 332129

Heavily discounted publisher overruns/remaindered stock, largely focusing on celeb biographies, gift books and *Strictly Come Dancing* spin-offs.

A STUDENT'S GUIDE TO BATH

NIA EVANS TAKES YOU ON A STUDENT BUDGET TOUR OF BATH

If you are looking for a raving party scene and endless streets of night clubs the size of department stores then to be honest Bath isn't really the place to be. On the other hand, with its quirky student hangouts, world-class sports facilities and an array of student-friendly traditional pubs, Bath is a great place to spend three unforgettable years of your life. With two universities (one science-based and the other more artsy), Bath has a strong and colourful student population adding to the vibrancy and atmosphere of this stunning city.

Freshers will have the comfort of staying on their respective campuses to ease them into a life of beans on toast and attempting to awake from deep, alcohol-fuelled slumbers for 9 o'clock lectures. Beyond first year however, the big wide world looms, as do the joys of finding rented accommodation in the city that doesn't blow the entire student loan in one month. The search will most likely end in Oldfield Park, just outside the city centre. With bus services to both university campuses and a train station with regular connections to Bristol, it certainly is the most convenient and affordable area for students. What's more, Moorland Road has everything a student might need right on their doorstep.

This bustling street of shops is the hub of the community and is definitely kind to the student budget. S & L Banable family butcher offers top-quality and reasonably priced local meat for all those hangover cure fry-ups and Stokes the greengrocers is a wonder of colour with fresh, seasonal produce always on offer.

Moorland Road's numerous charity shops are ideal when it comes to those last minute fancy dress parties – they have provided costumes for *Braveheart* and *Mrs Doubtfire* to name but two.

The Oldfield Park Bookshop is a great place to distract any student from essay writing and exam revision. This friendly neighbourhood bookstore stocks everything from the latest bestsellers and popular fiction to travel guides and the more quirky local interest reads.

If the thought of one more plate of beans on toast for dinner makes the stomach turn then Panahar Indian restaurant and takeaway is the ultimate solution. It is particularly popular with students thanks to its bring your own booze policy.

However, undoubtedly the most popular place in Oldfield Park is the Velo Lounge, a lively café bar enjoyed by families, OAPs and students alike. Complete with games, decent food and a chilled out atmosphere, students can get their caffeine fix, enjoy a laid-back revision session or take part in the weekly Sunday night quiz with the locals.

The only thing missing on Moorland Road is a student-friendly pub (we would steer clear of The Livingstone). The town centre however provides ample choice for any thirsty student. The Raven, famous for its Pieminister pies and wide selection of local ales, is definitely a favourite on a chilly winter weekend. The Crystal Palace beer garden is the place to be to enjoy a sunny summer's evening with a pitcher of Pimm's and The Pig and Fiddle has a fantastic atmosphere on rugby match days in Bath. All are well within staggering distance from Oldfield Park so there really is no excuse not to make the most of them.

So Bath is not just Jane Austen and cream teas after all. It has to be one of the most chilled out cities in Britain to study. With so much to do in such a modest-sized city, it's surprising that the students of Bath actually get any work done. Here are five top tips for Bath students:

1 Moles night club at first glance is grimy, cramped and a bit stinky but Cheese Night every Tuesday is not to be missed. With cheap drinks and the cheesiest of

...nes from the likes of S Club 7 and the Backstreet Boys, Moles will take you back to the cringeworthy days of school discos and become a firm favourite with everyone who wants to throw some mad shapes to *Build Me Up Buttercup*. On other nights here you'll find something to tickle almost every musical taste bud – including live acts.

2 If you are the superstitious type then it's probably best not to set foot in the Abbey before you graduate. Rumour has it that if you do you won't graduate at all.

3 Students are residents of Bath and are entitled to a Discovery Card, which allows locals to visit all the main tourist attractions such as the Roman Baths and the Royal Crescent Museum for free.

4 Go for the independent rather than mainstream. Bath has a fantastic range of independent shops, restaurants and entertainment venues, including the Little Theatre Cinema, the Real Italian Pizza Place and Jika Jika café bar, so make the most of them while you're here.

5 On a warm summer's day the ultimate student's day out has to be rowing (or punting if you're a bit posh) on the River Avon. Grab some mates, a picnic and a few cans of beer and follow the river to Bathampton, where you'll find the George – a cracking country pub. Oh, and try not to fall into the water, it's a bit grim.

The best advice anyone could give though is ENJOY IT!

THE NAKED GUIDE TO BATH MAP

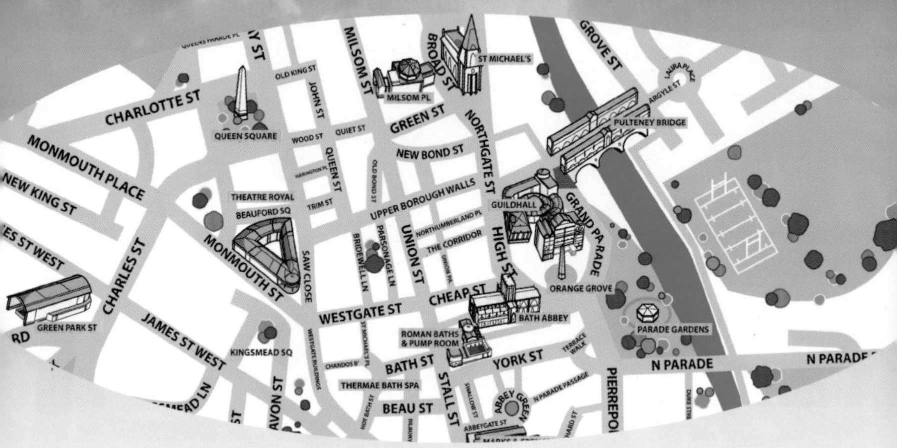

Bath Visitor Information Centre

The Bath Visitor Information Centre is by the Abbey in Abbey Chambers, off York Street (Bath BA1 1LY). Open Monday-Saturday 9.30-5.30 all year round except for Christmas Day, Boxing Day and New Year's Day. Tel: UK callers – 0906 711 2000 (50p/min), overseas callers – +44 (0)844 847 5257.

Email: tourism@bathtourism.co.uk. www.visitbath.co.uk

Also available in the Naked Guides series

Naked Guide to Bristol

The only guidebook to get under the skin of Bristol, the UK's centre of creativity. Now in its third edition, this book includes a complete area guide to Central Bristol as well as sections on music, politics, street art, history, celebrities plus complete listings for pubs, clubs, bars, restaurants and a lot more.

Naked Guide to Cider

A celebration of the juice of the fermented apple delivered with the wit, panache and attention to detail that sets the Naked Guides apart. Author James Russell takes you on a tour of all the UK's cider-making areas, explains how to make your own cider and tells you about the best places to drink and buy cider.

Coming Soon...

The *Naked Guide to Cardiff* a complete guide to the capital city of Wales, its history, culture and curiosities. Contains extensive eating, drinking and shopping listings.

FREE delivery online at www.tangentbooks.co.uk